Discovery Through the Humanities
THE SEARCH FOR MEANING

Discovery Through the Humanities
THE SEARCH FOR MEANING

Richard F. Hettlinger
in collaboration with Grace Worth

Walker and Company
720 Fifth Avenue
New York, N.Y. 10019

Discovery Through the Humanities

THE NATIONAL COUNCIL ON THE AGING, INC.
Washington, D.C.
1988

Authors' Note:

Richard F. Hettlinger, Professor of Religion, is presently Director of the Integrated Program in Humane Studies at Kenyon College, Gambier, Ohio.

Grace Worth, previous Humanities Program Field Representative, taught literature and child psychology at Chatfield College, St. Martin, Ohio.

Library of Congress Cataloging-in-Publication Data

Hettlinger, Richard Frederick.
  The search for meaning.

  Bibliography: p.
  1. Literature—Collections. 2. Self-perception—
Literary collections. 3. Conduct of life—Literary
collections. I. Worth, Grace. II. Title.
PN6014.H49   1988   808.8′035   88-27667
ISBN 0-8027-2628-3

Cover: *The Thinker* by Auguste Rodin (1840-1917). French, Sculpture, Bronze.

The Discovery Through the Humanities Program, a program of The National Council on the Aging, Inc., is supported by The National Endowment for the Humanities.

THE SEARCH FOR MEANING
1988

Distributed by Walker and Company

TABLE OF CONTENTS

PREFACE

"Discovery Through the Humanities" is a program based on the assumption that the humanities offer mature Americans unlimited opportunities for self-discovery and personal growth. Older persons will find their rich fund of experiences illuminated and clarified in literature, philosophy and history. And in turn, their recollections and critical, creative vision can contribute to understanding in these fields. Exploring the humanities can help make the later years a time of expansion of interest as well as one for reflection and synthesis.

We discover and define ourselves in many ways—through our work, our family relationships and our ethnic or national heritage, for example. This book goes beyond everyday experience to explore humankind's deepest beliefs and yearnings. It provides insights into the ways people give meaning to their lives in a world often full of anxiety and purposelessness.

In this age of rapid social and technological change, unsettling new ideas and conflicting values, the quest to find a meaning or purpose to life may seem all the more urgent. Many questions about life, though, remain timeless, as you will see from the rich diversity of readings and art taken from ancient and contemporary sources. Yet, answers to these fundamental questions usually evolve during the course of one's life.

It is hoped that this book will challenge you to contemplate new understandings, to continue your own search for meaning and to share your beliefs with your contemporaries, family and community.

Section 1

INTRODUCTION

Searching for a meaning to life seems to be a distinctively human characteristic. We now know that other animals are capable of thinking and reasoning to some degree, but there is no evidence to suggest that even the most intelligent of them—dolphins, for example—ask questions like: "What is the purpose of my life?" Loren Eiseley, scientist and poet, writes:

> It is man's folly, as it is perhaps a sign of his spiritual aspirations, that he is forever scrutinizing and redefining himself. A mole, as far as we can determine, is content with its dim world below the grass roots, a snow leopard with being what he is—a drifting ghost in a blizzard. Man, by contrast, is marked by a restless inner eye, which, in periods of social violence, such as characterize our age, grows clouded with anxiety.

One sign of this peculiarly human concern is the hope for life after death which will make sense of apparently pointless suffering in this life. It has been reported that baby chimpanzees sometimes die of grief over the death of their mothers, but there is nothing to suggest that they imagine the possibility of a reunion in another world. On the other hand, human beings—as long as 100,000 years ago—buried their dead surrounded by flowers, apparently because they thought of death as the entrance into a happier condition.

Many psychiatrists think that an ability to see our lives as part of a greater purpose is essential to human survival. Without it, there is a question as to whether social behavior and creative activity would continue. If

_____
The Hebrew lesson.

3

we merely recorded the events of our daily experience as facts and nothing else, and lacked the ability to relate them to an overarching principle or meaning, would we even have the motivation to survive? Viktor Frankl's experience in a Nazi concentration camp led him to say "No." Without what Frankl calls the "will to meaning," human personality tends to disintegrate:

> A man who could not see the end of his "provisional existence" was not able to aim at an ultimate goal in life. He ceased living for the future, in contrast to a man in normal life. Therefore, the whole structure of his inner life changed; signs of decay set in which we know from other areas of life. The unemployed worker, for example, is in a similar position. His existence has become provisional, and in a certain sense he cannot live for the future or aim at a goal.

There are times when we would gladly be free of this need for meaning, particularly when we find it difficult or impossible to see any point to life. At such times we would happily live in the present moment without any anxiety or questions. But the quest for purpose or understanding is as unavoidable as our need for food and drink. James Agee, studying the lives of a group of people in extreme poverty, barely able to subsist, wrote about "certain normal predicaments of human divinity" which remain even when human beings are abused and humilitated. As one French writer put it, we are "condemned to meaning."

In the following selection of readings we shall consider many (though by no means all) of the responses human beings have given to the question, "What is life all about and how can I make sense of it?" For many, an answer is found in the joy and challenge of relationships with people (Section 2). Others see their individual lives as meaningful because they contribute to a larger whole—as part of a continuing human group (Section 3) or as part of the complex unity of nature (Section 4). Many believe that the world we see can be understood through an awareness of the invisible, eternal realities on which it depends (Section 5). Some people accept things as they are and develop an inner peace that external events cannot disturb (Section 6). Many are confident that the injustices and suffering of this life will be explained in a richer life after this one (Section 7). Others conclude that, if life is to have meaning, it is up to us to *create* that meaning rather than merely to *search* for it; they achieve this through a wide range of creative activities (Section 8) or different kinds of service for other people (Section 9).

It is important to note that these various ways of finding meaning are

The Labyrinth *by Robert Vickrey (1926-   ). Casein on composition board.*

Nuns and walls often create ominous spaces in Vickrey's paintings. Closed in by corners and barriers, his people seem confused and disoriented as they seek their way.

not necessarily contradictory. Many of them can be combined, and few of us employ one way to the exclusion of all others. At different times in our lives, one approach will help us more than another. Each of us has to develop her or his own answer to the questions that our own personal experience puts to us. To quote Frankl again, "Every situation is distinguished by its uniqueness, and there is only one right answer to the problem posed by the situation in hand."

The arrangement of the materials in the following sections is not intended, then, to encourage you to choose one among the various types of answers as your own. It is intended rather to help you to clarify your own answers to the questions posed by *your* life as *you* live it. At the same time, by sharing personal experiences and discoveries with others in your life, you can learn from and contribute to the distinctive, individual self-understanding of all.

Every section contains a rich variety of readings and artwork. Tackling readings from less familiar cultures can open pathways to new ideas. Also, take time to enjoy and reflect on the illustrations that form an integral part of each session. They offer another dimension to the search for meaning, and often evoke deeper emotional responses than those prompted by the readings. While the pictures are intended to illuminate and expand on each session's theme, many of them will also enhance your understanding of other sections. A good painting, sculpture or drawing has many levels of meaning—some intended by the artist, others discovered by the viewer.

The readings for this introductory section illustrate the ways in which people understand the nature of the human predicament, rather than offer any resolution of it. In reading the selections, ask yourself whether the author's questions or anxieties are like your own.

Carl Sandburg's poem, "A Father Sees His Son Nearing Manhood," looks with insight at the dilemmas confronting a young man or woman, but we know that these challenges face us throughout life. We can ask ourselves how we have responded to them. E.B. White's story, "The Second Tree from the Corner," raises the question of what each of us wants from life. Are we satisfied with a nice house, money and leisure, or do we seek something else "both inexpressible and unattainable"? Finally Keats expresses the fears that we all have at times—fears that we shall never realize all our dreams and fulfill our potentialities.

A Father Sees His Son Nearing Manhood

Carl Sandburg
(1878-1976)

Carl Sandburg, born of Swedish immigrants in Illinois, was a poet of the common people. When he was obliged to leave school and go to work as a boy of 13, he saw many aspects of the lives of ordinary people firsthand. His work as a migratory worker throughout the Midwest included jobs as a milkman, harvest hand, hotel dishwasher, stagehand, brickmaker and sign painter.

Sandburg's poems present a panorama of the real-life situations and daily problems of the people of America. In the selection below, the poet dramatizes the inner thoughts of a father pondering the question every father faces as his son grows into manhood: "What shall I tell him?"

A father sees his son nearing manhood.
What shall he tell that son?
"Life is hard; be steel; be a rock."
And this might stand him for the storms
and serve him for humdrum and monotony
and guide him amid sudden betrayals
and tighten him for slack moments.
"Life is a soft loam; be gentle; go easy."
And this too might serve him.
Brutes have been gentled where lashes failed.
The growth of a frail flower in a path up
has sometimes shattered and split a rock.
A tough will counts. So does desire.
So does a rich soft wanting.
Without rich wanting nothing arrives.
Tell him too much money has killed men
and left them dead years before burial:
the quest of lucre beyond a few easy needs
has twisted good enough men
sometimes into dry thwarted worms.
Tell him time as a stuff can be wasted.
Tell him to be a fool every so often
and to have no shame over having been a fool
yet learning something out of every folly
hoping to repeat none of the cheap follies

thus arriving at intimate understanding
of a world numbering many fools.
Tell him to be alone often and get at himself
and above all tell himself no lies about himself
whatever the white lies and protective fronts
he may use amongst other people.
Tell him solitude is creative if he is strong
and the final decisions are made in silent rooms.
Tell him to be different from other people
if it comes natural and easy being different.
Let him have lazy days seeking his deeper motives.
Let him seek deep for where he is a born natural.
    Then he may understand Shakespeare
    and the Wright brothers, Pasteur, Pavlov,
    Michael Faraday and free imaginations
Bringing changes into a world resenting change.
    He will be lonely enough
    to have time for the work
    he knows as his own.

The Second Tree from the Corner

E. B. White
(1899-   )

E. B. White is one of America's finest essayists. Contributor to The New Yorker *magazine for many years, White has collected his essays and stories in book form and published several books of humor. He is also known for his beloved children's books,* Stuart Little *and* Charlotte's Web.

"The Second Tree from the Corner" is included in a collection of the same title. White has said this book is filled with revelations and contains farewells of many kinds. The excerpt below is taken from the conclusion of the story, when Trexler experiences a revelation about where the meaning of life is not *to be found. He then bids farewell to the psychiatrist who had been trying to help him pin down and define that which defies naming and definition.*

It was on the fifth visit, about halfway through, that the doctor turned to Trexler and said, suddenly, "What do you want?" He gave the word "want" special emphasis.

"I d'know," replied Trexler uneasily. "I guess nobody knows the answer to that one."

"Sure they do," replied the doctor.

"Do *you* know what you want?" asked Trexler narrowly.

"Certainly," said the doctor. Trexler noticed that at this point the doctor's chair slid slightly backward, away from him. Trexler stifled a small, internal smile. Scared as a rabbit, he said to himself. Look at him scoot!

"What *do* you want?" continued Trexler, pressing his advantage, pressing it hard.

The doctor glided back another inch away from his inquisitor. "I want a wing on the small house I own in Westport. I want more money, and more leisure to do the things I want to do."

Trexler was just about to say, "And what are those things you want to do, Doctor?" when he caught himself. Better not go too far, he mused. Better not lose possession of the ball. And besides, he thought, what the hell goes on here, anyway—me paying fifteen bucks a throw for these seances and then doing the work myself, asking the questions, weighing the answers. So he wants a new wing! There's a fine piece of theatrical gauze for you! A new wing.

Trexler settled down again and resumed the role of patient for the rest of the visit. It ended on a kindly, friendly note. The doctor reassured him that his fears were the cause of his sickness, and that his fears were unsubstantial. They shook hands, smiling.

Trexler walked dizzily through the empty waiting room and the doctor followed along to let him out. It was late; the secretary had shut up shop and gone home. Another day over the dam. "Goodbye," said Trexler. He stepped into the street, turned west toward Madison, and thought of the doctor all alone there, after hours, in that desolate hole—a man who worked longer hours than his secretary. Poor, scared, overworked bastard, thought Trexler. And that new wing!

It was an evening of clearing weather, the Park showing green and desirable in the distance, the last daylight applying a high lacquer to the brick and brownstone walls and giving the street scene a luminous and intoxicating splendor. Trexler meditated, as he walked, on what he wanted. "What do you want?" he heard again. Trexler knew what he wanted, and what, in general, all men wanted; and he was glad, in a way, that it was both inexpressible and unattainable, and that it wasn't a wing. He was satisfied to remember that it was deep, formless, enduring, and impossible of fulfillment, and that it made men sick, and that when you sauntered along Third Avenue and looked through the doorways into the dim saloons, you could sometimes pick out from the unregenerate ranks the ones who had not forgotten, gazing steadily into the bottoms of the glasses on the long chance that they could get another little peek at it. Trexler found himself renewed by the remembrance that what he wanted was at once great and microscopic, and that although it borrowed from the nature of large deeds and of youthful love and of old songs

and early intimations, it was not any one of these things, and that it had not been isolated or pinned down, and that a man who attempted to define it in the privacy of a doctor's office would fall flat on his face.

Trexler felt invigorated. Suddenly his sickness seemed health, his dizziness stability. A small tree, rising between him and the light, stood there saturated with the evening, each gilt-edged leaf perfectly drunk with excellence and delicacy. Trexler's spine registered an ever so slight tremor as it picked up this natural disturbance in the lovely scene. "I want the second tree from the corner, just as it stands," he said, answering an imaginary question from an imaginary physician. And he felt a slow pride in realizing that what he wanted none could bestow, and that what he had none could take away. He felt content to be sick, unembarrassed at being afraid; and in the jungle of his fear he glimpsed (as he had so often glimpsed them before) the flashy tail feathers of the bird courage.

Then he thought once again of the doctor, and of his being left there all alone, tired, frightened. (The poor, scared guy, thought Trexler.) Trexler began humming "Moonshine Lullaby," his spirit reacting instantly to the hypodermic of Merman's healthy voice. He crossed Madison, boarded a downtown bus, and rode all the way to Fifty-second Street before he had a thought that could rightly have been called bizarre.

Wadsworth Atheneum, Hartford, Connecticut.

Nooning *by Winslow Homer (1836-1910). Oil.*

Homer, who first achieved fame as a magazine illustrator, devoted his talents in midlife exclusively to painting, mostly watercolors and oils of seacoasts, boats at sea and rural settings.

When I Have Fears

John Keats
(1795-1821)

John Keats, one of the most renowned of the English poets, gained his fame in a brief life of only 25 years. Poetry, for him, meant a serious responsibility to use the creative power with which everyone is blessed—the power to see into the meaning of things as well as the power to share that meaning with others.

Several tragedies marked the poet's life. His father died when he was eight years old, his mother when he was 15, and he then personally nursed his brother Tom through the last stages of tuberculosis.

The poem below was written when Keats was only 22 years of age. Overwhelmed by his own ill health and financial difficulties, he found himself thrown into a depression in which he was unable to pursue the writing he valued so much. At this time, also, he realized that his sickness, tuberculosis, would prevent him from ever marrying the woman he loved. The concern of this poem, a meditation on one's own death, can occur at various times during a person's life.

When I have fears that I may cease to be
Before my pen has gleaned my teeming brain,
Before high-piléd books, in charactery,
hold like rich garners the full ripened grain.
When I behold, upon the night's starr'd face,
   Huge cloudy symbols of a high romance
And think that I may never live to trace
   Their shadows, with the magic hand of chance;
And when I feel, fair creature of an hour!
   That I shall never look upon thee more,
Never have relish in the faery power
   Of unreflecting love!—then on the shore
Of the wide world I stand alone, and think
Till Love and Fame to nothingness do sink.

Further Readings

Berry, Wendell. *The Memory of Old Jack.* 1974. A novel about a farmer bound to the land and his own high standards. Old Jack relives his life in memory, trying to find its meaning and purpose.

Hesse, Hermann. *Siddhartha.* 1951. The spirituality of the East and West meet in this short novel, the story of a soul's long quest in search of the ultimate meaning of our role on this earth.

Lindbergh, Anne Morrow. *Gift from the Sea.* 1955. A contemplative journal in which the author strives to "think out my own particular pattern of living, my own individual balance of life, work and human relationships."

McCarthy, Colman. *Inner Companions.* 1975. Fifty-three essays—on poets, philosophers, artists, saints and dissenters, each committed to meaningful living.

Rogers, Carl R. "To Be That Self Which One Truly Is: A Therapist's View of Personal Goals" in *On Becoming A Person.* 1961. A well-known psychotherapist shares his understanding of personal growth and creativity.

Scott-Maxwell, Florida. *Measure of My Days.* 1973. A notebook of philosophical musings about the essence and the experience of aging by an 82-year-old woman, a former analytical psychologist.

Section 2

PERSONAL RELATIONSHIPS

Many people find meaning and strength in life through their relationships with others. For these persons, whatever loss or tragedy is encountered, nothing can destroy or nullify the uniquely rich human experience of encountering other human beings. To them, to have known love, compassion, fellowship and common purpose is to have found something so valuable and inextinguishable that all else pales beside it. The times we have been close to another human being as child, parent, friend or lover remain with us forever and sustain us long after the relationship has been interrupted by separation, sickness or death. As long as we remain capable of remembering such occasions, we possess the capacity to enjoy them and the potential to renew them. No larger purpose is needed to give meaning to the lives of those who consider personal relationships central to the definition of life.

Viktor Frankl, writing of his experience in the horror and degradation of a Nazi concentration camp, expressed this conviction very well in *Man's Search for Meaning:*

> My mind still clung to the image of my wife. A thought crossed my mind: I didn't even know if she were still alive. I knew only one thing—which I have learned well by now: Love goes very far beyond the physical person of the beloved. It finds its deepest meaning in his spiritual being, his inner self. Whether or not he is actually present, whether or not he is alive at all, ceases somehow to be of importance. I did not know whether my wife was alive, and I had no means of finding out . . . but at that moment it ceased to matter. There was no need for me to know; nothing

Conversation by Henry Schnakenberg (1892-1934). Oil on canvas.

15

could touch the strength of my love, my thoughts, and the image of my beloved.

The first four selections of this section illustrate the potential quality and value of personal relationships between members of a family. Margaret Drabble's description of a young mother's love for her baby and James Agee's account of a young boy's happy relationship with his father raise two questions: Is it true that women in our culture find it easier to establish personal relationships than men; and, is it easier for a child to establish them than an adult? These questions raise another: Is it ever too late for a man or woman to develop intimacies that give meaning to life? Margaret Mead's autobiography suggests that there is a special kind of opportunity available to grandparents. N. Scott Momaday, from the perspective of a child, recalls the profound impression made by a visit to an elderly relative.

The centrality of relationships to an understanding of human life was the major concern of the influential Jewish philosopher, Martin Buber. He maintained that our inner being or self (the "I") is affected for good or ill by the way we respond to people. If we are open to others, accepting them as free, equal persons, we enter into relationships with them that are creative, rich and exciting. At the same time, such relationships are potentially demanding and filled with risk, for we ourselves may be changed by the effects of the other person on us. Buber calls this the *I-Thou* relationship.

On the other hand, we can treat people as *things,* thus having only an *I-It* experience. In this situation we use them for our purposes, control them and classify them as impersonal units. As a result, our own personhood is diminished, says Buber. The selection from *All Real Life is Meeting,* a book that attempts to summarize Buber's philosophy, should raise some interesting questions about the quality of our own lives. We might ask if there are times when an *I-It* experience is more appropriate than an *I-Thou* encounter. Or, what circumstances prevent us from engaging in deep human relationships? Can we sometimes change these situations so that our personal encounters are enriched?

The two final selections in this section explore another aspect of the *I-Thou* relationship: Sexuality as an expression of personal response and openness. The reading by Anthony Storr illustrates how profoundly enriching sexuality can be for human relationships. D. H. Lawrence, in his poem, "We Are Transmitters," describes genuine sexual love as the creative source of life and meaning—the antithesis of an *I-It* experience. Each of us can consider whether we share the views of these writers about the value of sexuality and how far—in our experience—physical intimacy has contributed to deeper human encounters.

Thank You All Very Much

Margaret Drabble
(1939-   )

Margaret Drabble, a contemporary English author, has the special skill of illuminating ordinary situations and conveying the essence of everyday relationships. In her novel, Thank You All Very Much, *the protagonist, Rosamund, describes her experience as an unwed mother bringing up a baby daughter. She becomes pregnant as the result of a single, uncharacteristic lapse with a man she knows well but does not love. She decides to raise Octavia by herself, telling neither the father, George, nor her parents about the decision. When the baby is only a few months old, she is found to have a congenital defect that requires surgery. In the final passage of the excerpt that follows, Rosamund is visited by George, who is blissfully unaware of the fact that he is the child's father. The contrast of his indifferent attitude with Rosamund's total commitment to the child pointedly demonstrates the wide range of personal relationships and the intensity of the parent-child bond that gives special meaning to Rosamund's life.*

Octavia was an extraordinarily beautiful child. Everyone said so, in shops and on buses and in the park, wherever we went. I took her to Regent's Park as often as I could face getting the pram up and down in the lift. It was a tolerable summer, and we both got quite brown. I was continually amazed by the way in which I could watch for hours nothing but the small movements of her hands, and the fleeting expressions of her face. She was a very happy child, and once she learned to smile, she never stopped; at first she would smile at anything, at parking meters and dogs and strangers, but as she grew older she began to favour me, and nothing gave me more delight than her evident preference. I suppose I had not really expected her to dislike and resent me from birth, though I was quite prepared for resentment to follow later on, but I certainly had not anticipated such wreathing, dazzling gaiety of affection from her whenever I happened to catch her eye. Gradually I began to realize that she liked me, that she had no option to liking me, and that unless I took great pains to alienate her she would go on liking me, for a couple of years at least. It was very pleasant to receive such uncritical love, because it left me free to bestow love; my kisses were met by small warm rubbery unrejecting cheeks and soft dovey mumblings of delight.

Indeed, it must have been in expectation of this love that I had insisted upon having her, or rather refrained from not having her: something in me had clearly known before I did that there would be compensations. I was not of course treated to that phrase which greets all reluctant married mothers, "I bet you wouldn't be without her now," so often repeated after the event, in the full confidence of nature, because I suppose people feared I might turn on them and say, Yes I certainly would, which would be mutually distressing for questioner and me. And in many ways I thought that I certainly would prefer to be without her, as one might reasonably prefer to lack beauty or intelligence or riches, or any other such sources of mixed blessing and pain. Things about life with a baby drove me into frenzies of weeping several times a week, and not only having milk on my clean jerseys. As so often in life, it was impossible to choose, even theoretically, between advantage and disadvantage, between profit and loss: I was up quite unmistakably against No Choice. So the best one could do was to put a good face on it, and to avoid adding to the large and largely discussed number of sad warnings that abounded in the part of the world that I knew. I managed very well, and the general verdict was, Extraordinary Rosamund, she really seems happy, she must have really wanted one after all.

. . . . .

I had thought, dimly, that after the birth I would once more become interested in men, as such, but nothing like this seemed to happen. I did from time to time think that it would be comforting to have a little adult affection, but in some strange way I did not seem to like anyone enough any more. I felt curiously disenchanted, almost as I

might have felt had I been truly betrayed and deceived and abandoned. The only person of whom I thought with any tenderness, apart from my small pliant daughter, was George. I still listened to his voice on the radio, comforted to know he was still so near, however pointlessly, and wondering what he was doing. Occasionally, when roused to a pitch of peculiar transport by Octavia's charm, I felt like ringing him up and telling him about her, but I never did; I fancied that I knew enough about human nature to know that no amount of charm could possibly balance the quite unjustified sense of obligation, financial, personal, and emotional, that such a revelation would instantly set to work. So I spared him and myself. Sometimes I thought I saw a likeness to him in Octavia, and more often I thought I caught a glimpse of George himself, but it was never him, it was always smooth young men selling things in antique shops or expensive tailors, who might have been him.

. . . . .

The night before Octavia's operation I lay awake, enduring what might have been my last battle with the vast shadowy monsters of doubt. Some on such occasions must doubt the existence of God; it does not seem to be natural to survive such disasters with faith unimpaired. I find it more honourable to take events into consideration, when speaking of the mercy of God. But, in fact, the subject of God did not much cross my mind, for I had never given it much thought, having been brought up a good Fabian rationalist, and notions such as the afterlife and heaven seemed to me crude quite literally beyond belief. Justice, however, preoccupied me. I could not rid myself of the notion that if Octavia were to die, this would be a vengeance upon my sin. The innocent shall suffer for the guilty. What my sin had been I found difficult to determine, for I could not convince myself that sleeping with George had been a sin; on the contrary, in certain moods I tended to look on it as the only virtuous action of my life. A sense of retribution nevertheless hung heavily over me, and what I tried to preserve that night was faith not in God but in the laws of chance.

Towards morning, I began to think that my sin lay in my love for her. For five minutes or so, I almost hoped that she might die, and thus relieve me of the corruption and the fatality of love. Ben Jonson said of his dead child, my sin was too much hope of thee, loved boy. We too easily take what the poets write as figures of speech, as pretty images, as strings of *bons mots*. Sometimes perhaps they speak the truth.

In the morning, when it was time to get up and get dressed and gather together her pitiably small requirements, I got out of bed and got down on my knees and said, Oh God, let her survive, let her live, let her be all right, and God was created by my need, perhaps.

We went to the hospital and I handed her over, and she smiled at me, then cried when they took her away. The world had contracted to the small size of her face and her clenching, waving hands. The poignancy was intolerable: her innocence, her gaiety, her size. I

went away, and I walked up and down Marylebone Road. I cannot think what I did with the hours. I did not go back till half an hour after they had told me to inquire, and when I got there I did not dare to ask. I stood there, waiting, till someone recognized me and came over smiling and told me that everything had gone extremely well, and that Mr. Protheroe sent his regards and hoped to see me, and that there was every hope of complete success. As on the day when I had first guessed at her condition, I could not believe that a mere recital of facts could thus change my fate: I stood there, dumbly, wondering if it could be the truth that she had told me, or whether she had got the wrong name, the wrong data, the wrong message. But she went on smiling and reassuring me, and soon I believed her, for it became suddenly clear that it was quite out of the question that anything should have gone wrong, that of course we had been lucky, Octavia and I. When I got round to speaking, I asked if I could see her, and they said to come back in the morning, as she was still unconscious and not to be disturbed. Of course, I said humbly, and backed away, full of gratitude towards the lot of them: then I went and wept copiously in the cloakroom, and then I went home.

It was only when I got home that I began to be preoccupied by certain details upon which I had not previously dared to exercise my mind. What would Octavia think when she woke in the hospital? Would she be in terrible pain from the operation? Would they feed her properly? Would she cry? Earlier it had seemed presumptuous to have considered these things, but now their importance swelled minute by minute in my mind. The threat of fatality removed, the conditions of life at once resumed their old significance. It was the strangeness, I thought, more than the pain that would afflict her, for she liked nobody but me; even Mrs. Jennings and Lydia she regarded only with tolerance, and strangers she disliked with noisy vehemence. Lord knows what incommunicable small terrors infants go through, unknown to all. We disregard them, we say they forget, because they have not the words to make us remember, because they cannot torment our consciences with a recital of their woes. By the time they learn to speak they have forgotten the details of their complaints, and so we never know. They forget so quickly, we say, because we cannot contemplate the fact that they never forget.

. . . . .

"Why don't you come and have a look at my baby?" I said.

"Wouldn't it waken her?" [George] said, reluctant.

"She never wakes," I said, and I led him along the corridor for my amusement and not for his, and opened the door of her room. There she lay, her eyes closed, her fists sweetly composed upon the pillow, and I looked from her face to George, and I acknowledged that it was too late, much much too late. It was no longer in me to feel for anyone what I felt for my child; compared with the perplexed fitful illuminations of George, Octavia shone there with a faint, constant and pearly brightness quite strong enough to eclipse any more garish future blaze. A bad investment, I knew, this affection, and one that would leave me in the dark and the cold in years to come; but then what warmer passion ever lasted longer than six months?

"She's beautiful," said George.

"Yes, isn't she?" I said.

But it was these words of apparent agreement that measured our hopeless distance, for he had spoken for my sake and I because it was the truth. Love had isolated me more securely than fear, habit or indifference. There was one thing in the world that I knew about, and that one thing was Octavia. I had lost the taste for half-knowledge. George, I could see, knew nothing with such certainty. I neither envied nor pitied his indifference, for he was myself, the self that but for accident, but for fate, but for chance, but for womanhood, I would still have been.

Excerpt from

A Death in the Family

James Agee
(1909-1955)

When James Agee died suddenly in 1955, his novel, A Death in the Family, *was unfinished. The book was published very much as the author had left it. In 1958 the novel won the Pulitzer Prize for fiction, the highest literary award in the United States.*

In the selection that follows, Rufus and his father share an evening together as they have done many times before. The narrator records the child's thoughts and feelings as if he were looking back at the scene years later, knowing more in the remembering than he could have known as a child. As the story develops, Jay, the child's father, is killed in an automobile accident the following evening. Thus, this shared experience is the last time Rufus sees his father alive. In learning this later in the novel, the reader is made aware of the specialness of this one night and why Rufus remembers it in such detail.

They turned through the swinging doors into a blast of odor and sound. There was no music: only the density of bodies and of the smell of a market bar, of beer, whiskey and country bodies, salt and leather; no clamor; only the thick quietude of crumpled talk. Rufus stood looking at the light on a damp spittoon and he heard his father ask for whiskey, and knew he was looking up and down the bar for men he might know. But they seldom come from so far away as the Powell River Valley; and Rufus soon realized that his father had found, tonight, no one he knew. He looked up his father's length and watched him bend backwards, tossing one off in one jolt in a lordly manner, and a moment later heard him say to the man next him, "That's my boy"; and felt a warmth of love. Next moment he felt his father's hands under his arm-pits, and he was lifted, high, and seated on the bar, looking into a long row of huge bristling and bearded red faces. The eyes of the men nearest him were interested, and kind; some of them smiled; further away, the eyes were impersonal and questioning, but now even some of these began to smile. Somewhat timidly, but feeling assured that his father was proud of him and that he was liked, and liked these men, he smiled back; and suddenly many of the men laughed. He was disconcerted by their laughter and lost his smile a moment; then, realizing it was friendly, smiled again; and again they laughed. His father smiled at him. "That's my boy," he said warmly. "Six years old, and he can already read like I couldn't read when I was twice his age."

Rufus felt a sudden hollowness in his voice, and all along the bar, and in his

The Banjo Lesson *by Henry O. Tanner (1786-1858). Oil on canvas.*

Tanner painted landscapes and biblical themes, as well as moments of family life. He traveled to Europe and the Holy Land to develop his artistic training and insights. How would you describe the personal bond that unites the teacher and his pupil in The Banjo Lesson? *What details in the painting suggest the relationship you perceive?*

own heart. But how does he fight, he thought. You don't brag about smartness if your son is brave. He felt the anguish of shame, but his father did not seem to notice, except that as suddenly as he had lifted him up to the bar, he gently lifted him down again. "Reckon I'll have another," he said, and drank it more slowly; then, with a few good nights, they went out.

His father proffered a Life Saver, courteously, man to man; he took it with a special sense of courtesy. It sealed their contract. Only once had his father felt it necessary to say to him, "I wouldn't tell your mama, if I were you"; he had known, from then on, that he could trust Rufus; and Rufus had felt gratitude in this silent trust. They walked away from Market Square, along a dark and nearly empty street, sucking their Life Savers; and Rufus' father reflected, without particular concern, that Life Savers were not quite life saver enough; he had better play very tired tonight, and turn away the minute they got in bed.

The deaf and dumb asylum was deaf and dumb, his father observed very quietly, as if he were careful not to wake it, as he always did on these evenings; its windows showed black in its pale brick, as the nursing woman's eyes, and it stood deep and silent among the light shadows of its trees. Ahead, Asylum Avenue lay bleak beneath its lamps. Latticed in pawnshop iron, an old saber caught the glint of a street lamp, a mandolin's belly glowed. In a closed drug store stood Venus de Milo, her golden body laced in elastic straps. The stained glass of the L&N Depot smoldered like

an exhausted butterfly, and at the middle of the viaduct they paused to inhale the burst of smoke from a switch engine which passed under; Rufus, lifted, the cinders stinging his face, was grateful no longer to feel fear at this suspension over the tracks and the powerful locomotives. Far down the yard, a red light flicked to green; a moment later, they heard the thrilling click. It was ten-seven by the depot clock. They went on, more idly than before.

If I could fight, thought Rufus. If I were brave; he would never brag how I could read: Brag. Of course. "Don't you brag." That was it. What it meant. Don't brag you're smart if you're not brave. You've got nothing to brag about. Don't you brag.

The young leaves of Forest Avenue wavered against street lamps and they approached their corner.

It was a vacant lot, part rubbed bare clay, part over-grown with weeds, rising a little from the sidewalk. A few feet in from the sidewalk there was a medium-sized tree and, near enough to be within its shade in daytime, an outcrop of limestone like a great bundle of dirty laundry. If you sat on a certain part of it the trunk of the tree shut off the weak street lamp a block away, and it seemed very dark. Whenever they walked downtown and walked back home, in the evenings, they always began to walk more slowly, from about the middle of the viaduct, and as they came near this corner they walked more slowly still, but with purpose; and paused a moment, at the edge of the sidewalk; then, without speaking, stepped into the dark lot and sat down on the rock, looking out over the steep face of the hill and at the lights of North Knoxville. Deep in the valley an engine coughed and browsed; couplings settled their long chains, and the empty cars sounded like broken drums. A man came up the far side of the street, walking neither slow nor fast, not turning his head, as he paused, and quite surely not noticing them; they watched him until he was out of sight, and Rufus felt, and was sure that his father felt, that though there was no harm in the man and he had as good a right as they did to be there, minding his own business, their journey was interrupted from the moment they first saw him until they saw him out of sight. Once he was out of sight they realized more pleasure in their privacy than before; they really relaxed in it. They looked across the darkness at the lights of North Knoxville. They were aware of the quiet leaves above them, and looked into them and through them. They looked between the leaves into the stars. Usually on these evening waits, or a few minutes before going on home, Rufus' father smoked a cigarette through, and when it was finished, it was time to get up and go on home. But this time he did not smoke. Up to recently he had always said something about Rufus' being tired, when they were still about a block away from the corner; but lately he had not done so, and Rufus realized that his father stopped as much because he wanted to, as on Rufus' account. He was just not in a hurry to get home, Rufus realized; and, far more important, it was clear that he liked to spend these few minutes with Rufus. Rufus had come recently to feel a quiet kind of anticipation of the corner, from the moment they finished crossing the viaduct; and, during the ten to twenty minutes they sat on the rock, a particular kind of contentment, unlike any other that he knew. He did not know what this was, in words or ideas, or what the reason was; it was simply all that he saw and felt. It was, mainly, knowing that his father, too, felt a particular kind of contentment, here, unlike any other, and that their kinds of contentment were much alike, and depended on each other. Rufus seldom had at all sharply the feeling that he and his father were estranged, yet they must have been, and he must have felt it, for always during these quiet moments on the rock a part of his sense of complete contentment lay in the feeling that they were reconciled, that there was really no division, no estrangement, or none so strong, anyhow, that it could mean much, by comparison with the unity that was so firm and assured, here. He felt that although his father loved their home and loved all of them, he was more lonely than the contentment of this family love could help; that it even increased his loneliness, or made it hard for him not to be lonely. He felt that sitting out here, he was not lonely; or if he was, that he felt on good terms with the loneliness; that he was a homesick man, and that here on the rock, though he might be more homesick than ever, he was well. He knew that a very important part of his well-being came of staying a few minutes away from home, very quietly, in the dark, listening to the leaves if they moved, and looking at the stars; and that his own, Rufus' own presence, was fully as indispensable to this well-being. He knew that each of them knew of the other's well-being, and of the reasons for it, and knew how each depended on the other, how each meant more to the other, in this most important of all ways, then anyone or anything else in the world; and that the best of this well-being lay in this mutual knowledge, which was neither concealed nor revealed. He knew these things very distinctly, but not, of course, in any such way as we have of suggesting them in words. There were no words, or even ideas, or formed emotions, of the kind that have been suggested here, no more in the man than in the boy child. These realizations moved clearly through the senses, the memory, the feelings, the mere feeling of the place they paused at, about a quarter of a mile from home, on a rock under a stray tree that had grown in the city, their feet on undomesticated clay, facing north through the night over the Southern Railway tracks and over North Knoxville, towards the deeply folded small mountains and the Powell River Valley, and above them, the trembling lanterns of the universe, seeming so near, so intimate, that when air stirred the leaves and their hair, it seemed to be the breathing, the whispering of the stars. Sometimes on these evenings his father would hum a little and the humming would break open into a word or two, but he never finished even a part of a tune, for silence was even more pleasurable, and sometimes he would say a few words, of very little consequence, but would never seek to say much, or to finish what he was say-

ing, or to listen for a reply; for silence again was even more pleasurable. Sometimes, Rufus had noticed, he would stroke the wrinkled rock and press his hand firmly against it; and sometimes he would put out his cigarette and tear and scatter it before it was half finished. But this time he was much quieter than ordinarily. They slackened their walking a little sooner than usual and walked a little more slowly, without a word, to the corner; and hesitated, before stepping off the sidewalk into the clay, purely for the luxury of hesitation; and took their place on the rock without breaking silence. As always, Rufus' father took off his hat and put it over the front of his bent knee, and as always, Rufus imitated him, but this time his father did not roll a cigarette. They waited while the man came by, intruding on their privacy, and disappeared, as someone nearly always did, and then relaxed sharply into the pleasure of their privacy; but this time Rufus' father did not hum, nor did he say anything, nor even touch the rock with his hand, but sat with his hands hung between his knees and looked out over North Knoxville, hearing the restive assemblage of the train; and after there had been silence for a while, raised his head and looked up into the leaves and between the leaves into the broad stars, not smiling, but with his eyes more calm and grave and his mouth strong and more quiet, than Rufus had ever seen his eyes and his mouth; and as he watched his father's face, Rufus felt his father's hand settle, without groping or clumsiness, on the top of his bare head; it took his forehead and smoothed it, and pushed the hair backward from his forehead, and held the back of his head while Rufus pressed his head backward against the firm hand, and, in reply to that pressure, clasped over his right ear and cheek, over the whole side of his head, and drew Rufus' head quietly and strongly against the sharp cloth that covered his father's body, through which Rufus could feel the breathing ribs; then relinquished him, and Rufus sat upright, while the hand lay strongly on his shoulder, and he saw that his father's eyes had become still more clear and grave and that the deep lines around his mouth were satisfied; and looked up at what his father was so steadily looking at, at the leaves which silently breathed and at the stars which beat like hearts. He heard a long, deep sigh break from his father, and then his father's abrupt voice: *"Well . . ."* and the hand lifted from him and they both stood up. The rest of the way home they did not speak, or put on their hats. When he was nearly asleep Rufus heard once more the crumpling of freight cars, and deep in the night he heard the crumpling of subdued voices and the words, "Naw: I'll probly be back before they're asleep"; then quick feet creaking quietly downstairs. But by the time he heard the creaking and departure of the Ford, he was already so deeply asleep that it seemed only a part of a dream, and by next morning, when his mother explained to them why his father was not at breakfast, he had so forgotten the words and the noises that years later, when he remembered them, he could never be sure that he was not making them up.

Excerpt from

Blackberry Winter

Margaret Mead
(1901-1978)

Margaret Mead, one of the pioneers in anthropology, spent her early career studying tribal and family customs among the primitive peoples of the South Sea Islands. She published the results of her research in books that contributed important insights to understanding the modern family.

In her autobiography, Blackberry Winter, *Margaret Mead tells about her own family, from whom she received her first strong sense of family ties. In the following excerpt, she recounts how she grew into the role of grandmother, having learned from her own grandmother and mother. She gives a delightful view of herself as both granddaughter and grandmother in the continuing human family. One reviewer called the entire book "a grandmother's tale for a time that needs grandmothers very badly."*

My mother was trustworthy in all matters that concerned our care. Grandma was trustworthy in a quite different way. She meant exactly what she said, always. If you borrowed her scissors, you returned them. In like case, Mother would wail ineffectually, "Why does everyone borrow my scissors and never return them?" and Father would often utter idle threats. But Grandma never threatened. She never raised her voice. She simply commanded respect and obedience by her complete expectation that she would be obeyed. And she never gave silly orders. She became my model when, in later life, I tried to formulate a role for the modern parent who can no longer exact obedience merely by virtue of being a parent and yet must be able to get obedience when it is necessary. Grandma never said, "Do this because Grandma says so," or "because Grandma wants you to do it."

She simply said, "Do it," and I knew from her tone of voice that it was necessary.

. . . . .

As the years went by, I had carefully not let myself hope that I would have grandchildren, as I knew before Catherine had children I would be old enough to be a great-grandmother. Great-grandmotherhood is something we do not think of as a likely possibility of the human condition, even now when it is becoming more common.

But I did think how delightful it would be, if it happened, to see my daughter with a child. And I wondered what kind of child Catherine and Barkev Kassarjian would have—she with her long ancestry from the British Isles and he with his long Armenian heritage in the Middle East, she with her English fairness and he with his dark eyes and black hair. Thinking back to my grandmother and my mother and the kind of mother I had tried to be and remembering all the different kinds of mothering people who had cared for my daughter in her childhood—her English nanny, her lovely young aunt Mary, and her devoted godmother, Aunt Marie, who brought in the generation of my grandmother's day when people respected heirlooms and passed their dolls on from generation to generation—I wondered what kind of child my daughter would have and what kind of mother she would be.

. . . . .

When the news came that Sevanne Margaret was born, I suddenly realized that through no act of my own I had become biologically related to a new human being. This was one thing that had never come up in discussions of grandparenthood and had never before occurred to me. In many primitive societies grandparents and grandchildren are aligned together. A child who has to treat his father with extreme respect may joke with his grandfather and playfully call his grandmother "wife." The tag that grandparents and grandchildren get along so well because they have a common enemy is explicitly faced in many societies. In our own society the point most often made is that grandparents can enjoy their grandchildren because they have no responsibility for them, they do not have to discipline them, and they lack the guilt and anxiety of parenthood. All these things were familiar. But I had never thought how strange it was to be

involved at a distance in the birth of a biological descendant.

I always have been acutely aware of the way one life touches another—of the ties between myself and those whom I have never met, but who read *Coming of Age in Samoa* and decided to become anthropologists. From the time of my childhood I was able to conceive of my relationship to all my forebears, some of whose genes I carry, both those I did not know even by name and those who helped to bring me up, particularly my paternal grandmother. But the idea that as a grandparent one was dealing with action at a distance—that somewhere, miles away, a series of events occurred that changed one's own status forever—I had not thought of that and I found it very odd.

I felt something like the shock that must be felt by those who have lived all their lives secure in their citizenship in the nation of their birth and who then, suddenly, by the arbitrary act of some tyrannical government, find that they are disenfranchised—as happened to the old aristocracy in Russia after the revolution, to the Jews in Germany in the 1930's, and to the Turkish Armenians in Turkey. But of course what happened to me was not an arbitrary denial of something I had regarded as irreversibly given, but rather an arbitrary confirmation of a state which I felt that I myself had done nothing to bring about. Scientists and philosophers have speculated at length about the source of man's belief that he is a creature with a future life or, somewhat less commonly, with a life that preceded his life on earth. Speculation may be the only kind of answer that is possible, but I would now add to the speculations that are more familiar another of my own: the extraordinary sense of having been transformed not by any act of one's own but by the act of one's child.

Then, as a new grandmother, I began both to relive my own daughter's infancy and to observe the manifestations of temperament in the tiny creature who was called Vanni—to note how she learned to ignore the noisy carpentry as the house was finished around her but was so sensitive to changes in the human voice that her mother had to keep low background music playing to mask the change in tone of voice that took place when someone who had been speaking then answered the telephone. I remarked how she responded to pattern in the brightly colored chintzes and the mobiles that had been prepared for her. I showed the movies of Cathy's birth and early childhood, to which my daughter commented, "I think my baby is brighter"—or prettier, or livelier—"than your baby!"

However, I felt none of the much trumpeted freedom from responsibility that grandparents are supposed to feel. Actually, it seems to me that the obliga-tion to be a resource but not an inter-ference is just as preoccupying as the at-tention one gives to one's own children. I think we do not allow sufficiently for the obligation we lay on grandparents to keep themselves out of the picture— not to interfere, not to spoil, not to in-sist, not to intrude—and, if they are old and frail, to go and live apart in an old people's home (by whatever name it may be called) and to say that they are happy when, once in a great while, their children bring their grandchildren to visit them.

Most American grandparents are supported in their laborious insistence on not being a nuisance by the way they felt toward their own parents and by the fierceness with which, as young adults, they resented interference by their parents and grandparents. But I had none of this. I had loved my grand-mother and I had valued the way my mother nursed and loved her children. My only complaint when I took Cathy home as a baby was that Mother could not remember as much as I would have liked about the things it was useful to know. And I had quite gladly shared my baby with her nurse and with my closest friends.

Hirshhorn Museum and Sculpture Garden, Smithsonian Institution, Washington, D.C.

Family Group *by Henry Moore (1898-   ). British. Sculpture, bronze.*

Moore, an influential modern sculptor, shapes not only solid masses but voids (hollows and holes) that may represent the roundness of a chest or head or emphasize relations between persons. In this sculpture, a hollowed torso symbolizes a place of shelter for the child.

Excerpt from

The Names

N. Scott Momaday
(1934-   )

Momaday, a Kiowa Indian, grew up on the Southwest plains of Oklahoma. He often writes of the rich cultural heritage that played such an important part in shaping his life. In his Pulitzer Prize-winning novel, House Made of Dawn, *he describes both the beauty and the chaos of growing up between two cultures. In* The Names, *from which the following excerpt is taken, Momaday tells his own story and affectionately traces the lives of his ancestors over the past century. Currently, Momaday is a professor of English at Stanford University.*

It seems reasonable to suppose that I visited my great-grandmother on other occasions, but I remember only this once, and I remember it very well. My father leads me into her room. It is dark and close inside, and I cannot see until my eyes become accustomed to the dim light. There is a certain odor in the room and not elsewhere in the house, the odor of my great-grandmother's old age. It is not unpleasant, but it is most particular and exclusive, as much hers as is her voice or her hair or the nails of her hands. Such a thing has not only the character of great age but something also of the deep self, of one's own dignity and well-being. Because of this, I believe, this old blind woman is like no one I have ever seen or shall ever see. To a child her presence is formidable. My father is talking to her in Kiowa, and I do not understand what is being said, only that the talk is of me. She is seated on the side of her bed, and my father brings me to stand directly in front of her. She reaches out for me and I place my hands in hers. *Eh neh neh neh neh.* She begins to weep very softly in a high, thin, hollow voice. Her hands are little and soft, so soft that they seem not to consist in flesh and bone, but in the softest fiber, cotton or fine wool. Her voice is so delicate, so surely expressive of her deep feelings. Long afterwards I think: That was a wonderful and beautiful thing that happened in my life. There, on that warm, distant afternoon: an old woman and a child, holding hands across the generations. There is great good in such a remembrance; I cannot imagine that it might have been lost upon me.

31

Excerpt from

All Real Life is Meeting

J. H. Oldham
(1874-1969)

We all relate to two worlds, the world of things and the world of persons. Theologian Martin Buber, in his influential work I and Thou *(1923), first emphasized this distinction, calling the former the world of "It" and the latter the world of "Thou." But it is the manner in which we relate to these separate worlds that makes us what we are. When we feel, observe, experience or use something—and that "something" may be a person—we are in the realm of "It," the world of things. If a genuine encounter or meeting occurs between ourselves and another person, we are in a different realm entirely, the world of "Thou." It is this response, this "I-Thou" relationship, that Buber says makes us persons.*

His theory about human relationships, described by J. H. Oldham in the selection below, offers a stimulating context for understanding the ways people relate to each other and ultimately to the "pulsating life of the universe." We can apply this theory to our own lives as well as to the other selections in this session and study unit.

Martin Buber made outstanding contributions to religion, philosophy, education and sociology. A leader of the Jewish community in Germany in the 1930s, he participated in the early Zionist movement and was a professor of social philosophy in Israel from 1938 to 1951.

The world, Buber tells us, has a twofold meaning. Man's attitude to it is dual. The two attitudes are different and uninterchangeable. To understand this twofold nature of human existence is the beginning of wisdom.

This twofold attitude is expressed in the fundamental difference between our relation to persons and our relation to things or objects. That is not precisely Buber's language. He speaks of the difference between our relation to the world of "Thou" and our relation to the world of "It." But the term "Thou" has disappeared in English as a form of address to a human person, though it survives in the language of the most personal of all relations—the language of prayer. For our present purpose Buber's meaning can sufficiently be expressed by the contrast between persons and things, provided we understand clearly that, in the sense in which the words are here used, persons are not always persons nor things always things. Persons may be, and for certain purposes must be, treated as things, as when we organize them or discipline them or care for their health of body or of mind; and even in the most personal meeting the "Thou" who addresses us and to whom we respond is continually passing over into a "He" or "She" (which in respect of the twofold attitude is the same as an

Vanity Fair *by Henry Koerner (1915-   ). Oil on composition board.*

The style of this painting is similar to that of Flemish painters such as Brueghel (see The Fall of Icarus *in Session 6) because of its panorama of social activities and landscape details. The composition of the painting is basically a circle, which leads our eyes around to scenes of vanity and self-indulgence. No sign of happiness or contentment can be perceived. Why do you think the older couple and the children on the bridge are situated outside the center of activity?*

"It"). We become aware, for example, of the tone of our friend's voice or of the colour of his hair or of his individual characteristics, and he no longer confronts us as a person, but has become an object among other objects. Every human person is at the same time an "It." On the other hand, both animate and inanimate nature can meet us in a personal approach—confront us, that is to say, not as something to be experienced and used, but as entering into relation with us, making demands on us and evoking from us a full personal response of our whole being.

This distinction between two fundamental attitudes may appear at first sight difficult and abstruse. But in reality what Buber is talking about is the common stuff of our ordinary experience. If it seems difficult, it can only be because we have not been in the habit of reflecting on our experience; and partly also because, as we shall see, our experience has become distorted. Things have gained so strong a hold over us as to blunt our sensitiveness to the personal.

The World of Things

Let us look first at the world of things. I observe something, I imagine something, I feel something, I think something, I will something. These activities have all to do with "It," and taken together they seem to include the whole range of our experience. To the world of objects belongs the whole of the vast domain over which science reigns. To it belong also the spheres of industry and commerce, the tasks of the economist and statesman. All organiza-

tion, all arranging and ordering have to do with things. From the mechanization of life, from the pressure of institutions, men seek an escape into the region of feeling, hoping there to find the meaning of personal life. But feelings, as the feelings of an individual, belong also to the world of "It." It might seem as though we had included the whole of life in the world of things. It is true that everything that we *experience* and everything that we *use* belong to that world. Just as the whole of life is functional, so it is embedded inextricably in a world of "It" and lived in an unbroken relation to things.

The World of Persons

Yet nothing could be farther from the truth than that man's life consists only in activities which have some *thing* for an object. From out of this infinite, inexhaustible world of things which he is so eager to explore, to taste, to appropriate and to bend to his purposes there may come to him unexpectedly a voice. What that voice may say to him he cannot himself control; he can only listen and respond. In relation to the world of things man is master; he observes, measures, weighs, judges, arranges, and orders. But in the encounter with another person he is no longer the sole arbiter; he does not alone control the situation. He is addressed and has to respond. The situation to which he has to respond is not created by him, but created for him. He *meets* the other. He has passed from his solitariness into community, where there is not one point of view, but two or more.

Things exist, events take place, in the

context of space and time. Each is bounded by something else. But a person is not a thing among other things. We do not *experience* a person—so far as we experience another person it is as a "He" or "She"—but enter into relation with him. He gives himself to us; we give ourselves to him. Meeting takes place not in a fixed and stable world of unalterable law, but in the free and living present in which the world is continually born anew.

The meeting is unforeseeable. It comes unexpectedly. It is not found by seeking. We can, of course, make a date, and keep it, but that does not in itself ensure the personal meeting. The other meets us by grace; our response to the meeting is our destiny. We cannot "order" the world of personal meeting; only things can be ordered and planned.

It is through our responses to other persons that we become persons. It is others who challenge, enlighten and enrich us. There is no such thing as the isolated individual. We are persons only in our relation with other persons. How greatly this has been forgotten is evident when one picks up almost any modern work or statement on education. So strong is the humanist, individualistic tradition that the starting-point is almost always the individual child, and the question is discussed how he may rightly relate himself to other persons— how he may become social. But in reality the relation comes first; only out of it is personality born.

Reality is the lived relation. Through sharing in the giving and receiving of mutual being the "I" becomes real. "Reality is an activity in which I share

without being able to appropriate it for myself. Where there is no sharing there is no reality. Where there is appropriation by the self there is no reality." *All real life is meeting.*

Every day the meeting awaits us. But whether it takes place depends on our choice. Our egoism continually tempts us to evade it. We prefer to wrap ourselves in our solitariness and pursue our solitary purposes. As a protection against the meeting we build round us a wall of ideas—a philosophy, a theology, a tradition, a point of view. Nothing can reach us that does not get through its meshes. We take refuge in an imagined world where we are safe from the disturbing challenge of the "Thou."

Not only those about us but the great ones of the past are ready to meet us. They are willing to become alive again and enter into contemporary life. But we are content too often to pile up information about them rather than allow them really to speak to us. Day by day opportunities of meeting touch us with their wings and, finding no eagerness of response, pass us by. The windows through which we might have caught glimpses of eternity remain closed, and our life narrows and hardens into death.

The difference between the lonely world in which the individual in his isolation experiences and uses and the living world of relation is no new discovery. Raymond Lull understood it, when he wrote in the thirteenth century, "He who loves not lives not"; the writer of the First Epistle of St. John knew it, when he wrote, "He that loveth not, abideth in *death.*"

In both the life of the individual and

The Subway *by George Tooker (1920-   ). Egg tempera on composition board.*

The themes in Tooker's paintings explore the kinds of anxieties we all know—such as being among strangers in a place where we do not know the rules. The woman in The Subway *seems to be looking without success for clues to help her reach her destination. What emotions are invoked in the woman by the half-hidden figures in the corridors and the barbed aspect of the turnstile? What relationship, if any, exists between the persons in the painting? What is the viewer's reaction?*

the history of the race there is a progressive increase in the extent and dominion of the world of things. The ability to experience the world and to use what it contains steadily grows. With this growing capacity in the one direction there is apt to go a decrease in man's power to enter into relation.

. . . . .

How May We Be Saved?
. . . How may the fundamental change come about, which will free society

Whitney Museum of American Art, New York, New York.

from the baleful incubus of "It" and restore the healthy and life-giving intercourse of persons living in community? Buber's answer is an arresting one. It was once believed that power could be obtained over an evil spirit by addressing it by its real name. In the same way the seemingly all-powerful world of "It" which threatens to crush the spirit of man will fade into nothingness before those who know it for what it really is—something which is separated and alienated from true life. The word "It" is a word of separation. The thing stands over against you in its separateness; you may take it, and use it, but it does not give itself to you. The word "Thou" is a word of union. When you utter it—when you are addressed and you respond—you are re-united with the pulsating life of the universe. For in every "Thou" that addresses us and calls us to a responsible decision, there speaks the voice of the eternal "Thou," the source of all life, the creative, living spirit of God.

37

The answer to our question is, then, the answer of religion. There is that in the universe which is waiting to meet us. Let us go forth to meet it. What will come from the meeting is not in our hands. If it were, there would be no meeting; we should be still in the prison-house of our own self-chosen purposes in which we control and order things.

What comes out of the meeting is God's affair. In every real encounter with life and with our fellow-men we meet the living Spirit, the Creator of life. God is not to be found by leaving the world. He is not found by staying in the world. But those who in their daily living respond with their whole being to the "Thou" by whom they find themselves addressed are caught up into union with the true life of the world. "Inasmuch as ye did it unto one of these My brethren, even these least, ye did it unto *Me*."

Those who meet—who answer in responsible decision to the word addressed to them by another—are already sharers in eternal life. They are already bound together in community. They are allied with the power of the eternal Spirit—a power that can destroy the domination of things, overturn the proudest monuments of ambition and acquisitiveness and restore man to his true life which is realized only in community.

Sexuality and Personality

Anthony Storr
(1920-   )

Anthony Storr is a leading British psychiatrist who attempts to help people understand sexuality in the wider context of total personal growth. In his view, impersonal and deviant sexual behavior is directly related to a lack of love, particularly in early childhood experiences. He believes that being comfortable with our sexuality (which is not the same as parading it or giving it indiscriminate physical expression) is important for the development of a mature and balanced personal life.

One important emphasis in the following excerpt is that the quality of sexual life (by which he does not mean technical prowess, but the degree to which it reflects a deeply human union with another person) has implications for the quality of all our relationships—even those that might otherwise be purely It experiences ("simply to exchange information, or to discuss ideas, or in some professional setting").

In Western society today we are only just beginning to study sexuality objectively, despite the fact that the sexual impulse is a basic and integral part of human nature which deeply affects the character and conduct of each one of us. The way in which an individual has or has not come to terms with his sexual instinct determines many aspects of his character, including both his confidence in himself and also his capacity for making relationships with other human beings. . . .

This statement may be disputed; since many people would like to dissociate their erotic behaviour from the rest of their life and, in attempting to do so, treat sex as a fundamentally unimportant part of their existence. This is especially true of those who either have sexual difficulties which they are ashamed to acknowledge, or a secret sexual life which they feel bound to conceal. Such people find it a relief to pretend that sex can be relegated to a separate compartment of their lives, stored away in a safe deposit to which no other person is ever allowed access. But the front which people of this kind are compelled to present to the world is a dull, unemotional façade; for sex is so important, so pervasive, and so intimately connected with every aspect of personality that it cannot be separated from the person as a whole without impoverishing even superficial relationships. There are times when we meet other human beings simply to exchange information, or to discuss ideas, or in some professional setting. On such occasions the sexual aspect of ourselves is of minimal importance. But directly we meet people socially as people, our attitude to our own sexuality and to theirs becomes significant; for the kind of contact which we make with each other in ordinary social exchanges at a superficial level is determined by the capacity we possess for making deeply intimate relationships; and the ideal sexual relationship is probably the deepest and most intimate which we can experience.

The very words we use express the fact that, fundamentally, it is impossible to separate physical from mental in inter-personal relations. For do we not talk of *making contact* with another; of a person's *warmth* or *coldness;* of being *close* to someone or *distant;* and of being touched by another's interest or thoughtfulness? We are not, and cannot be, disembodied; and so our attitude to our own bodies and to those of other people is an important part of our total feeling towards even those with whom we may never exchange any more intimate gesture than a handshake. It is because of this that those who are ill-at-ease with their own sexuality are often detached and remote; for they are unable to allow their sexual selves to be manifest, and thus withdraw, both physically and psychologically, from the possibility of close contact. On the other hand, those who have been able to find sexual happiness are not generally afraid of intimacy, and are thus less guarded and more able to interchange

experience at even purely social levels of relationship.

. . . . .

Sexual intercourse may be said to be one aspect, perhaps the most basic and most important aspect, of a relationship between persons. In ideally mature form it is a relationship between a man and a woman in which giving and taking is equal, and in which the genitals are the most important channel through which love is expressed and received. It is one of the most natural, and certainly the most rewarding and the most life-enhancing of all human experiences. It is also the only one which both has a completely satisfying ending and yet can be endlessly repeated. Not even the greatest works of literature and music can stand such iteration. But this wonderfully enriching experience is only possible when the two people concerned have achieved a relationship in which, at least during the actual process of love-making, each is able to confront the other exactly as they are, with no reserves and no pretenses, and in which there is no admixture of childish dependence or fear.

In this most intimate relation, we are all vulnerable, and we all reveal ourselves for what we are.

The Kiss *by Edvard Munch (1863-1944). Norwegian. Watercolored etching.*

Munch's mother and sister died of tuberculosis when he was a child. In his early adult years, he also lost the two women he came to love, who died prematurely. Many of his paintings reflect a mood of impending doom; anxiety and tentativeness mark his subjects' faces. Yet The Kiss, *one of his best known works, deviates from the pattern by its affirmation of beauty, grace and fulfillment.*

We Are Transmitters

D. H Lawrence
(1885-1930)

D. H. Lawrence, who was born in England and raised among coal miners, deplored the depression and isolation that marked the lives of the people around him, as he observed them go about their daily routines with little or no real feeling. In his novels, written during the first part of the 20th century, he was one of the first to speak openly about the problems experienced in sexual relationships: "But giving life is not so easy." His writings focus on the difficulty we have in our struggle to know and understand each other, and he portrays this struggle between man and woman in terms of the simple happenings of daily life. In the poem below, Lawrence expresses one of his deepest convictions: That the life-giving force of sexuality permeates every area of our life.

As we live, we are transmitters of life.
And when we fail to transmit life, life fails to flow through us.

That is part of the mystery of sex, it is a flow onwards.
Sexless people transmit nothing.

And if, as we work, we can transmit life into our work,
life, still more life, rushes into us to compensate, to be ready
and we ripple with the life through the days.

Even if it is a woman making an apple dumpling, or a man a
    stool,
if life goes into the pudding, good is the pudding,
good is the stool,
content is the woman, with fresh life rippling in to her,
content is the man.

Give, and it shall be given unto you
is still the truth about life.
But giving life is not so easy.
It doesn't mean handing it out to some mean fool, or letting
    the living dead eat you up.
It means kindling the life-quality where it was not,
even if it's only in the whiteness of a washed pocket-handkerchief.

Further Readings

Browning, Elizabeth Barrett. *Sonnets from the Portuguese*. Considered some of the most beautiful love poems in the English language.

Fromm, Erich. *The Art of Loving*. 1958. Fromm believes that "love is the only sane and satisfying answer to the problem of human existence." A challenging essay that addresses romantic love, the love of parent for child, brotherly love, erotic love and the love of God.

Jansson, Tove. *Summer Book*. 1974. A day-by-day account of a summer on a Scandinavian island, as a little girl and her grandmother explore their surroundings and share themselves.

Laurence, Margaret. *The Stone Angel*. 1964. Ninety-year-old Hagar Shipley, querulous and independent, reviews her life and realizes that her pride and sense of propriety have been the cause of her unhappiness.

Sarton, May. *Kinds of Love*. 1970. The touching friendship of two old women and their circle of friends and family in a small New England town.

Tyler, Anne. *Search for Caleb*. 1975. Daniel Peck is obsessed with the idea of finding his long lost brother Caleb.

Walster, Elaine and G. William. *A New Look at Love*. 1975. Short essays on the psychology of love. What people look for and how they secure romance or escape it.

W. Glackens

Section 3

PART OF A SOCIAL WHOLE

In earlier times, people largely satisfied their need for meaning by thinking of themselves as members of a structured social group rather than as separate individuals. One's role as a contributor to the activity and survival of the group was sufficient to explain life's purpose. Membership in the extended family, the village, the tribe, the "working" or "ruling" class, the nation or some other larger whole provided a basic sense of belonging. The individual's handicaps, failures or inevitable death, however important for the person concerned and his close relatives, were somehow overshadowed and made understandable in the context of the continuing health and survival of the larger group. To find fulfillment and completion, the individual had to play his assigned role in society, conforming to laws and customs and participating in public rituals.

Throughout most of the Old Testament period, people did not expect a worthwhile life after death. In ancient Israel hope for the future meant—as it does for many Jews today—hope for the growth and health of the community. A person's life had meaning if he had children through whom he could continue to live as part of the chosen People of God.

Many of us can recall having known, in our childhood, a deep sense of belonging to a tangible community. The *Autobiography of a Papago Woman* reflects that feeling of satisfaction and comfort in the life of a close-knit family and tribal group. John Updike's "Family Meadow" conveys the same sense of belonging but in a different ethnic context.

These accounts, however, describe experiences which, while real enough and worth recalling, do not totally reflect family life today. Perhaps George Moore's short story, "Home Sickness," comes closer to

---

Washington Square (A Holiday in the Park) (1913) *by William Glackens (1870-1938).*
Pencil and wash, touched with white, over blue crayon outlines.

the mark as it describes an individual who yearns for a sense of belonging and place but is not sure how to achieve it. The vast size of a modern nation such as our own, the breakdown of strong community ties, the impersonality of industry and the ugly fact of unemployment have contributed to people's sense of isolation and to a profound doubt about their usefulness. How many of us feel—or have felt—that the world would go on just as well without us, that we are not a needed part of any whole?

The Preamble to the United States Constitution sets forth a great ideal: "We the People of the United States, in order to form a more perfect Union, establish justice, insure domestic tranquillity, provide for the common defense, promote the general welfare, and secure the blessings of liberty to ourselves and our posterity, do ordain and establish this Constitution for the United States of America." In practice, this whole has been divided, and this union has been far from perfect. Thus the dream of Martin Luther King, Jr., described in the famous speech included in this session, remains far from realized today.

Religion and ritual have often provided a powerful source of the sense of social unity. A sociologist described the practice of a Jewish lady in this way: "Though she eats alone, she always spreads a white linen handkerchief on her table because 'this my mother taught me to do. No matter how poor, we would eat off clean white linen, and say the prayers before touching anything to the mouth. And so I do it still. Whenever I sit down, I eat with God, my mother, and all the Jews who are doing these same things even if I can't see them.'" St. Paul compared the church to the body of Christ, of which each individual is a member, fulfilling an appointed and necessary task (I Corinthians 12). The central act of Christian worship is a sharing in the bread that is Christ's body.

Two selections in this section demonstrate ways that ritual and religion contribute to a sense of social unity. Betty Nickerson writes about festivals and holidays—times when we celebrate nature's wonder and rhythms as well as our communion with one another, giving us a sense of being part of a universal, timeless company. James Baldwin's description of a Sunday service depicts the way in which, each week, individual worshipers are caught up in the inspiration of the congregation.

The Family Meadow

John Updike
(1932-   )

"The Family Meadow," a short story appearing here in its entirety, is a marvelous mosaic of sensory objects: Sights, smells ("watermelons smelling of childhood cellars") and sounds ("the rhythmic chunking of thrown quoits"). Seldom resorting to dialogue to describe the family gathering, the author creates a picture so vivid in detail that we seem to know the members of the clan as they gather to affirm their part in this large and sprawling family.

John Updike focuses on family relationships in many of his novels and short stories, though his subject matter is more often the nuclear family than the extended family portrayed in the story that follows.

The family always reconvenes in the meadow. For generations it has been traditional, this particular New Jersey meadow, with its great walnut tree making shade for the tables and its slow little creek where the children can push themselves about in a rowboat and nibble watercress and pretend to fish. Early this morning, Uncle Jesse came down from the stone house that his father's father's brother had built and drove the stakes, with their carefully tied rag flags, that would tell the cars where to park. The air was still, inert with the post-dawn laziness that foretells the effort of a hot day, and between blows of his hammer Jesse heard the breakfast dishes clinking beneath the kitchen window and the younger collie barking behind the house. A mild man, Jesse moved scrupulously, mildly through the wet grass that he had scythed yesterday. The legs of his gray workman's pants slowly grew soaked with dew and milkweed spittle. When the stakes were planted, he walked out the lane with the REUNION signs, past the houses. He avoided looking at the houses, as if glancing into their wide dead windows would wake them.

By nine o'clock Henry has come up from Camden with a carful—Eva, Mary, Fritz, Fred, the twins, and, incredibly, Aunt Eula. It is incredible she is still alive, after seven strokes. Her shrivelled head munches irritably and her arms twitch, trying to shake off assistance, as if she intends to dance. They settle her in an aluminum chair beneath the walnut tree. She faces the creek, and the helpless waggle of her old skull seems to establish itself in sympathy with the oscillating shimmer of the sunlight on the slow water. The men, working in silent pairs whose unison is as profound as blood, carry down the tables from the barn, where they are stacked from one year to the next. In truth, it has been three summers since the last reunion, and it was feared that there might never be another. Aunt Jocelyn, her gray hair done up in braids, comes out of her kitchen to say hello on the dirt drive. Behind her lingers her granddaughter, Karen, in white Levi's and bare feet, with something shadowy and doubtful about her dark eyes, as if she had been intensely watching television. The girl's father—not here; he is working in Philadelphia—is Italian, and as she matures an alien beauty estranges her, so that during her annual visits to her grandparents' place, which when she was a child had seemed to her a green island, it is now she herself, at thirteen, who seems the island. She feels surrounded by the past, cut off from the images—a luncheonette, a civic swimming pool, an auditorium festooned with crepe paper—that represent life to her, the present, her youth. The air around her feels brown, as in old photographs. These men greeting her seem to have stepped from an album. The men, remembering their original prejudice against her mother's marrying a Catholic, are especially cordial to her, so jovially attentive that Jocelyn suddenly puts her arm around the girl, expressing a strange multitude of things; that she loves her, that she is one of them, that she needs to be shielded, suddenly, from the pronged kidding of men.

By ten-thirty Horace's crowd has come down from Trenton, and the Oranges clan is arriving, in several cars. The first car says it dropped Cousin Claude in downtown Burlington because he was sure that the second car, which had faded out of sight behind them, needed to be told the way. The second car, with a whoop of hilarity, says it took the bypass and never saw him. He arrives in a third car, driven by Jimmy and Ethel Thompson from Morristown, who say they saw his forlorn figure standing along Route 130 trying to thumb a ride and as they were passing him Ethel cried, "Why, I think that's Claude." Zealous and reckless, a true believer in good deeds, Claude is always getting into scrapes like this, and enjoying it. He stands surrounded by laughing women, a typical man of this family, tall, with a tribal boyishness, a stubborn refusal to look his age, to lose his hair. Though his face is pitted and gouged by melancholy, Claude looks closer to forty than the sixty he is, and, though he works in Newark, he still speaks with the rural softness and slide of middle New Jersey. He has the gift—the privilege—of making these women laugh; the women uniformly run to fat and their laughter has a sameness, a quality both naive and merciless, as if laughter meant too much to them. Jimmy and Ethel Thompson, whose name is not the family name, stand off to one side, in the unscythed grass, a fragile elderly couple whose links to family have all died away but who come because they received a mimeographed postcard inviting them. They are like those isolated corners of interjections and foreign syllables in a poorly planned crossword puzzle.

The twins bring down from the barn the horseshoes and the quoits. Uncle Jesse drives the stakes and pegs in the places that, after three summers, still show as spots of depressed sparseness in the grass. The sun, reaching toward noon, domineers over the meadow; the

Remains of the bean day festival, Wagon Mound, New Mexico *by Russell Lee (1903-   ). Photograph.*

shade of the walnut tree grows smaller and more noticeably cool. By noon, all have arrived, including the Dodge station wagon from central Pennsylvania, the young pregnant Wilmington cousin who married an airline pilot, and the White Plains people, who climb from their car looking like clowns, wearing red-striped shorts and rhinestone-studded sunglasses. Handshakes are exchanged that feel to one man like a knobbed wood carving and to the other like a cow's slippery, unresisting teat. Women kiss, kiss stickily, with little overlapping patches of adhesive cheek and clicking conflicts of spectacle rims, under the white unslanting sun. The very insects shrink toward the shade. The eating begins. Clams steam, corn steams, salad wilts, butter runs, hot dogs turn, torn chicken shines in the savage light. Iced tea, brewed in forty-quart milk cans, chuckles when sloshed. Paper plates buckle on broad laps. Plastic butter knives, asked to cut cold ham, refuse. Children underfoot in the pleased frenzy eat only potato chips. Somehow, as the first wave of appetite subsides, the long tables turn musical, and a murmur rises to the blank sky, a cackle rendered harmonious by a remote singleness of ancestor; a kind of fabric is woven and hung, a tapestry of the family fortunes, the threads of which include milkmen, ministers, mailmen, bankruptcy, death by war, death by automobile, insanity—a strangely prevalent thread, the thread of insanity. Never far from a farm or the memory of a farm, the family has hovered in honorable obscurity, between poverty and wealth, between jail and high office.

Real-estate dealers, schoolteachers, veterinarians are its noblemen; butchers, electricians, door-to-door salesmen its yeomen. Protestant, teetotalling, and undaring, ironically virtuous and mildly proud, it has added to America's statistics without altering their meaning. Whence, then, this strange joy?

Watermelons smelling of childhood cellars are produced and massively sliced. The sun passes noon and the shadows relax in the intimate grass of this antique meadow. To the music of reminiscence is added the rhythmic chunking of thrown quoits. They are held curiously between a straight thumb and four fingers curled as a unit, close to the chest, and thrown with a soft constrained motion that implies realms of unused strength. The twins and the children, as if superstitiously, have yielded the game to the older men, Fritz and Ed, Fred and Jesse, who, in pairs, after due estimation and measurement of the fall, pick up their four quoits, clink them together to clean them, and alternately send them back through the air on a high arc, floating with a spin-held slant like that of gyroscopes. The other pair measures, decides, and stoops. When they tap their quoits together, decades fall away. Even their competitive crowing has something measured about it, something patient, like the studied way their shirtsleeves are rolled up above their elbows. The backs of their shirts are ageless. Generations have sweated in just this style, under the arms, across the shoulder blades, and wherever the suspenders rub. The younger men and the teen-age girls play a softball game along the base paths that Jesse has scythed. The children discover the rowboat and, using the oars as poles, bump from bank to bank. When they dip their hands into the calm brown water, where no fish lives, a mother watching from beneath the walnut tree shrieks, "Keep your hands inside the boat! Uncle Jesse says the creek's polluted!"

And there is a stagnant fragrance the lengthening afternoon, strains from the happy meadow. Aunt Eula nods herself asleep, and her false teeth slip down, so her face seems mummified and the children giggle in terror. Flies, an exploding population, discover the remains of the picnic and skate giddily on its odors. The softball game grows boring, except to the airline pilot, a rather fancy gloveman excited by the admiration of Cousin Karen in her tight white Levis. The Pennsylvania and New York people begin to pack their cars. The time has come for the photograph. Their history is kept by these photographs of timeless people in changing costumes standing linked and flushed in a moment of midsummer heat. All line up, from resurrected Aunt Eula, twitching and snapping like a mud turtle, to the unborn baby in the belly of the Delaware cousin. To get them all in, Jesse has to squat, but in doing so he brings the houses into his view-finder. He does not want them in the picture, he does not want them there at all. They surround his meadow on three sides, raw ranch shacks built from one bastard design but painted in a patchwork of pastel shades. Their back yards, each nurturing an aluminum clothes tree, come right to the far bank of the creek, polluting it, and though a tall link fence holds back the children who have gathered in these yards to watch the picnic as if it were a circus or a zoo, the stare of the houses—mismatched kitchen windows squinting above the gaping cement mouth of a garage—cannot be held back. Not only do they stare, they speak, so that Jesse can hear them even at night. *Sell,* they say. *Sell.*

Excerpt from

Autobiography of a Papago Woman

Ruth Underhill
(1884-   )

Native Americans have maintained a relatively stable relationship to the land and to their tribes for thousands of years. In the selection below, a woman of the Papago tribe from Arizona recounts two episodes from her childhood, revealing a simple but profound sense of unity with her family and tribe. The legends and histories of families and tribes were handed down from one generation to the next in the form of unwritten songs and stories. The persons entrusted with this task possessed the power of clear memory, the gift of song and the talent to recite trivial lore in an eternally fresh fashion. The necessity for a people to gather together to hear about their past and their customs may have helped them to achieve the solidarity of family and tribe.

On winter nights, when we had finished our gruel or rabbit stew and lay back on our mats, my brothers would say to my father: "My father, tell us something."

My father would lie quietly upon his mat with my mother beside him and the baby between them. At last he would start slowly to tell us about how the world began. This is a story that can be told only in winter when there are no snakes about, for if the snakes heard they could crawl in and bite you. But in winter when snakes are asleep, we tell these things. Our story about the world is full of songs, and when the neighbors heard my father singing they would open our door and step in over the high threshold. Family by family they came, and we made a big fire and kept the door shut against the cold night. When my father finished a sentence we would all say the last word after him. If anyone went to sleep he would stop. He would not speak any more. But we did not go to sleep. . . .

My father was a song maker, and he had visions even if he was not a medicine man. He always made a song for the big harvest festival, the one that keeps the world going right and that only comes every four years.

We all went then from all over our country to the Place of the Burnt Seeds. We camped together, many, many families, and we made images of the beautiful things that make life good for the desert people, like clouds and corn and squash and deer. The men sang about these things and my father made songs. When I was about eight years old, my father once made an image of a mountain out of cactus ribs covered with white cloth. He had dreamed about this mountain and this is the song he made:

There is a white shell mountain in the
   ocean
Rising half out of the water.
Green scum floats on the water

And the Mountain turns around.

The song is very short because we understand so much. We can understand how tall and white the mountain was, and that white shell is something precious, such as the handsome men of old used to have for their necklaces, and it would shine all across the earth as they walked. We understand that as that mountain turns, it draws the clouds and the birds until they all float around it.

. . . . .

At last the giant cactus grew ripe on all the hills. It made us laugh to see the fruit on top of all the stalks. . . . We

Delaware Doll Dance *by Ruthe Balock Jones (1939-* *). Shawnee/Delaware—Oklahoma. Casein on* *illustration board.*

The doll dance, an annual ritual performed by the Delaware Indians until the 1930s, sought to protect the family owning the doll from disease. Each year the doll was provided with new clothes for the event.

went to pick it, to the same place where we always camped, and every day my mother and all the women went out with baskets. They knocked the fruit down with cactus poles. It fell on the ground and all the red pulp came out. Then I picked it up and dug it out of the shell with my fingers, and put it in my mother's basket. She told me always to throw down the skins with the red inside uppermost, because that would bring the rain.

It was good at cactus camp. When my father lay down to sleep at night he would sing a song about the cactus liquor. And we could hear songs in my uncle's camp across the hill. Everybody sang. We felt as if a beautiful thing was coming. Because the rain was coming and the dancing and the songs.

Where on Quijota Mountain a cloud
   stands
There my heart stands with it.
Where the mountain trembles with
   the thunder
My heart trembles with it.

That was what they sang. When I sing that song yet it makes me dance.

Then the little rains began to come. We had jugs of the juice my mother had boiled. . . . And we drank it to pull down the clouds, for that is what we call it.

Excerpt from

Home Sickness

George Moore
(1852-1933)

In addressing a universal theme in his short story, "Home Sickness," George Moore suggests that, for some, being part of a social whole has as much to do with physical surroundings as it does with other persons. In the excerpt that follows we meet Bryden, a New York bartender, who decides to visit Ireland, the place of his birth, after living in America for 13 years. A succession of events causes him to reflect on what he means by "home."

Moore was born in Ireland and spent nine years of his adult life in Dublin writing and working to establish the new Irish theater; the rest of his life he spent in Paris and London. He was a significant force in introducing European and Russian writers to an Irish readership.

He told the doctor he was due in the barroom at eight o'clock in the morning; the barroom was in a slum in the Bowery; and he had only been able to keep himself in health by getting up at five o'clock and going for long walks in Central Park.

"A sea voyage is what you want," said the doctor. "Why not go to Ireland for two or three months? You will come back a new man."

"I'd like to see Ireland again."

And then he began to wonder how the people at home were getting on. The doctor was right. He thanked him, and three weeks afterwards he landed in Cork.

As he sat in the railway carriage he recalled his native village—he could see it and its lake, and then the fields one by one, and the roads. He could see a large piece of rocky land—some three or four hundred acres of headland stretching out into the winding lake. Upon this headland the peasantry had been given permission to build their cabins by former owners of the Georgian house standing on the pleasant green hill. The present owners considered the village a disgrace, but the villagers paid high rents for their plots of ground, and all the manual labour that the Big House required came from the village: the gardeners, the stable helpers, the house and the kitchen maids.

He had been thirteen years in America, and when the train stopped at his station, Bryden looked round to see if there were any changes in it. It was just the same blue limestone station-house as it was thirteen years ago. The platform and the sheds were the same, and there were five miles of road from the station to Duncannon. The sea voyage had done him good, but five miles were too far for him today; the last time he had walked the road, he had walked it in an hour and a half, carrying

Hirshhorn Museum and Sculpture Garden, Smithsonian Institution, Washington, D.C.

Bus Riders *by George Segal (1924-   ). Sculpture: plaster, metal and vinyl.*

Like other American "pop" artists, Segal is interested in contemporary experiences and scenes. He uses living models to make rough plaster casts which he then places in ordinary public environments such as an elevator, a lunch counter or a bus. In this sculpture, the unnatural whiteness of the figures and the lack of specific details contrast with the familiar setting and natural poses. His people seem to be standing still in time, close in the physical sense, perhaps, but separated in countless other ways.

a heavy bundle on a stick.

He was sorry he did not feel strong enough for the walk; the evening was fine, and he would meet many people coming home from the fair, some of whom he had known in his youth, and they would tell him where he could get a clean lodging. But the carman would be able to tell him that; he called the car that was waiting at the station, and soon he was answering questions about America. But Bryden wanted to hear of those who were still living in the old country, and after hearing the stories of many people he had forgotten, he heard that Mike Scully, who had been away in a situation for many years as a coachman in the King's County, had come back and built a fine house with a concrete floor. Now there was a good loft in Mike Scully's house, and Mike would be pleased to take in a lodger.

Bryden remembered that Mike had been in a situation at the Big House; he had intended to be a jockey, but had suddenly shot up into a fine tall man, and had had to become a coachman instead. Bryden tried to recall the face, but he could only remember a straight nose, and a somewhat dusky complexion. Mike was one of the heroes of his childhood, and his youth floated before him, and he caught glimpses of himself, something that was more than a phantom and less than a reality. Suddenly his reverie was broken: the carman pointed with his whip, and Bryden saw a tall, finely-built, middle-aged man coming through the gates, and the driver said:

"There's Mike Scully."

Mike had forgotten Bryden even more completely than Bryden had for-

gotten him, and many aunts and uncles were mentioned before he began to understand.

"You've grown into a fine man, James," he said, looking at Bryden's great width of chest. "But you are thin in the cheeks, and you're sallow in the cheeks too."

"I haven't been very well lately—that is one of the reasons I have come back; but I want to see you all again."

Bryden paid the carman, wished him "God-speed," and he and Mike divided the luggage between them, Mike carrying the bag and Bryden the bundle, and they walked round the lake, for the townland was at the back of the demesne; and while they walked, James proposed to pay Mike ten shillings a week for his board and lodging.

. . . . .

The cackling of some geese in the road kept him awake, and the loneliness of the country seemed to penetrate to his bones, and to freeze the marrow in them. There was a bat in the loft—a dog howled in the distance—and then he drew the clothes over his head. Never had he been so unhappy, and the sound of Mike breathing by his wife's side in the kitchen added to his nervous terror. Then he dozed a little; and lying on his back he dreamed he was awake, and the men he had seen sitting round the fireside that evening seemed to him like spectres come out of some unknown region of morass and reedy tarn. He stretched out his hands for his clothes, determined to fly from this house, but remembering the lonely road that led to the station he fell back on his pillow.

The geese still cackled, but he was too tired to be kept awake any longer. He seemed to have been asleep only a few minutes when he heard Mike calling him. Mike had come half way up the ladder and was telling him that breakfast was ready. "What kind of breakfast will he give me?" Bryden asked himself as he pulled on his clothes. There were tea and hot griddle cakes for breakfast, and there were fresh eggs; there was sunlight in the kitchen and he liked to hear Mike tell of the work he was going to do in the fields. Mike rented a farm of about fifteen acres, at least ten of it was grass; he grew an acre of potatoes and some corn, and some turnips for his sheep. He had a nice bit of meadow, and he took down his scythe, and as he put the whetstone in his belt Bryden noticed a second scythe, and he asked Mike if he should go down with him and help him to finish the field.

"You haven't done any mowing this many a year; I don't think you'd be of much help. You'd better go for a walk by the lake, but you may come in the afternoon if you like and help to turn the grass over."

Bryden was afraid he would find the lake shore very lonely, but the magic of returning health is the sufficient distraction for the convalescent, and the morning passed agreeably. The weather was still and sunny. He could hear the ducks in the reeds. The hours dreamed themselves away, and it became his habit to go to the lake every morning. One morning he met the landlord, and they walked together, talking of the country, of what it had been, and the ruin it was slipping into. James Bryden told him

that ill health had brought him back to Ireland; and the landlord lent him his boat, and Bryden rowed about the islands, and resting upon his oars he looked at the old castles, and remembered the pre-historic raiders that the landlord had told him about. He came across the stones to which the lake dwellers had tied their boats, and these signs of ancient Ireland were pleasing to Bryden in his present mood.

As well as the great lake there was a smaller lake in the bog where the villagers cut their turf. This lake was famous for its pike, and the landlord allowed Bryden to fish there, and one evening, when he was looking for a frog with which to bait his line, he met Margaret Dirken driving home the cows for the milking. Margaret was the herdsman's daughter, and she lived in a cottage near the Big House; but she came up to the village whenever there was a dance, and Bryden had found himself opposite to her in the reels. But until this evening he had had little opportunity of speaking to her, and he was glad to speak to someone, for the evening was lonely, and they stood talking together.

"You're getting your health again," she said. "You'll soon be leaving us."

"I'm in no hurry."

"You're grand people over there; I hear a man is paid four dollars a day for his work."

"And how much," said James, "has he to pay for his food and for his clothes?"

Her cheeks were bright and her teeth small, white and beautifully even; and a woman's **soul** looked at Bryden out of her soft Irish eyes. He was troubled and turned aside, and catching sight of a frog looking at him out of a tuft of grass he said:

"I have been looking for a frog to put upon my pike line."

The frog jumped right and left, and nearly escaped in some bushes, but he caught it and returned with it in his hand.

"It is just the kind of frog a pike will like," he said. "Look at its great white belly and its bright yellow back."

And without more ado he pushed the wire to which the hook was fastened through the frog's fresh body, and dragging it through the mouth he passed the hooks through the hind legs and tied the line to the end of the wire.

. . . . .

They had not met very often when she said, "James, you had better not come here so often calling to me."

"Don't you wish me to come?"

"Yes, I wish you to come well enough, but keeping company is not the custom of the country, and I don't want to be talked about."

"Are you afraid the priest would speak against us from the altar?"

"He has spoken against keeping company, but it is not so much what the priest says, for there is no harm in talking."

"But if you are going to be married there is no harm in walking out together."

"Well, not so much, but marriages are made differently in these parts; there is not much courting here."

And the next day it was known in the village that James was going to marry Margaret Dirken.

His desire to excel the boys in dancing had aroused much gaiety in the parish, and for some time there had been dancing in every house where there was a floor fit to dance upon; and if the cottager had no money to pay for a barrel of beer, James Bryden, who had money, sent him a barrel, so that Margaret might get her dance. She told him that they sometimes crossed over into another parish where the priest was not so adverse to dancing, and James wondered. And next morning at Mass he wondered at their simple fervour. Some of them held their hands above their heads as they prayed, and all this was very new and very old to James Bryden. But the obedience of these people to their priest surprised him. When he was a lad they had not been so obedient, or he had forgotten their obedience; and he listened in mixed anger and wonderment to the priest who was scolding his parishioners, speaking to them by name, saying that he had heard there was dancing going on in their homes. Worse than that, he said he had seen boys and girls loitering about the roads, and the talk that went on was of one kind—love. He said that newspapers containing love-stories were finding their way into the people's houses, stories about love, in which there was nothing elevating or ennobling. The people listened, accepting the priest's opinion without question. And their submission was pathetic. It was the submission of a primitive people clinging to religious authority, and Bryden contrasted the weakness and incompetence of the people about him with the modern restlessness and cold energy of the people he had left behind him.

One evening, as they were dancing, a knock came to the door, and the piper stopped playing, and the dancers whispered:

"Some one has told on us; it is the priest."

And the awe-stricken villagers crowded round the cottage fire, afraid to open the door. But the priest said that if they did not open the door he would put his shoulder to it and force it open. Bryden went towards the door, saying he would allow no one to threaten him, priest or no priest, but Margaret caught his arm and told him that if he said anything to the priest, the priest would speak against them from the altar, and they would be shunned by the neighbours. It was Mike Scully who went to the door and let the priest in, and he came in saying they were dancing their souls into hell.

"I've heard of your goings on," he said—"of your beer-drinking and dancing. I will not have it in my parish. If you want that sort of thing you had better go to America."

"If that is intended for me, sir, I will go back tomorrow. Margaret can follow."

"It isn't the dancing, it's the drinking I'm opposed to," said the priest, turning to Bryden.

"Well, no one has drunk too much, sir," said Bryden.

"But you'll sit here drinking all night," and the priest's eyes went towards the corner where the women had gathered, and Bryden felt that the priest looked on the women as more dangerous than the porter.

"It's after midnight," he said, taking out his watch.

By Bryden's watch it was only half-past eleven, and while they were arguing about the time Mrs. Scully offered Bryden's umbrella to the priest, for in his hurry to stop the dancing the priest had gone out without his; and, as if to show Bryden that he bore him no ill-will, the priest accepted the loan of the umbrella, for he was thinking of the big marriage fee that Bryden would pay him.

"I shall be badly off for the umbrella tomorrow," Bryden said, as soon as the priest was out of the house. He was going with his father-in-law to a fair. His father-in-law was learning him how to buy and sell cattle. And his father-in-law was saying that the country was mending, and that a man might become rich in Ireland if he only had a little capital. Bryden had the capital, and Margaret had an uncle on the other side of the lake who would leave her all he had, that would be fifty pounds, and never in the village of Duncannon had a young couple begun life with so much prospect of success as would James Bryden and Margaret Dirken.

Some time after Christmas was spoken of as the best time for the marriage; James Bryden said that he would not be able to get his money out of America before the spring. The delay seemed to vex him, and he seemed anxious to be married, until one day he received a letter from America, from a man who had served in the bar with him.

This friend wrote to ask Bryden if he were coming back. The letter was no more than a passing wish to see Bryden again. Yet Bryden stood looking at it, and everyone wondered what could be in the letter. It seemed momentous, and they hardly believed him when he said it was from a friend who wanted to know if his health were better. He tried to forget the letter, and he looked at the worn fields, divided by walls of loose stones, and a great longing came upon him.

The smell of the Bowery slum had come across the Atlantic, and had found him out in this western headland; and one night he awoke from a dream in which he was hurling some drunken customer through the open doors into the darkness. He had seen his friend in his white duck jacket throwing drink from glass into glass amid the din of voices and strange accents; he had heard the clang of money as it was swept into the till, and his sense sickened for the barroom. But how should he tell Margaret Dirken that he could not marry her? She had built her life upon this marriage. He could not tell her that he would not marry her . . . yet he must go. He felt as if he were being hunted; the thought that he must tell Margaret that he could not marry her haunted him day after day as a weasel hunts a rabbit. Again and again he went to meet her with the intention of telling her that he did not love her, that their lives were not for one another, that it had all been a mistake, and that happily he had found out it was a mistake soon enough. But Margaret, as if she guessed what he was about to speak of, threw her arms

about him and begged him to say he loved her, and that they would be married at once. He agreed that he loved her, and that they would be married at once. But he had not left her many minutes before the feeling came upon him that he could not marry her—that he must go away. The smell of the barroom hunted him down. Was it for the sake of the money that he might make there that he wished to go back? No, it was not the money. What then? His eyes fell on the bleak country, on the little fields divided by bleak walls; he remembered the pathetic ignorance of the people, and it was these things he could not endure. It was the priest who came to forbid the dancing. Yes, it was the priest. As he stood looking at the line of the hills the barroom seemed by him. He heard the politicians, and the excitement of politics was in his blood again. He must go away from this place—he must get back to the barroom. Looking up he saw the scanty orchard, and he hated the spare road that led to the village, and he hated the little hill at the top of which the village began, and he hated more than all other places the house where he was to live with Margaret Dirken—if he married her. He could see it from where he stood—by the edge of the lake, with twenty acres of pasture land about it, for the landlord had given up part of his demesne land to them.

He caught sight of Margaret, and he called her to come through the stile.

"I have just had a letter from America."

"About the money?" she said.

"Yes, about the money. But I shall

have to go over there."

He stood looking at her, seeking for words; and she guessed from his embarrassment that he would say to her that he must go to America before they were married.

"Do you mean, James, you will have to go at once?"

"Yes," he said, "at once. But I shall come back in time to be married in August. It will only mean delaying our marriage a month."

They walked on a little way talking; every step he took James felt that he was a step nearer the Bowery slum. And when they came to the gate Bryden said:

"I must hasten or I shall miss the train."

"But," she said, "you are not going now—you are not going today?"

"Yes, this morning. It is seven miles. I shall have to hurry not to miss the train."

And then she asked him if he would ever come back.

"Yes," he said, "I am coming back."

"If you are coming back, James, why not let me go with you?"

"You could not walk fast enough. We should miss the train."

"One moment, James. Don't make me suffer; tell me the truth. You are not coming back. Your clothes—where shall I send them?"

He hurried away, hoping he would come back. He tried to think that he liked the country he was leaving, that it would be better to have a farmhouse and live there with Margaret Dirken than to serve drinks behind a counter in the Bowery. He did not think he was telling her a lie when he said he was

coming back. Her offer to forward his clothes touched his heart, and at the end of the road he stood and asked himself if he should go back to her. He would miss the train if he waited another minute, and he ran on. And he would have missed the train if he had not met a car. Once he was on the car he felt himself safe—the country was already behind him. The train and the boat at Cork were mere formulae; he was already in America.

The moment he landed he felt the thrill of home that he had not found in his native village, and he wondered how it was that the smell of the bar seemed more natural than the smell of the fields, and the roar of crowds more welcome than the silence of the lake's edge. However, he offered up a thanksgiving for his escape, and entered into negotiations for the purchase of the barroom.

He took a wife, she bore him sons and daughters, the barroom prospered, property came and went; he grew old, his wife died, he retired from business, and reached the age when a man begins to feel there are not many years in front of him, and that all he has had to do in life has been done. His children married, lonesomeness began to creep about him; in the evening, when he looked into the fire-light, a vague, tender reverie floated up, and Margaret's soft eyes and name vivified the dusk. His wife and children passed out of mind, and it seemed to him that a memory was the only real thing he possessed, and the desire to see Margaret again grew intense. But she was an old woman, she had married, maybe she was dead. Well, he would like to be buried in the village where he was born.

There is an unchanging, silent life within every man that none knows but himself, and his unchanging, silent life was his memory of Margaret Dirken. The barroom was forgotten and all that

concerned it, and the things he saw most clearly were the green hillside, and the bog lake and the rushes about it, and the greater lake in the distance, and behind it the blue lines of wandering hills.

I Have a Dream

Martin Luther King, Jr.
(1929-1968)

On August 28, 1963, more than 200,000 persons took part in a march on Washington intended to challenge Congress and the nation to deal more effectively with issues of civil rights and poverty. In a moving mass gathering before the Lincoln Memorial, outstanding speakers appealed for the implementation of Lincoln's ideals. But the most eloquent address was that of Martin Luther King, Jr., president of the Southern Christian Leadership Conference. He appealed for a social fabric in which all Americans are united and equal.

Five score years ago, a great American, in whose symbolic shadow we stand, signed the Emancipation Proclamation. This momentous decree came as a great beacon light of hope to millions of Negro slaves who had been seared in the flames of withering injustice. It came as a joyous daybreak to end the long night of captivity.

But one hundred years later, we must face the tragic fact that the Negro is still not free. One hundred years later, the life of the Negro is still sadly crippled by the manacles of segregation and the chains of discrimination. One hundred years later, the Negro lives on a lonely island of poverty in the midst of a vast ocean of material prosperity. One hundred years later, the Negro is still languishing in the corners of American society and finds himself an exile in his own land. So we have come here today to dramatize an appalling condition.

. . . . .

I say to you today, my friends, that in spite of the difficulties and frustrations of the moment I still have a dream. It is a dream deeply rooted in the American dream.

I have a dream that one day this nation will rise up and live out the true meaning of its creed: "We hold these truths to be self-evident; that all men are created equal."

I have a dream that one day on the red hills of Georgia the sons of former slaves and the sons of former slave-owners will be able to sit down together at the table of brotherhood.

I have a dream that one day even the state of Mississippi, a desert state sweltering with the heat of injustice and oppression, will be transformed into an oasis of freedom and justice.

I have a dream that my four little children will one day live in a nation where they will not be judged by the color of their skin but by the content of their character.

I have a dream today.

I have a dream that one day the state of Alabama, whose governor's lips are presently dripping with the words of

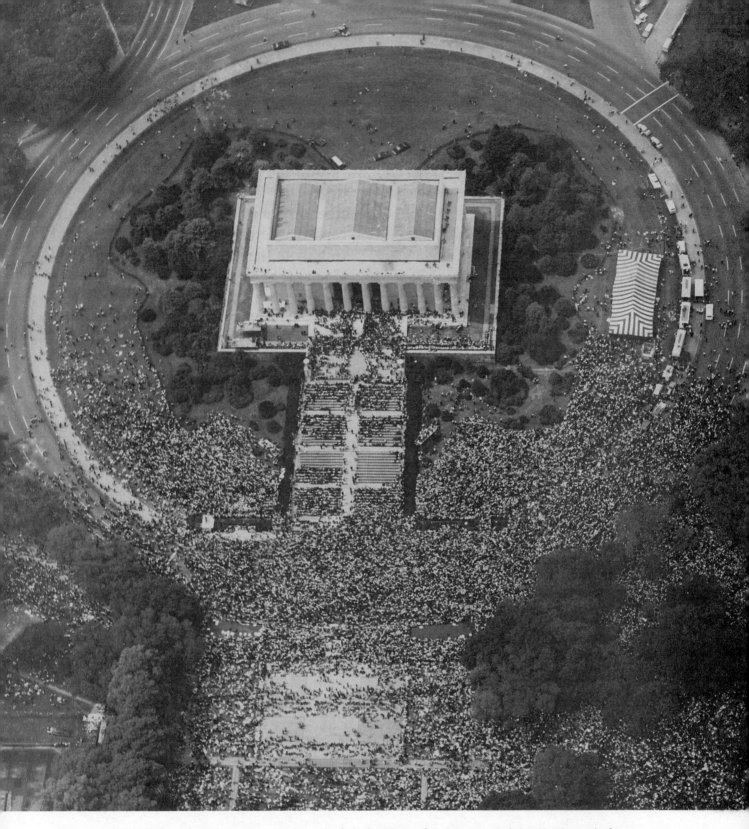

Throngs of citizens, united by the common goal of civil rights reform, came to the nation's capital on August 28, 1963, to take part in the "March on Washington." The climax of the event was the delivery of the memorable "I Have a Dream" speech by Martin Luther King, Jr. This aerial photograph shows the crowd assembled on the mall at the Lincoln Memorial.

interposition and nullification, will be transformed into a situation where little black boys and black girls will be able to join hands with little white boys and white girls and walk together as sisters and brothers.

I have a dream today.

I have a dream that one day every valley shall be exalted, every hill and mountain shall be made low, the rough places will be made plains, and the crooked places will be made straight, and the glory of the Lord shall be revealed, and all flesh shall see it together.

This is our hope. This is the faith with which I return to the South. With this faith we will be able to hew out of the mountain of despair a stone of hope. With this faith we will be able to transform the jangling discords of our nation into a beautiful symphony of brotherhood.

With this faith we will be able to work together, to pray together, to struggle together, to go to jail together, to stand up for freedom together, knowing that we will be free one day.

This will be the day when all of God's children will be able to sing with new meaning, "My country 'tis of thee, sweet land of liberty, of thee I sing.

Land where my fathers died, land of the Pilgrims' pride, from every mountainside, let freedom ring."

And if America is to be a great nation, this must become true. So let freedom ring from the prodigious hilltops of New Hampshire. Let freedom ring from the mighty mountains of New York. Let freedom ring from the heightening Alleghenies of Pennsylvania.

Let freedom ring from the snow-capped Rockies of Colorado! Let freedom ring from the curvaceous peaks of California! But not only that; let freedom ring from Stone Mountain of Georgia! Let freedom ring from Lookout Mountain of Tennessee!

Let freedom ring from every hill and molehill of Mississippi. From every mountainside, let freedom ring.

When we let freedom ring, when we let it ring from every village and every hamlet, from every state and every city, we will be able to speed up that day when all of God's children, black men and white men, Jews and Gentiles, Protestants and Catholics, will be able to join hands and sing in the words of the old Negro spiritual, "Free at last! Free at last! Thank God Almighty, we are free at last!"

Celebrate the Sun
Betty Nickerson

Not only is there a basic human need to relate to other persons and to see oneself as part of a social whole, there is also a yearning to express publicly the commonality of our existence and to mark the important events of our lives. When we do these things, we are celebrating. In earlier times, when the forces of nature and the seasonal changes directly affected human existence and survival, people focused their celebrations—religious and secular—on the sun, the moon and the elements of nature. Traces of these rites can still be seen in modern-day customs and traditions. In the following excerpt, the author discusses festivals, holidays and other times we set aside to "bring [our] joy and love of life into public view and share them with the larger community."

Man is the creature who celebrates. He dances, sings, feasts, fasts and dramatizes important moments in his life. He celebrates as a member of a community of people and finds joy. From most primitive tribe to most sophisticated nation, all people have holidays that have special meaning for them. Traditional festivals have ancient roots springing from mankind's very early ideas of life, the world and the heavens. Most annual celebrations originated from seasonal changes in the lives of agricultural people, and they can be traced back through uncharted years to a time when human survival depended directly on natural events. The festivals are usually related to the movement of the earth around the sun, and the changes this made in the lives of human beings whose behavior was governed by it.

For some of us technology obscures the rhythm of the world by turning night into day and winter into indoor summer. Children often live closer to nature, and feel the wonder of the changing seasons. They have painted their festivals in a bright profusion of color. Some will take us back to the very beginning.

A celebration is the joy of time passing, marking the achievement of a milestone in the cycle of time. The cycle most generally observed, the year of 365 1/4 days which the earth now requires to complete its orbit around the sun, is not the only time cycle. There is fascinating evidence in old records, on ancient temple walls and surviving shadow clocks to show that the year was 360 days long in the second millennium before the present era. The people of Moslem faith follow the lunar time cycle which makes the year 11 days shorter than the sun cycle. Calendars, which must frequently be changed, are simply a convenient way of keeping track of time. Our ancestors knew the new year had come when the fields turned green. They knew it was summer when the sun was at its highest overhead, and autumn arrived with the golden grains and ripe fruits of the field. Winter with its cold and fear was a time of waiting.

. . . . .

Celebrations probably began with a primitive form of the dance, perhaps as the group moved sympathetically together imitating the stalking of game. Dancing together must have been an extremely early expression of the emotional and rhythmic unity of the group, which is what celebrations are all about—doing things together. In pre-Paleolithic times one person did not or could not exist outside the group. Only after an uncountable length of time did a sense of personal individuality develop, and it is still far from certain that a human being can remain human unless he is part of some group. Modern man in his festivals returns for a moment to a semblance of the closeness of group existence.

If we listen today, we will hear a large part of the world's youth pleading for some means of creating community, this sense of belonging. Festival celebrations can lighten the loneliness that burdens so many of us. In the act of celebration the individual must come in contact with other people. The traditional communal festivals that celebrate nature's wonders belong to everyone. One doesn't pay admission to spring, or subscribe to a particular faith to see the full moon of August, or the meeting of two stars on the Milky Way. One need only look up to the sky and feel how its beauty touches the spirit and illuminates the quality of life.

A man does not celebrate alone. Celebration must be shared. The stereotype of loneliness in Christian countries is the image of one person alone at Christmas. Even if his surroundings are comfortable and his table heaped with food and gifts, the fact that he is alone still suffuses his situation with tragedy. In contrast, harmony with other people is what festivals are all about. At festivals mankind brings his joy and love of life into public view, and shares them with the larger community.

Excerpt from

Go Tell It on the Mountain

James Baldwin
(1924-   )

*James Baldwin began to plot novels at about the time he learned to read. His mother
was delighted with his early writings, but his father wanted him to be a preacher.
When he was 14 he followed his father's direction, but at 17 he gave up preaching to
begin his long struggle to become a writer.*

*Baldwin draws upon the enormous resources of black American speech and life in
order to portray authentically the context in which his characters live out their lives.
His early stories are based on his own experience because that was "the gate I had to
unlock before I could hope to write about anything else."*

*The excerpt that follows describes a Sunday morning worship service so vividly
that the reader feels like an onlooker, standing at the door of the storefront church.
The selection dramatizes the importance of the church community in the lives of the
novel's main characters.*

On Sunday mornings and Sunday
nights the church was always full;
on special Sundays it was full all day.
The Grimes family arrived in a body,
always a little late, usually in the middle
of Sunday school, which began at nine
o'clock. This lateness was always their
mother's fault—at least in the eyes of
their father; she could not seem to get
herself and the children ready on time,
ever, and sometimes she actually remained behind not to appear until the
morning service. When they all arrived
together, they separated upon entering
the doors, father and mother going to sit
in the Adult Class, which was taught by
Sister McCandless, Sarah going to the
Infant's Class, John and Roy sitting in
the Intermediate, which was taught by
Brother Elisha.

When he was young, John had paid
no attention in Sunday school, and always forgot the golden text, which
earned him the wrath of his father.
Around the time of his fourteenth birth-
day, with all the pressures of church and
home uniting to drive him to the altar,
he strove to appear more serious and
therefore less conspicuous. But he was
distracted by his new teacher, Elisha,
who was the pastor's nephew and who
had but lately arrived from Georgia. He
was not much older than John, only sev-
enteen, and he was already saved and
was a preacher. John stared at Elisha all
during the lesson, admiring the timbre
of Elisha's voice, much deeper and
manlier than his own, admiring the
leanness, and grace, and strength, and
darkness of Elisha in his Sunday suit,
wondering if he would ever be holy as
Elisha was holy. But he did not follow
the lesson, and when, sometimes, Elisha
paused to ask John a question, John was

ashamed and confused, feeling the palms of his hands become wet and his heart pound like a hammer. Elisha would smile and reprimand him gently, and the lesson would go on.

Roy never knew his Sunday school lesson either, but it was different with Roy—no one really expected of Roy what was expected of John. Everyone was always praying that the Lord would change Roy's heart, but it was John who was expected to be good, to be a good example.

When Sunday school service ended there was a short pause before morning service began. In this pause, if it was good weather, the old folks might step outside a moment to talk among themselves. The sisters would almost always be dressed in white from crown to toe. The small children, on this day, in this place, and oppressed by their elders, tried hard to play without seeming to be disrespectful of God's house. But sometimes, nervous or perverse, they shouted, or threw hymn-books, or began to cry, putting their parents, men or women of God, under the necessity of proving—by harsh means or tender—who, in a sanctified household, ruled. The older children, like John or Roy, might wander down the avenue, but not too far. Their father never let John and Roy out of his sight, for Roy had often disappeared between Sunday school and morning service and had not come back all day.

The Sunday morning service began when Brother Elisha sat down at the piano and raised a song. This moment and this music had been with John, so it seemed, since he had first drawn breath.

It seemed that there had never been a time when he had not known this moment of waiting while the packed church paused—the sisters in white, heads raised, the brothers in blue, heads back; the white caps of the women seeming to glow in the charged air like crowns, the kinky, gleaming heads of the men seeming to be lifted up—and the rustling and the whispering ceased and the children were quiet; perhaps someone coughed, or the sound of a car horn, or a curse from the streets came in; then Elisha hit the keys, beginning at once to sing, and everybody joined him, clapping their hands, and rising, and beating the tambourines.

> The song might be: *Down at the cross where my Saviour died!*
> Or : *Jesus, I'll never forget how you set me free!*
> Or : *Lord, hold my hand while I run this race!*

They sang with all the strength that was in them, and clapped their hands for joy. There had never been a time when John had not sat watching the saints rejoice with terror in his heart, and wonder. Their singing caused him to believe in the presence of the Lord; indeed, it was no longer a question of belief, because they made that presence real. He did not feel it himself, the joy they felt, yet he could not doubt that it was, for them, the very bread of life—could not doubt it, that is, until it was too late to doubt. Something happened to their faces and their voices, the rhythm of their bodies, and to the air they breathed; it was as though wherever they might be became the up-

Assembly Church *by Prentiss Taylor (1907-   ). Lithograph.*

per room, and the Holy Ghost were riding on the air. His father's face, always awful, became more awful now; his father's daily anger was transformed into prophetic wrath. His mother, her eyes raised to heaven, hands arced before her, moving, made real for John that patience, that endurance, that long suffering, which he had read of in the Bible and found so hard to imagine.

On Sunday mornings the women all seemed patient, all the men seemed mighty. While John watched, the Power struck someone, a man or woman; they cried out, a long, wordless crying, and, arms outstretched like wings, they began the Shout. Someone moved a chair a little to give them room, the rhythm paused, the singing stopped, only the pounding feet and the clapping hands were heard; then another cry, another dancer; then the tambourines began again, and the voices rose again, and the music swept on again, like fire, or flood, or judgment. Then the church seemed to swell with the Power it held, and, like a planet rocking in space, the temple rocked with the Power of God. John watched, watched the faces, and the weightless bodies, and listened to the timeless cries. One day, so everyone said, this Power would possess him; he would sing and cry as they did now, and dance before his King. He watched young Ella Mae Washington, the seventeen-year-old granddaughter of Praying Mother Washington, as she began to dance. And then Elisha danced.

At one moment, head thrown back, eyes closed, sweat standing on his brow, he sat at the piano, singing and playing; and then, like a great black cat in trouble in the jungle, he stiffened and trembled, and cried out. *Jesus Jesus, oh Lord Jesus!* He struck on the piano one last, wild note, and threw up his hands, palms upward, stretched wide apart. The tambourines raced to fill the vacuum left by his silent piano, and his cry drew answering cries. Then he was on his feet, turning, blind, his face congested, contorted with this rage, and the muscles, leaping and swelling in his long, dark neck. It seemed that he could not breathe, that his body could not contain this passion, that he would be, before their eyes, dispersed into the waiting air. His hands, rigid to the very fingertips, moved outward and back against his hips, his sightless eyes looked upward, and he began to dance. Then his hands closed into fists, and his head snapped downward, his sweat loosening the grease that slicked down his hair; and the rhythm of all the others quickened to match Elisha's rhythm; his thighs moved terribly against the cloth of his suit, his heels beat on the floor, and his fists moved beside his body as though he were beating his own drum. And so, for a while, in the center of the dancers, head down, fists beating, on, on, unbearably, until it seemed the walls of the church would fall for very sound; and then, in a moment, with a cry, head up, arms high in the air, sweat pouring from his forehead, and all his body dancing as though it would never stop. Sometimes he did not stop until he fell—until he dropped like some animal felled by a hammer—moaning, on his face. And then a great moaning filled the church.

Further Readings

Baskin, John. *New Burlington: The Life and Death of an American Village.* 1976. A portrait of a small Ohio town and its people, living and dead, whose lives were part of that place yet uniquely their own. The author recorded the voices of townspeople and unearthed the letters and diaries of the past to create this mosaic of rural America.

Brand. Millen. *Fields of Peace: A Pennsylvania German Album.* 1973. Text and photographs describing the life of the Amish people in Pennsylvania.

Gordon, Suzanne. *Lonely in America.* 1976. Present-day American society, says the author, promotes loneliness, alienating even the closest of families, friends and colleagues. The old ties of kinship, church and community are eroding without being replaced by a satisfactory alternative.

Kroeber, Theodora. *Ishi in Two Worlds.* 1961. This biography of the last surviving member of the Yahi Indian tribe describes his boyhood in the context of a close-knit family following ancient tribal traditions, and his lonely adulthood among white society.

Section 4

ONE WITH NATURE

Section 3 focused on various expressions of meaning found in being part of a social unity. In this session, we consider an extension of that view—the awareness of being part of an even greater whole: Nature and the universe. Such a feeling is not necessarily inconsistent with being one with family, race or nation. Indeed, the sense of communal unity may be closely tied to that of unity with nature, as the reading from *Black Elk Speaks* makes clear. But for some persons there is an order, a permanence, a cohesion, a timelessness about the physical world and our individual role in that scheme of things that provides a meaning to life independent of the changes and chances of history and social structures. For them, the vast and beautiful context of the world, the solar system and the universe communicates a strong support when human associations fail.

A contemporary American poet, Robinson Jeffers, articulates this perspective clearly in his poem, "The Answer."

A severed hand
Is an ugly thing, and man dissevered from the earth and stars
   and his history . . . for contemplation or in fact . . .
Often appears atrociously ugly. Integrity is wholeness,
   the greatest beauty is
Organic wholeness, the wholeness of life and things, the divine beauty
   of the universe. Love that, not man
Apart from that, or else you will share man's pitiful confusions,
   or drown in despair when his days darken.

The modern concern for conservation and ecology reflected in the Jeffers' poem takes much of its inspiration from the conviction that human exist-

---

Hermit Fishing on River in Autumn *by Ma Yuan (flourished early 13th century). Chinese.*
The peace of the river lulls the fisherman into harmony with all that is about him.

ence is only worthwhile when understood in the setting of nature, and that disregard for our oneness with "the divine beauty of the universe" is an invitation to chaos and disaster. Do you agree with this view? If so, is it one you have been made aware of only recently, or can you and members of your discussion group draw on memories of similar attitudes earlier in the century?

Many artists perceive their work as a reflection of nature's creative process. French impressionist painter Pierre Auguste Renoir was such an artist. The excerpt from his biography, written by his son, illustrates another level at which participation in nature gives meaning to life. Renoir thought of himself as carried like a "cork in the flow of the stream," but, as the author points out, he actually helped to *create* the world through his painting.

Most people who depend on the land are attuned from childhood to the ways of nature and sense a personal harmony with the universe. A case in point is Black Elk, revered holy man of the Oglala Sioux Indians, who describes his calling to the leadership of his tribe. In a childhood vision, he is taken before the six Grandfathers (representing the past history of the tribe) and given the sacred tree symbolizing the life of his people. The Grandfathers are the powers of the world, the sky and the earth, "older than men can ever be—old like hills, like stars." They appear magically in the form of animals. The sixth Grandfather turns out to be Black Elk himself. In his vision he is an eagle soaring over the people, who are transformed into elks, bison and other animals. The health of the nation is inextricably linked with the flowering of the sacred tree, and the whole universe is caught up in the final dance of nature led by the singing of Black Elk's stallion—that is, by the "good nation" delivered from danger and confident in its future. Thus the common life of the Oglala Sioux and the religious faith on which it is based are part of a universal whole, with man, animals, nature and the supernatural interwoven.

The effect on us of discovering our oneness with nature and the universe can be inspiring, liberating or even overpowering. From the many beautiful poems celebrating the aesthetic response to nature, we have included "Once More, the Round," "The Lake Isle of Innisfree" and an excerpt from "Endymion." In his short story, "The Adulterous Woman," Albert Camus portrays a woman whose sense of mystical union with nature is so intense that she feels it has involved a betrayal of her marriage vows.

Science, another field of human endeavor, often suggests that human life is best understood when it is viewed as a small part of a larger whole. The fact that human history has existed only a small fraction of the billions of years in which the universe has been in the making is a frightening concept for some people. For just as many others, however, there is a meaning to human existence *because* it represents a remarkable outcome of the complex process of evolution and *because* it constitutes a small part of the great stream of life.

Loren Eiseley, a scientist of remarkable perception, reflects the position of those who see human life in the larger context of cosmic life. On one occasion, he tells us in *The Unexpected Universe,* he tripped in the street and smashed his nose on the sidewalk, spilling blood profusely. His response was to talk to the blood cells he was losing, asking their forgiveness for his own clumsiness. Eiseley was instinctively expressing his dependence on the tiny, living entities escaping from his body. "I was made up of millions of these tiny creatures, their toil, their sacrifices, as they hurried to seal and repair the rent fabric of this vast being whom they had unknowingly, but in love, compounded." This profoundly reverent attitude toward nature also characterizes *The Immense Journey,* from which our selection is taken.

Excerpt from

Renoir, My Father

Jean Renoir
(1894-1979)

Pierre Auguste Renoir (1841-1919) was originally a member of the French Impressionists, a group of painters whose style was marked by vivid colors conveying the impression of light on objects. In other words, they painted directly from nature as it appeared to the human eye. Simple photographic representation was not their intent but rather an interpretation of the essence of nature. To capture the inner secrets of nature, Renoir had to feel and be in total harmony with it.

Renoir brilliantly coordinated all the elements of his paintings—colors, brushwork and composition—to create the same unity he saw in nature. Viewing his paintings, therefore, enables people to sense and appreciate the fact that "the world is one"—the components of the painting, nature itself and all of humankind are one.

The selection below is taken from a biography written by the painter's son. Jean Renoir excelled at a new and different art form from his father's—motion pictures; he was a well-known movie director.

Naturally, Renoir did portraits of women who differed from one another physically. His interest in human beings made him strive to achieve real likenesses in his portraits. Yet whenever he painted subjects of his own choosing, he returned to the physical characteristics which were essentially those of his future wife. No one knows whether he deliberately chose such models or whether his imagination guided his hand. Oscar Wilde, whom he was to meet in later years, offered a much simpler explanation when he made the quip apropos of Turner: "Before him, there was no London fog." The theory that painters "create the world" is borne out strikingly in Renoir. For it was not only my mother who was to be born in Renoir's pictures, but we, his children also. He had done our portraits even before we came into the world, even before we were conceived, physically. He had represented us all hundreds of times; and all children, as well; all the young girls with whom he was unconsciously to people a universe which was to become his own.

That Renoir's world has come into being can no longer be doubted. I am constantly being waylaid by parents who show me their children and say: "Don't you think they are perfect little Renoirs?" And the extraordinary part is that they are! Our world which before him was filled with people with elongated pale faces has since his time seen an influx of little round, plump beings with beautiful red cheeks. And the similarity is carried further by the choice of colors for their clothing. He is responsible for that too. His contempo-

The Phillips Collection, Washington, D.C.

Luncheon of the Boating Party *by Pierre Auguste Renoir (1841-1919). French. Oil.*

It is not simply the shared meal that creates an air of naturalness, abandon and festivity in Renoir's painting but the meal in this special setting and at this time of day. Like other Impressionists, Renoir painted scenes only after carefully studying the way the color of an object varies as the light of day changes.

raries have ranted enough about "the gaudy finery with which he decked out the cooks and maids who served as his models." This criticism by a forgotten journalist was repeated to me by my father himself. Renoir let them talk. Anyone able to create a world filled with health and color is beyond criticism. "Let the literary crowd indulge their passion for anemia and 'whites.'" And then, to point up his remark, he added, "You'd have to pay me to sleep with the Dame aux Camélias." He would have resented anyone telling him the exact nature of the task he was so humbly to accomplish. To create even a little corner of the universe was the work of God, and not that of a capable painter who had become a good workman in painting. On the contrary, he was convinced that it was the world which was creating him; and that he was merely reproducing this life of ours, which enraptured him like a passage in a great symphony. "The cork in the flow of the stream." He only wanted to interpret faithfully the marvels he perceived so clearly for the benefit of those unable to perceive them. He would have been incensed if anyone had dared to tell him that the life which he filled his pictures with so abundantly came from within him. He would have felt just as insulted as if someone had called him an intellectual. He only wanted to be a mechanism to take in and to give out, and to that end he was careful not to squander his strength, and to keep his vision clear and his hand sure. "If it came from me alone, it would be merely the creation of my brain. And the brain,

of itself, is an ugly thing. It has no value except what you put into it."

. . . . .

The world of Renoir is a single entity. The red of the poppy determines the pose of the young woman with the umbrella. The blue of the sky harmonizes with the sheepskin the young shepherd wears. His pictures are demonstrations of an over-all unity. The backgrounds are as important as the foregrounds. It is not just flowers, faces, mountains, which are put in juxtaposition to each other: it is an ensemble of elements which go to make one central theme, and they are bound together by a feeling of love which unites the differences between them. When one evokes Renoir, one always comes back to that vital point. In his world mind is liberated from matter, not by ignoring it but by penetrating it. The blossom of the linden tree and the bee sipping the honey from it follow the same rhythm as the blood circulating under the skin of the young girl sitting on the grass. This is also the current in which the symbolic "cork" is carried along. The world is one. The linden, the bees, the young girl, the light and Renoir are all part of the same thing, and of equal importance. And the same holds true of the seas, the cities, the eagle soaring above the mountains, the miner deep in the mine, Aline Charigot feeding her little son Pierre at her breast. In this compact whole each of our gestures, each of our thoughts, has its repercussions. A forest fire will bring on a flood. A tree transformed into paper, and then into words, can drive men to war, or awaken them to what is great and beautiful. Renoir believed in the Chinese legend that a mandarin can be killed at a distance by an unconsciously lethal gesture made in Paris.

. . . . .

To help us to understand Renoir's creative process better, I must quote one of his cryptic remarks: "I am not God the Father. He created the world, and I am content to copy it." And to show that he did not mean copying in the literal sense of the word, he told us the classic story of the ancient Greek painter Apelles. In a competition that took place on the Acropolis, a rival of the Athenian master had submitted a picture which seemed to surpass any of the other entries. The subject of the pic-

ture was grapes, which were so realistically depicted that the birds came and pecked at them. Then Apelles, with a knowing wink, as though to say "Now you're going to see something!" presented his masterpiece. "It is hidden behind this drapery." The judges wanted to lift the drapery, but they could not—for it was the subject of the picture!

. . . . .

Among seekers of truth, painters perhaps come closest to discovering the secret of the balance of forces in the universe, and hence of man's fulfillment. That is why they are so important in modern life. I mean real painters: the great ones. They spring up in little groups in periods of high civilization.

Excerpt from

Black Elk Speaks

John G. Neihardt
(1881-1973)

In 1930, Black Elk was interviewed by John G. Neihardt, who was researching a massacre that had taken place in the mid-1880s. The holy man of the Oglala Sioux was able to describe how he survived this terrible experience and also to recount, in vivid detail, his earlier visions of the role he would come to assume as tribal leader. These prophecies form the subject matter of the excerpt that follows.

This selection invites readers to share the image-filled visions of the youthful Black Elk: A world where men become animals, sticks turn into blossoming trees, and old men are transformed into the Powers of the World—North, South, East, West, Earth and Sky. The future leader is endowed with the power to bring life and the power to destroy. He will lead his nation with "the power that is peace." His destiny and that of the tribe are linked to the symbolism of the sacred tree that blossoms in times of prosperity.

Later sections of the book record the tragic destruction of his people by white soldiers. "A people's dream died there . . . ," says Black Elk. "It was a beautiful dream. And I, to whom so great a vision was given in my youth—you see now a pitiful old man who has done nothing, for the nation's hoop is broken and scattered. There is no center any longer, and the sacred tree is dead."

What happened after that until the summer I was nine years old is not a story. There were winters and summers, and they were good; for the Wasichus [white men] had made their iron road [the Union Pacific Railway] along the Platte and traveled there. This had cut the bison herd in two, but those that stayed in our country with us were more than could be counted, and we wandered without trouble in our land. . . .

It was the summer when I was nine years old, and our people were moving slowly towards the Rocky Mountains. We camped one evening in a valley beside a little creek just before it ran into the Greasy Grass [the Little Big Horn River], and there was a man by the name of Man Hip who liked me and asked me to eat with him in his tepee.

While I was eating, a voice came and said: "It is time; now they are calling you." The voice was so loud and clear that I believed it, and I thought I would just go where it wanted me to go. So I got right up and started. As I came out of the tepee, both my thighs began to hurt me, and suddenly it was like waking from a dream, and there wasn't any voice. So I went back into the tepee, but I didn't want to eat. Man Hip looked at me in a strange way and asked me what was wrong. I told him that my legs were hurting me.

The next morning the camp moved again, and I was riding with some boys. We stopped to get a drink from a creek, and when I got off my horse, my legs crumpled under me and I could not walk. So the boys helped me up and put me on my horse; and when we camped again that evening, I was sick. The next day the camp moved on to where the different bands of our people were coming together, and I rode in a pony drag, for I was very sick. Both my legs and both my arms were swollen badly and my face was all puffed up.

When we had camped again, I was lying in our tepee and my mother and father were sitting beside me. I could see out through the opening, and there two men were coming from the clouds, headfirst like arrows slanting down, and I knew they were the same that I had seen before. Each now carried a long spear, and from the points of these a jagged lightning flashed. They came clear down to the ground this time and stood a little way off and looked at me and said: "Hurry! Come! Your Grandfathers are calling you!"

Then they turned and left the ground like arrows slanting upward from the bow. When I got up to follow, my legs did not hurt me any more and I was very light. I went outside the tepee, and yonder where the men with flaming spears were going, a little cloud was coming very fast. It came and stooped and took me and turned back to where it came from, flying fast. And when I looked down I could see my mother and my father yonder, and I felt sorry to be leaving them.

Then there was nothing but the air and the swiftness of the little cloud that bore me and those two men still leading up to where white clouds were piled like mountains on a wide blue plain, and in them thunder beings lived and leaped and flashed.

. . . . .

Then as we walked, there was a heaped up cloud ahead that changed into a tepee, and a rainbow was the open door of it; and through the door I saw six old men sitting in a row.

The two men with the spears now stood beside me, one on either hand, and the horses took their places in their quarters, looking inward four by four. And the oldest of the Grandfathers spoke with a kind voice and said: "Come right in and do not fear." And as he spoke, all the horses of the four quarters neighed to cheer me. So I went in and stood before the six, and they looked older than men can ever be—old like hills, like stars.

The oldest spoke again: "Your Grandfathers all over the world are having a council, and they have called you here to teach you." His voice was very kind, but I shook all over with fear now, for I knew that these were not old men, but the Powers of the World. And the first was the Power of the West; the second, of the North; the third, of the East; the fourth, of the South; the fifth, of the Sky; the sixth, of the Earth. I knew this, and was afraid, until the first Grandfather spoke again: "Behold them yonder where the sun goes down, the thunder beings! You shall see, and have from them my power; and they shall take you to the high and lonely center of the earth that you may see; even to the place where the sun continually shines, they shall take you there to understand."

And as he spoke of understanding, I looked up and saw the rainbow leaping with flames of many colors over me.

Now there was a wooden cup in his hand and it was full of water and in the water was the sky.

"Take this," he said. "It is the power to make live, and it is yours."

Now he had a bow in his hands. "Take this," he said. "It is the power to destroy, and it is yours."

Then he pointed to himself and said: "Look close at him who is your spirit now, for you are his body and his name is Eagle Wing Stretches."

And saying this, he got up very tall and started running toward where the sun goes down; and suddenly he was a black horse that stopped and turned and looked at me, and the horse was very poor and sick; his ribs stood out.

Then the second Grandfather, he of the North, arose with a herb of power in his hand, and said: "Take this and hurry." I took and held it toward the black horse yonder. He fattened and was happy and came prancing to his place again and was the first Grandfather sitting there.

The second Grandfather, he of the North, spoke again: "Take courage, younger brother," he said; "on earth a nation you shall make live, for yours shall be the power of the white giant's wing, the cleansing wing." Then he got up very tall and started running toward the north; and when he turned toward me, it was a white goose wheeling. I looked about me now, and the horses in the west were thunders and the horses of the north were geese.

. . . . .

And now it was the third Grandfather who spoke, he of where the sun shines continually. "Take courage, younger brother," he said, "for across the earth they shall take you!" Then he pointed to where the daybreak star was shining, and beneath the star two men were flying. "From them you shall have power," he said, "from them who have awakened all the beings of the earth with roots and legs and wings." And as he said this, he held in his hand a peace pipe which had a spotted eagle outstretched upon the stem; and this eagle seemed alive, for it was poised there, fluttering, and its eyes were looking at me. "With this pipe," the Grandfather said, "you shall walk upon the earth, and whatever sickens there you shall make well." Then he pointed to a man who was bright red all over, the color of good and of plenty, and as he pointed the red man lay down and rolled and changed into a bison that got up and galloped toward the sorrel horses of the east, and they too turned to bison, fat and many.

And now the fourth Grandfather spoke, he of the place where you are always facing [the south], whence comes the power to grow. "Younger brother," he said, "with the powers of the four quarters you shall walk, a relative.

Behold the living center of a nation I shall give you, and with it many you shall save." And I saw that he was holding in his hand a bright red stick that was alive, and as I looked it sprouted at the top and sent forth branches, and on the branches many leaves came out and murmured and in the leaves the birds began to sing. And then for just a little while I thought I saw beneath it in the shade the circled villages of people and every living thing with roots or legs or wings, and all were happy. "It shall stand in the center of the nation's circle," said the Grandfather, "a cane to walk with and a people's heart; and by your powers you shall make it blossom."

Then when he had been still a little while to hear the birds sing, he spoke again: "Behold the earth!" So I looked down and saw it lying yonder like a hoop of peoples, and in the center bloomed the holy stick that was a tree, and where it stood there crossed two roads, a red one and a black. "From where the giant lives [the north] to where you always face [the south] the red road goes, the road of good," the Grandfather said, "and on it shall your nation walk. The black road goes from where the thunder beings live [the west] to where the sun continually shines [the east], a fearful road, a road of troubles and of war. On this also you shall walk, and from it you shall have the power to destroy a people's foes. In four ascents you shall walk the earth with power."

I think he meant that I should see four generations, counting me, and now I am seeing the third.

Then he rose very tall and started running toward the south, and was an elk; and as he stood among the buckskins yonder, they too were elks.

Now the fifth Grandfather spoke, the oldest of them all, the Spirit of the Sky. "My boy," he said, "I have sent for you and you have come. My power you shall see!" He stretched his arms and turned into a spotted eagle hovering. "Behold," he said, "all the wings of the air shall come to you, and they and the winds and the stars shall be like relatives. You shall go across the earth with my power." Then the eagle soared above my head and fluttered there; and suddenly the sky was full of friendly wings all coming toward me.

Now I knew the sixth Grandfather was about to speak, he who was the Spirit of the Earth, and I saw that he was very old, but more as men are old. His hair was long and white, his face was all in wrinkles and his eyes were deep and dim. I stared at him, for it seemed I knew him somehow; and as I stared, he slowly changed, for he was growing backwards into youth, and when he had become a boy, I knew that he was myself with all the years that would be mine at last. When he was old again, he said: "My boy, have courage, for my power shall be yours, and you shall need it, for your nation on the earth will have great troubles. Come."

He rose and tottered out through the rainbow door, and as I followed I was riding on the bay horse who had talked to me at first and led me to that place.

Then the bay horse stopped and faced the black horses of the west, and a

Peaceable Kingdom *by Edward Hicks (1870-1949). Oil on canvas.*

The theme of the "peaceable kingdom" was painted dozens of times by Hicks, often as gifts for friends. Its source is a quotation from The Bible *(Isaiah 11:6-8) that begins: "The wolf shall also dwell with the lamb and the leopard shall lie down with the kid; and the calf and the young lion and fatling together; and a little child shall lead them." In the background, Hicks has included another favorite subject, William Penn signing the historic treaty with the Indians.*

voice said: "They have given you the cup of water to make live the greening day, and also the bow and arrow to destroy." The bay neighed, and the twelve black horses came and stood behind me, four abreast.

The bay faced the sorrels of the east, and I saw that they had morning stars upon their foreheads and they were very bright. And the voice said: "They have given you the sacred pipe and the power that is peace, and the good red day." The bay neighed, and the twelve sorrels stood behind me, four abreast.

My horse now faced the buckskins of the south, and a voice said: "They have given you the sacred stick and your nation's hoop, and the yellow day; and in the center of the hoop you shall set the stick and make it grow into a shielding tree, and bloom." The bay neighed, and the twelve buckskins came and stood behind me, four abreast.

. . . . .

So I rode to the center of the village, with the horse troops in their quarters round about me, and there the people gathered. And the Voice said: "Give them now the flowering stick that they may flourish, and the sacred pipe that they may know the power that is peace, and the wing of the white giant that they may have endurance and face all winds with courage."

So I took the bright red stick and at the center of the nation's hoop I thrust it in the earth. As it touched the earth it leaped mightily in my hand and was a waga chun, the rustling tree [the cottonwood], very tall and full of leafy

branches and of all birds singing. And beneath it all the animals were mingling with the people like relatives and making happy cries. The women raised their tremolo of joy, and the men shouted all together: "Here we shall raise our children and be as little chickens under the mother sheo's [prairie hen] wing."

. . . . .

Then I looked up and saw that there were four ascents ahead, and these were generations I should know. Now we were on the first ascent, and all the land was green. And as the long line climbed, all the old men and women raised their hands, palms forward, to the far sky yonder and began to croon a song together, and the sky ahead was filled with clouds of baby faces.

When we came to the end of the first ascent we camped in the sacred circle as before, and in the center stood the holy tree, and still the land about us was all green.

Then we started on the second ascent, marching as before, and still the land was green, but it was getting steeper. And as I looked ahead, the people changed into elks and bison and all four-footed beings and even into fowls, all walking in a sacred manner on the good red road together. And I myself was a spotted eagle soaring over them. But just before we stopped to camp at the end of that ascent, all the marching animals grew restless and afraid that they were not what they had been, and began sending forth voices of trouble, calling to their chiefs. And when they camped at the end of that ascent, I looked down and saw that leaves were falling from the holy tree.

And the Voice said, "Behold your nation, and remember what your Six Grandfathers gave you, for thenceforth your people walk in difficulties."

Then the people broke camp again, and saw the black road before them towards where the sun goes down, and black clouds coming yonder; and they did not want to go but could not stay. And as they walked the third ascent all the animals and fowls that were the people ran here and there, for each one seemed to have his own little vision that he followed and his own rules; and all over the universe I could hear the winds at war like wild beasts fighting.

And when we reached the summit of the third ascent and camped, the nation's hoop was broken like a ring of smoke that spreads and scatters and the holy tree seemed dying and all its birds were gone. And when I looked ahead I saw that the fourth ascent would be terrible.

Then when the people were getting ready to begin the fourth ascent, the Voice spoke like someone weeping, and it said: "Look there upon your nation." And when I looked down, the people were all changed back to human, and they were thin, their faces sharp, for they were starving. Their ponies were only hide and bones, and the holy tree was gone.

And as I looked and wept, I saw that there stood on the north side of the starving camp a sacred man who was painted red all over his body, and he held a spear as he walked into the center

of the people, and there he lay down and rolled. And when he got up, it was a fat bison standing there, and where the bison stood a sacred herb sprang up right where the tree had been in the center of the nation's hoop. The herb grew and bore four blossoms on a single stem while I was looking—a blue, a white, a scarlet, and a yellow—and the bright rays of these flashed to the heavens.

I know now what this meant, that the bison were the gift of a good spirit and were our strength, but we should lose them, and from the same good spirit we must find another strength. For the people all seemed better when the herb had grown and bloomed, and the horses raised their tails and neighed and pranced around, and I could see a light breeze going from the north among the people like a ghost; and suddenly the flowering tree was there again at the center of the nation's hoop where the four-rayed herb had blossomed.

I was still the spotted eagle floating, and I could see that I was already in the fourth ascent and the people were camping yonder at the top of the third long rise. It was dark and terrible about me, for all the winds of the world were fighting. It was like rapid gun-fire and like whirling smoke, and like women and children wailing and like horses screaming all over the world.

I could see my people yonder running about, setting the smoke-flap poles and fastening down their tepees against the wind, for the storm cloud was coming on them very fast and black, and there were frightened swallows without number fleeing before the cloud.

Then a song of power came to me and I sang it there in the midst of that terrible place where I was. It went like this:

A good nation I will make live.
This the nation above has said.
They have given me the power to make
*   over.*

And when I had sung this, a Voice said: "To the four quarters you shall run for help, and nothing shall be strong before you. Behold him!"

Now I was on my bay horse again, because the horse is of the earth, and it was there my power would be used. And as I obeyed the Voice and looked, there was a horse all skin and bones yonder in the west, a faded brownish black. And a Voice there said: "Take this and make him over"; and it was the four-rayed herb that I was holding in my hand. So I rode above the poor horse in a circle, and as I did this I could hear the people yonder calling for spirit power, "A-hey! a-hey! a-hey! a-hey!" Then the poor horse neighed and rolled and got up, and he was a big, shiny, black stallion with dapples all over him and his mane about him like a cloud. He was the chief of all the horses; and when he snorted, it was a flash of lightning and his eyes were like the sunset star. He dashed to the west and neighed, and the west was filled with a dust of hoofs, and horses without number, shiny black, came plunging from the dust. Then he dashed toward the north and neighed, and to the east and to the south, and the dust

clouds answered, giving forth their plunging horses without number— whites and sorrels and buckskins, fat, shiny, rejoicing in their fleetness and their strength. It was beautiful, but it was also terrible.

Then they all stopped short, rearing, and were standing in a great hoop about their black chief at the center, and were still. And as they stood, four virgins, more beautiful than women of the earth can be, came through the circle, dressed in scarlet, one from each of the four quarters, and stood about the great black stallion in their places; and one held the wooden cup of water, and one the white wing, and one the pipe, and one the nation's hoop. All the universe was silent, listening; and then the great black stallion raised his voice and sang. . . . His voice was not loud, but it went all over the universe and filled it. There was nothing that did not hear, and it was more beautiful than anything can be. It was so beautiful that nothing anywhere could keep from dancing. The virgins danced, and all the circled horses. The leaves on the trees, the grasses on the hills and in the valleys, the waters in the creeks and in the rivers and the lakes, the four-legged and the two-legged and the wings of the air—all danced together to the music of the stallion's song.

And when I looked down upon my people yonder, the cloud passed over, blessing them with friendly rain, and stood in the east with a flaming rainbow over it.

Poems

In their view of the natural world, John Keats and William Butler Yeats, poets writing in different eras, shared a reverence for the old stories and myths—Keats, the Greek, and Yeats, the Irish—in which ancient peoples discovered truth through contact with the rhythms of the cosmos. Yeats, however, felt that in the modern era the experience of nature as a source of peace and solace often degenerated to a mere romantic dream or wish. Innisfree, whose name so happily suggests freedom and inwardness, remains but a wishful dream for modern man, cut off from his roots and caught up in hectic daily affairs. Dream or reality, the natural world represented for both poets an infinite resource for getting in touch with one's own inner powers.

Theodore Roethke, author of the third poem "Once More, the Round," like Keats and Yeats, pursued a lifelong search for the meaning to be found in the works of nature.

Picnickers Along Highway 12A, Hanover, New Hampshire *by Jack Delano (1914-   ). Photograph.*

Excerpt from

Endymion

John Keats
(1795-1821)

John Keats is considered one of the greatest poets of the English romantic period, when nature was idealized as a source of innocence, peace and truth. He believed in the power of the human imagination to peer into the workings of nature and to discover there the truth of things. Keats attempted, particularly in his longer poems, to revive the ancient sense of awe and wonder that primitive peoples displayed toward the universe.

A thing of beauty is a joy for ever:
Its loveliness increases; it will never
Pass into nothingness; but still will keep
A bower quiet for us, and a sleep
Full of sweet dreams, and health, and quiet breathing.
Therefore, on every morrow, are we wreathing
A flowery band to bind us to the earth,
Spite of despondence, of the inhuman dearth
Of noble natures, of the gloomy days,
Of all the unhealthy and o'er-darken'd ways
Made for our searching: yes, in spite of all,
Some shape of beauty moves away the pall
From our dark spirits. Such the sun, the moon,
Trees old and young, sprouting a shady boon
For simple sheep; and such are daffodils
With the green world they live in; and clear rills
That for themselves a cooling covert make
'Gainst the hot season; the mid-forest brake,
Rich with a sprinkling of fair musk-rose blooms:
And such too is the grandeur of the dooms
We have imagined for the mighty dead;
All lovely tales that we have heard or read:
An endless fountain of immortal drink,
Pouring unto us from the heaven's brink.

Nor do we merely feel these essences
For one short hour; no, even as the trees
That whisper round a temple become soon
Dear as the temple's self, so does the moon,
The passion poesy, glories infinite,
Haunt us till they become a cheering light
Unto our souls, and bound to us so fast,
That, whether there be shine, or gloom o'ercast,
They always must be with us, or we die.

Abby Aldrich Rockefeller Folk Art Center, Williamsburg, Virginia.

The Residence of David Twining *by Edward Hicks (1870-1949). Oil.*

Hicks was a sign painter and well-known Quaker preacher in Pennsylvania. He painted scenes of farm life and biblical stories in which the fruitfulness and order of the earth are illustrated by the many types of animals and the productive work of man.

The Lake Isle of Innisfree

William Butler Yeats
(1865-1939)

Yeats's passionate love for his native Ireland and its legends drove him to extensive explorations of Irish mythology. He was a founder of the Irish National Theatre as well as a prime mover in the attempt to revive Ireland's culture and civilization. One of the most noted poets of the 20th century, Yeats is best known for his poems about love, nature and art.

I will arise and go now, and go to Innisfree,
And a small cabin build there, of clay and wattles made:
Nine bean-rows will I have there, a hive for the honeybee,
And live alone in the bee-loud glade.

And I shall have some peace there, for peace comes dropping slow,
Dropping from the veils of the morning to where the cricket sings;
There midnight's all a glimmer, and noon a purple glow,
And evening full of the linnet's wings.

I will arise and go now, for always night and day
I hear lake water lapping with low sounds by the shore;
While I stand on the roadway, or on the pavements grey,
I hear it in the deep heart's core.

Once More, the Round

Theodore Roethke
(1908-1963)

Born in Saginaw, Michigan, Theodore Roethke grew up in the environs of a greenhouse owned by his father and uncle. Many of his poems are based on his boyhood experiences working in the greenhouse.

Roethke taught at various colleges, including the University of Washington; he won the Pulitzer Prize in 1954 for The Waking: Poems 1933-1953, *as well as several other national awards for his poetry. He loved and admired William Blake, a romantic poet of 18th century England whose poetry protested the materialism and rationalism of the new industrial age. In his writings Roethke seeks to revive his own sense of cosmic oneness with all forms of life, and in the following poem he creates a ritual, a dance, for doing so.*

What's greater, Pebble or Pond?
What can be known? The Unknown.
My true self runs toward a Hill
More! O More! visible.

Now I adore my life
With the Bird, the abiding Leaf,
With the Fish, the questing Snail,
And the Eye altering all;
And I dance with William Blake
For love, for Love's sake;

And everything comes to One,
As we dance on, dance on, dance on.

Excerpt from

The Adulterous Woman

Albert Camus
(1913-1960)

On receiving the Nobel Prize for Literature in 1957, Albert Camus, Algerian-born novelist and playwright, spoke of two trusts the writer bears, "the service of truth and the service of freedom." All of his literary works reflect his own tireless search for meaning, with truth and freedom as companions on the journey. The story from which the following excerpt is taken focuses on a woman who yearns to be liberated from the "craziness or stuffiness of life, the long anguish of living and dying." She attains spiritual freedom and a new meaning in life as she gradually experiences an awareness of the world around her, ultimately achieving a brief but profound union with nature and the universe.

As the narrative opens, Janine and Marcel, a married couple, are riding through the desert on a bus. Their fatigue and annoyance at physical discomfort mar the journey. They stop at a hotel where they will stay for one night. Our selection begins as they take the hotel manager's advice and climb the stairs of a fort for a view of the desert.

When they climbed the stairs to the fort, it was five o'clock. The wind had died down altogether. The sky, completely clear, was now periwinkle blue. The cold, now drier, made their cheeks smart. Halfway up the stairs an old Arab, stretched out against the wall, asked them if they wanted a guide, but didn't budge, as if he had been sure of their refusal in advance. The stairs were long and steep despite several landings of packed earth. As they climbed, the space widened and they rose into an ever broader light, cold and dry, in which every sound from the oasis reached them pure and distinct. The bright air seemed to vibrate around them with a vibration increasing in length as they advanced, as if their progress struck from the crystal of light a sound wave that kept spreading out. And as soon as they reached the terrace and their gaze was lost in the vast horizon beyond the palm grove, it seemed to Janine that the whole sky rang with a single short and piercing note, whose echoes gradually filled the space above her, then suddenly died and left her silently facing the limitless expanse.

From east to west, in fact, her gaze swept slowly, without encountering a single obstacle, along a perfect curve. Beneath her, the blue-and-white terraces of the Arab town overlapped one another, splattered with the dark-red spots of peppers drying in the sun. Not a soul could be seen, but from the inner courts, together with the aroma of roasting coffee, there rose laughing voices or incomprehensible stamping of feet. Farther off, the palm grove, divided into uneven squares by clay walls, rustled its upper foliage in a wind that could not be felt up on the terrace. Still farther off and all the way to the horizon extended the ocher-and-gray realm of stones, in which no life was visible. At some distance from the oasis, however, near the wadi that bordered the palm grove on the west could be seen broad black tents. All around them a flock of motionless dromedaries, tiny at that distance, formed against the gray ground the black signs of a strange handwriting, the meaning of which had to be deciphered. Above the desert, the silence was as vast as the space.

Janine, leaning her whole body against the parapet, was speechless, unable to tear herself away from the void opening before her. Beside her, Marcel was getting restless. He was cold; he wanted to go back down. What was there to see here, after all? But she could not take her gaze from the horizon. Over yonder, still farther south, at that point where sky and earth met in a pure line—over yonder it suddenly seemed there was awaiting her something of which, though it had always been lacking, she had never been aware until now. In the advancing afternoon the light relaxed and softened; it was passing from the crystalline to the liquid. Simultaneously, in the heart of a woman brought there by pure chance a knot tightened by the years, habit, and boredom was slowly loosening. She was looking at the nomads' encampment. She had not even seen the men living in it; nothing was stirring among the black tents, and yet she could think only of them whose existence she had barely known until this day. Homeless, cut off from the world, they were a handful wandering over the vast territory she could see, which however was but a paltry part of an even greater expanse whose dizzying course stopped only thousands of miles farther south, where the first river finally waters the forest. Since the beginning of time, on the dry earth of this limitless land scraped to the bone, a few men had been ceaselessly trudging, possessing nothing but serving no one, poverty-stricken but free lords of a strange kingdom. Janine did not know why this thought filled her with such a sweet, vast melancholy that it closed her eyes. She knew that this kingdom had been eternally promised her and yet that it would never be hers, never again, except in this fleeting moment perhaps when she opened her eyes again on the suddenly motionless sky and on its waves of steady light, while the voices rising from the Arab town suddenly fell silent. It seemed to her that the world's course had just stopped and that, from that moment on, no one would ever age any more or die. Everywhere, henceforth, life was suspended—except in her heart, where, at the same moment, someone was weeping with affliction and wonder.

But the light began to move; the sun, clear and devoid of warmth, went down toward the west, which became slightly pink, while a gray wave took shape in the east ready to roll slowly over the vast expanse. A first dog barked and its distant bark rose in the now even colder air. Janine noticed that her teeth were chattering. "We are catching our death of cold," Marcel said. "You're a fool. Let's go back." But he took her hand awkwardly. Docile now, she turned away from the parapet and followed him. Without moving, the old Arab on the stairs watched them go down toward the town. She walked along without seeing anyone, bent under a tremendous and sudden fatigue, dragging her body, whose weight now seemed to her unbearable. Her exaltation had left her. Now she felt too tall, too thick, too white too for this world she had just entered. A child, the girl, the dry man, the furtive jackal were the only creatures who could silently walk that earth. What would she do there henceforth except to drag herself toward sleep, toward death?

She dragged herself, in fact, toward the restaurant with a husband suddenly taciturn unless he was telling how tired he was, while she was struggling weakly against a cold, aware of a fever rising within her. Then she dragged herself toward her bed, where Marcel came to join her and put the light out at once without asking anything of her. The room was frigid. Janine felt the cold creeping up while the fever was increasing. She breathed with difficulty, her blood pumped without warming her; a sort of fear grew within her. She turned over and the old iron bedstead groaned under her weight. No, she didn't want to fall ill. Her husband was already asleep; she too had to sleep; it was essential. The muffled sounds of the town reached her through the window-slit. With a nasal twang old phonographs in the Moorish cafés ground out tunes she

recognized vaguely; they reached her borne on the sound of a slow-moving crowd. She must sleep. But she was counting black tents; behind her eyelids motionless camels were grazing; immense solitudes were whirling within her. Yes, why had she come? She fell asleep on that question.

She awoke a little later. The silence around her was absolute. But, on the edges of town, hoarse dogs were howling in the soundless night. Janine shivered. She turned over, felt her husband's hard shoulder against hers, and suddenly, half asleep, huddled against him. She was drifting on the surface of sleep without sinking in and she clung to that shoulder with unconscious eagerness as her safest haven. She was talking, but no sound issued from her mouth. She was talking, but she herself hardly heard what she was saying. She could feel only Marcel's warmth. . . .

She called him with all her heart. After all, she too needed him, his strength, his little eccentricities, and she too was afraid of death. "If I could overcome that fear, I'd be happy. . . ." Immediately, a nameless anguish seized her. She drew back from Marcel. No, she was overcoming nothing, she was not happy, she was going to die, in truth, without having been liberated. Her heart pained her; she was stifling under a huge weight that she suddenly discovered she had been dragging around for twenty years. Now she was struggling under it with all her strength. She wanted to be liberated even if Marcel, even if the others, never were! Fully awake, she sat up in bed and listened to a call that seemed very close.

But from the edges of night the exhausted and yet indefatigable voices of the dogs of the oasis were all that reached her ears. A slight wind had risen and she heard its light waters flow in the palm grove. It came from the south, where desert and night mingled now under the again unchanging sky, where life stopped, where no one would ever age or die any more. Then the waters of the wind dried up and she was not even sure of having heard anything except a mute call that she could, after all, silence or notice. But never again would she know its meaning unless she responded to it at once. At once—yes, that much was certain at least!

She got up gently and stood motionless beside the bed, listening to her husband's breathing. Marcel was asleep. The next moment, the bed's warmth left her and the cold gripped her. She dressed slowly, feeling for her clothes in the faint light coming through the blinds from the street-lamps. Her shoes in her hand, she reached the door. She waited a moment more in the darkness, then gently opened the door. The knob squeaked and she stood still. Her heart was beating madly. She listened with her body tense and, reassured by the silence, turned her hand a little more. The knob's turning seemed to her interminable. At last she opened the door, slipped outside, and closed the door with the same stealth. Then, with her cheek against the wood, she waited. After a moment she made out, in the distance, Marcel's breathing. She faced about, felt the icy night air against her cheek, and ran the length of the balcony. The outer door was closed.

While she was slipping the bolt, the night watchman appeared at the top of the stairs, his face blurred with sleep, and spoke to her in Arabic. "I'll be back," said Janine as she stepped out into the night.

Garlands of stars hung down from the black sky over the palm trees and houses. She ran along the short avenue, now empty, that led to the fort. The cold, no longer having to struggle against the sun, had invaded the night; the icy air burned her lungs. But she ran, half blind, in the darkness. At the top of the avenue, however, lights appeared, then descended toward her zigzagging. She stopped, caught the whir of turning sprockets and, behind the enlarging lights, soon saw vast burnooses surmounting fragile bicycle wheels. The burnooses flapped against her; then three red lights sprang out of the black behind her and disappeared at once. She continued running toward the fort. Halfway up the stairs, the air burned her lungs with such cutting effect that she wanted to stop. A final burst of energy hurled her despite herself onto the terrace, against the parapet, which was now pressing her belly. She was panting and everything was hazy before her eyes. Her running had not warmed her and she was still trembling all over. But the cold air she was gulping down soon flowed evenly inside her and a spark of warmth began to flow amidst her shivers. Her eyes opened at last on the expanse of night.

Not a breath, not a sound—except at intervals the muffled crackling of stones that the cold was reducing to sand—disturbed the solitude and silence surrounding Janine. After a moment, however, it seemed to her that the sky above her was moving in a sort of slow gyration. In the vast reaches of the dry, cold night, thousands of stars were constantly appearing, and their sparkling icicles, loosened at once, began to slip gradually toward the horizon. Janine could not tear herself away from contemplating those drifting flares. She was turning with them, and the apparently stationary progress little by little identified her with the core of her being, where cold and desire were now vying with each other. Before her the stars were falling one by one and being snuffed out among the stones of the desert, and each time Janine opened a little more to the night. Breathing deeply, she forgot the cold, the dead weight of others, the craziness or stuffiness of life, the long anguish of living and dying. After so many years of mad, aimless fleeing from fear, she had come to a stop at last. At the same time, she seemed to recover her roots and the sap again rose in her body, which had ceased trembling. Her whole belly pressed against the parapet as she strained toward the moving sky; she was

merely waiting for her fluttering heart to calm down and establish silence within her. The last stars of the constellations dropped their clusters a little lower on the desert horizon and became still. Then, with unbearable gentleness, the water of night began to fill Janine, drowned the cold, rose gradually from the hidden core of her being and overflowed in wave after wave, rising up even to her mouth full of moans. The next moment, the whole sky stretched out over her, fallen on her back on the cold earth.

When Janine returned to the room, with the same precautions, Marcel was not awake. But he whimpered as she got back in bed and a few seconds later sat up suddenly. He spoke and she didn't understand what he was saying. He got up, turned on the light, which blinded her. He staggered toward the washbasin and drank a long draught from the bottle of mineral water. He was about to slip between the sheets when, one knee on the bed, he looked at her without understanding. She was weeping copiously, unable to restrain herself. "It's nothing, dear," she said, "it's nothing."

The Immense Journey

Loren Eiseley
(1907-1974)

In The Immense Journey, *Loren Eiseley, scientist and poet, imaginatively portrays the ways in which human life is linked to nature and to our animal forebears. He uses incidents from his own experience to illustrate the carefully constructed story. In the following selection, he feels a harmony with nature as he reflects on the complex process of evolution.*

Eiseley was a professor of anthropology at the University of Pennsylvania at the time of his death in 1974. A reviewer said of him recently, "He is every writer's writer, and every human's human." Among his other books are The Unexpected Universe, Darwin's Century *and* The Night Country.

The Slit

Some lands are flat and grass-covered, and smile so evenly up at the sun that they seem forever youthful, untouched by man or time. Some are torn, ravaged and convulsed like the features of profane old age. Rocks are wrenched up and exposed to view; black pits receive the sun but give back no light.

It was to such a land I rode, but I rode to it across a sunlit, timeless prairie over which nothing passed but antelope or a wandering bird. On the verge where that prairie halted before a great wall of naked sandstone and clay, I came upon the Slit. A narrow crack worn by some descending torrent had begun secretly, far back in the prairie grass, and worked itself deeper and deeper into the fine sandstone that led by devious channels into the broken waste beyond. I rode back along the crack to a spot where I could descend into it, dismounted, and left my horse to graze.

The crack was only about body-width and, as I worked my way downward, the light turned dark and green from the overhanging grass. Above me the sky became a narrow slit of distant blue, and the sandstone was cool to my hands on either side. The Slit was a little sinister—like an open grave, assuming the dead were enabled to take one last look—for over me the sky seemed already as far off as some future century I would never see.

I ignored the sky, then, and began to concentrate on the sandstone walls that had led me into this place. It was tight and tricky work, but that cut was a perfect cross section through perhaps ten million years of time. I hoped to find at least a bone, but I was not quite prepared for the sight I finally came upon. Staring straight out at me, as I slid farther and deeper into the green twilight, was a skull embedded in the solid sandstone. I had come at just the proper moment when it was fully to be seen, the white bone gleaming there in a kind of ashen splendor, water worn, and about to be ground away in the next long torrent.

It was not, of course, human. I was deep, deep below the time of man in a remote age near the beginning of the reign of mammals. I squatted on my heels in the narrow ravine, and we stared a little blankly at each other, the skull and I. There were marks of generalized primitiveness in that low, pinched brain case and grinning jaw that marked it as lying far back along those converging roads where, as I shall have occasion to establish elsewhere, cat and man and weasel must leap into a single shape.

It was the face of a creature who had spent his days following his nose, who was led by instinct rather than memory, and whose power of choice was very small. Though he was not a man, nor a direct human ancestor, there was yet about him, even in the bone, some trace of that low, snuffling world out of which our forebears had so recently emerged. The skull lay tilted in such a manner that it stared, sightless, up at me as though I, too, were already caught a few feet above him in the strata and, in my turn, were staring upward at that strip of sky which the ages were carrying farther away from me beneath the tumbling debris of falling mountains. The creature had never lived to see a man, and I, what was it I was never going to see?

I restrained a panicky impulse to hurry upward after that receding sky that was outlined above the Slit. Probably, I thought, as I patiently began the task of chiseling into the stone around the

skull, I would never again excavate a fossil under conditions which led to so vivid an impression that I was already one myself. The truth is that we are all potential fossils still carrying within our bodies the crudities of former existences, the marks of a world in which living creatures flow with little more consistency than clouds from age to age.

As I tapped and chiseled there in the foundations of the world, I had ample time to consider the cunning manipulability of the human fingers. Experimentally I crooked one of the long slender bones. It might have been

The marvelous continuity of nature is called to mind by this photograph of a dinosaur footprint large enough to hold a child and 18 gallons of water. In his essay "The Slit," Loren Eiseley describes an insight that came to him on excavating a fossil: "That we are all potential fossils still carrying within our bodies the crudities of former existences." What are your own feelings about being part of the earth's physical history?

silica, I thought, or aluminum, or iron—the cells would have made it possible. But no, it is calcium, carbonate of lime. Why? Only because of its history. Elements more numerous than calcium in the earth's crust could have been used to build the skeleton. Our history is the reason—we came from the water. It was there the cells took the lime habit, and they kept it after we came ashore.

It is not a bad symbol of that long wandering, I thought again—the human hand that has been fin and scaly reptile foot and furry paw. If a stone should fall (I cocked an eye at the leaning shelf above my head and waited, fatalistically), let the bones lie here with their message, for those who might decipher it, if they come down late among us from the stars.

Above me the great crack seemed to lengthen.

Perhaps there is no meaning in it at all, the thought went on inside me, save that of journey itself, so far as men can see. It has altered with the chances of life, and the chances brought us here; but it was a good journey—long, perhaps—but a good journey under a pleasant sun. Do not look for the purpose. Think of the way we came and be a little proud. Think of this hand—the utter pain of its first venture on the pebbly shore.

Further Readings

Carson, Rachel. *The Sea Around Us*. Revised edition, 1961. A work about the sea which combines scientific observation with poetic language. It has been called one of the most beautiful books of our time.

Dillard, Annie. *Pilgrim at Tinker Creek*. 1974. Mystical musings from detailed natural observations made during one year in the Blue Ridge Mountains. The author finds "grace tangled in a rapture with violence . . . mystery, newness and a kind of spendthrift energy" in nature.

Hamsun, Knut. *Growth of the Soil*. 1953. A novel about the dramatic relationship between the eternal tiller of the soil and the earth he works.

Krutch, Joseph Wood. *The Best Nature Writing of Joseph Wood Krutch*. 1970. Thirty-four essays by a distinguished naturalist about everything from spring peepers to the Grand Canyon.

Matthiessen, Peter. *The Snow Leopard*. 1978. Philosophical observations based on a journal Matthiessen kept during his journey to the Crystal Mountain in upper Nepal in 1973.

Porter, Eliot. *In Wildness Is the Preservation of the World*. 1967. The photographs of Eliot Porter are juxtaposed with selections from Henry David Thoreau. Wilderness as necessary for the health of the human spirit.

Saint-Exupéry, Antoine de. *Wind, Sand and Stars*. 1939. Reminiscences by a flyer of his flights in Africa, South America and Europe. Philosophy and poetry as well as information on aviation.

Schneider, Bruno. *Renoir*. 1967. Brief but well-documented account of the painter's life accompanied by 44 full color reproductions and 30 drawings.

Witt, Shirley Hill and Stan Steiner, eds. *The Way*. 1972. An anthology of American Indian writings from a variety of contexts: spiritual, cultural and political.

Section 5

TRUTH IN THE UNSEEN

The various ways of finding meaning in life examined in previous sections have one thing in common: They all try to find a value *within* the world of individual life. They do not exclude the idea of an invisible realm or purpose, but they do not *require* anything beyond the physical, historical world of experience to provide meaning. For many persons, the simple, unquestionable joy of knowing and loving others helps to offset the adversities in their experience. For others, the mere fact that everyone plays a part in the unity and continuance of a family or other group or of the ongoing life of the universe compensates for the ambiguities and brevity of individual existence.

Since the dawn of human civilization, such temporal answers to the search for meaning have in themselves often proved insufficient. In the past and still today, the satisfaction found in personal relationships, in participation in a larger social whole and in the contemplation of nature has usually depended on a conviction that those experiences make sense in a wider context. In this section we focus on the attempt to find meaning hidden behind or beyond the visible, tangible world. Understanding our existence in such a light, the questions and contradictions of the human situation are resolvable only if we realize that what we see, hear, feel and touch is not the whole truth. Furthermore, human relationships, social unity and even oneness with the universe itself are too fleeting to provide adequate fulfillment of our fundamental intellectual and spiritual needs. We can find relief from the uncertainties of time and space, birth and death and pain and sorrow only if we direct our thoughts and imaginations to an unseen, eternal, unchanging realm where truth is to be found.

Ripples in the sand in Death Valley, California, and a vista that seems to have no end.

TRUTH IN THE UNSEEN

The ancient Greek philosopher Plato believed that the soul is immortal and existed before birth, when it was capable of grasping the invisible truth. In this life, however, the soul is clouded and confused by its union with the physical body. As a result we have great difficulty in understanding the world and ourselves. Indeed, most of us often completely reverse the value of things. We grow up thinking that material, temporal things are real and important, whereas they are only shadows of reality. The real world is unseen by our physical eyes. It is eternal, perfect, unchanging. We can know the meaning of life, Plato argues, only when we see with our "mind's eye" the eternal "form" or "idea" of things—of which visible things are superficial and ultimately unimportant copies.

In the first reading from *The Republic*, Plato argues that the only people who can rule well in a society are philosophers (lovers of wisdom). They have achieved the proper balance between experience of the visible world and knowledge of the truly good but unseen realm. Try to determine what the different people and things in the Parable of the Cave correspond to in actual life. According to Plato, how might we begin to achieve the vision of truth? Do you agree with his devaluation of this world of "becoming" or change in favor of the unchanging and eternal?

Wordsworth's ode "Intimations of Immortality" picks up many of Plato's ideas, though the poet differs from the philosopher in at least two respects. First, Wordsworth thinks that the awareness of truth and beauty is lost not at birth but in adolescence when "shades of the prison-house begin to close upon the growing boy." Secondly, whereas Plato tends to look for truth by directing the mind *away* from the natural world, Wordsworth seems to direct us *toward* the depths in nature: "To me the meanest flower that blows can give/ thoughts that do often lie too deep for tears." Do you think that Wordsworth is right in implying that the "vision splendid" fades in adulthood? How does he suggest that we recover the "celestial light"? In a contemporary vein, D.H. Lawrence in *"Terra Incognita"* reminds us of the "vast realms of consciousness" within, but seems to question whether we can ever *know* the truth.

When people speak of finding meaning in the supernatural realm, they are almost inevitably using religious language. Thus Plato talks of "the contemplation of the divine," and Wordsworth can say that we come "trailing clouds of glory . . . from God, who is our home." But both authors differ in one respect from the emphasis of *The Bible*. They imply that the discovery of truth is a matter of *self*-discovery, of plumbing the depths of human knowledge of the unseen. In *The Bible*, knowledge of the unseen depends on God's act or word that reveals or discloses truth otherwise hidden from human wisdom. The meaning of life, or at least the assurance that there *is* meaning beyond our immediate understanding, is

106

given to us rather than attained by us.

In the selection from The Book of Job, God speaks "out of the whirlwind," and Job is reduced to silence. Human effort is negated rather than exalted; meaning is not discovered by human search but uncovered by divine grace. What does this suggest about the appropriate attitude for those who desire to find truth in the unseen? Are the revelation and conviction given to Job experiences common to many people? How does a direct encounter with God such as Job experienced help to satisfy the human need for meaning in *this* life?

The two poems by Emily Dickinson are on a less dramatic level than The Book of Job, but convey a restless confidence in the reality of the unseen and in the illumination that truth brings to ordinary experience. Like Plato, Wordsworth and Job, the poet recognizes that ambiguity and doubt are always involved in faith in the unseen: "Narcotics cannot still the Tooth that nibbles at the soul" . . . "And Life steps *almost* straight." You may want to recall times in your life when the certainty of ultimate meaning has been strong and times when holding on to faith in the unseen has been difficult. What factors seem to affect such variations?

The Republic

Plato
(412-347 BC)

Plato lived in the city-state of Athens, Greece, at the time of a remarkable flowering of human thought that was to lay the intellectual foundation of western civilization. He was the disciple of the philosopher Socrates who, in 399 B.C., was tried and executed for challenging the traditional ideas of Athenian society. Socrates held that the reasoning mind, if disciplined and challenged, will uncover the world's great truths. He taught by a question-and-answer method of logical argument called "dialectic." In the following passage, Plato has Socrates engaging in such a dialectic with a student named Glaucon.

This selection presents the famous Parable of the Cave. Socrates shows a man ascending from the dark cave of ignorance and illusion to the bright light of education, knowledge and truth. We do not know how much of what Plato attributes to Socrates is actually what Socrates taught. Nevertheless, while there is no reason to suppose that he contradicted Socrates' point of view, Plato undoubtedly developed and modified his teacher's ideas.

Next, I said, compare the effect of education and the lack of it upon our human nature to a situation like this: imagine men to be living in an underground cave-like dwelling place, which has a way up to the light along its whole width, but the entrance is a long way up. The men have been there from childhood, with their neck and legs in fetters, so that they remain in the same place and can only see ahead of them, as their bonds prevent them turning their heads. Light is provided by a fire burning some way behind and above them. Between the fire and the prisoners, some way behind them and on a higher ground, there is a path across the cave and along this a low wall has been built, like the screen at a puppet show in front of the performers who show their puppets above it. — I see it.

See then also men carry along that wall, so that they overtop it, all kinds of artifacts, statues of men, reproductions of other animals in stone or wood fashioned in all sorts of ways, and, as is likely, some of the carriers are talking while others are silent. — This is a strange picture, and strange prisoners.

They are like us, I said. Do you think, in the first place, that such men could see anything of themselves and each other except the shadows which the fire casts upon the wall of the cave in front of them? — How could they, if they have to keep their heads still throughout life?

And is not the same true of the objects carried along the wall?—Quite.

If they could converse with one

another, do you not think that they would consider these shadows to be the real things? — Necessarily.

What if their prison had an echo which reached them from in front of them? Whenever one of the carriers passing behind the wall spoke, would they not think that was the shadow passing in front of them which was talking? Do you agree? — By Zeus I do.

Altogether then, I said, such men would believe the truth to be nothing else than the shadows of the artifacts? — They must believe that.

Consider then what deliverance from their bonds and the curing of their ignorance would be if something like this naturally happened to them. Whenever one of them was freed, had to stand up suddenly, turn his head, walk, and look up toward the light, doing all that would give him pain, the flash of the fire would make it impossible for him to see the objects of which he had earlier seen the shadows. What do you think he would say if he was told that what he saw then was foolishness, that he was not somewhat closer to reality and turned to things that existed more fully, that he saw more correctly? If one then pointed to each of the objects passing by, asked him what each was, and forced him to answer, do you not think he would be at a loss and believe that the things which he saw earlier were truer than the things now pointed out to him?—Much truer.

If one then compelled him to look at the fire itself, his eyes would hurt, he would turn round and flee toward those things which he could see, and think that they were in fact clearer than those now shown to him — Quite so.

And if one were to drag him thence by force up the rough and steep path, and did not let him go before he was dragged into the sunlight, would he not be in physical pain and angry as he was dragged along? When he came into the light, with the sunlight filling his eyes, he would not be able to see a single one of the things which are now said to be true. — Not at once, certainly.

I think he would need time to get adjusted before he could see things in the world above; at first he would see shadows most easily, then reflections of men and other things in water, then the things themselves. After this he would see objects in the sky and the sky itself more easily at night, the light of the stars and the moon more easily than the sun and the light of the sun during the day. — Of course.

Then, at last, he would be able to see the sun, not images of it in water or in some alien place, but the sun itself in its own place, and be able to contemplate it. — That must be so.

After this he would reflect that it is the sun which provides the seasons and the years, which governs everything in the visible world, and is also in some way the cause of those other things which he used to see. — Clearly that would be the next stage.

What then? As he reminds himself of his first dwelling place, of the wisdom there and of his fellow prisoners, would he not reckon himself happy for the change, and pity them? — Surely.

And if the men below had praise and honours from each other, and prizes for the man who saw most clearly the shadows that passed before them, and who could best remember which usually came earlier and which later, and which came together and thus could most ably prophesy the future, do you think our man would desire those rewards and envy those who honoured and held power among the prisoners, or would he feel, as Homer put it, that he certainly wished to be "serf to another man without possessions upon the earth"* and go through any suffering, rather than share their opinions and live as they do? — Quite so, he said, I think he would rather suffer anything.

Reflect on this too, I said. If this man went down into the cave again and sat down in the same seat, would his eyes not be filled with darkness, coming suddenly out of the sunlight?—They certainly would.

And if he had to contend again with those who had remained prisoners in recognizing those shadows while his sight was affected and his eyes had not settled down—and the time for this adjustment would not be short—would he not be ridiculed? Would it not be said that he had returned from his upward journey with his eyesight spoiled, and that it was not worthwhile even to attempt to travel upward? As for the man who tried to free them and lead them upward, if they could somehow lay their hands on him and kill him, they would do so. — They certainly would.

This whole image, my dear Glaucon, I said, must be related to what we said before. The realm of the visible should be compared to the prison dwelling, and the fire inside it to the power of the sun.

Seen and yet unseen, the communication between the boy and the African sculpture is meaningful.

If you interpret the upward journey and the contemplation of things above as the upward journey of the soul to the intelligible realm, you will grasp what I surmise since you were keen to hear it. Whether it is true or not only the god knows, but this is how I see it, namely that in the intelligible world the Form of the Good is the last to be seen, and with difficulty; when seen it must be reckoned to be for all the cause of all that is right and beautiful, to have produced in the visible world both light and the fount of light, while in the intelligible world it is itself that which produces and controls truth and intelligence, and he who is to act intelligently in public or in private must see it. — I share your thought as far as I am able.

Come then, share with me this thought also: do not be surprised that those who have reached this point are unwilling to occupy themselves with human affairs, and that their souls are

_____

*Homer's *Odyssey,* written before 700 B.C.

always pressing upward to spend their time there, for this is natural if things are as our parable indicates. — That is very likely.

Further, I said, do you think it at all surprising that anyone coming to the evils of human life from the contemplation of the divine behaves awkwardly and appears very ridiculous while his eyes are still dazzled and before he is sufficiently adjusted to the darkness around him, if he is compelled to contend in court or some other place about the shadows of justice or the objects of which they are shadows, and to carry through the contest about these in the way these things are understood by those who have never seen Justice itself? — That is not surprising at all.

Anyone with intelligence, I said, would remember that the eyes may be confused in two ways and from two causes, coming from light into darkness as well as from darkness into light.

Realizing that the same applies to the soul, whenever he sees a soul disturbed and unable to see something, he will not laugh mindlessly but will consider whether it has come from a brighter life and is dimmed because unadjusted, or has come from greater ignorance into greater light and is filled with a brighter dazzlement. The former he would declare happy in its life and experience, the latter he would pity, and if he should wish to laugh at it, his laughter would be less ridiculous than if he laughed at a soul that has come from the light above. — What you say is very reasonable.

We must then, I said, if these things are true, think something like this about them, namely that education is not what some declare it to be; they say that knowledge is not present in the soul and that they put it in, like putting sight into blind eyes. — They surely say that.

Our present arguments shows, I said, that the capacity to learn and the organ with which to do so are present in every person's soul. It is as if it were not possible to turn the eye from darkness to light without turning the whole body; so one must turn one's whole soul from the world of becoming until it can endure to contemplate reality, and the brightest of realities, which we say is the Good. — Yes.

Education then is the art of doing this very thing, this turning around, the knowledge of how the soul can most easily and most effectively be turned around; it is not the art of putting the capacity of sight into the soul; the soul possesses that already but it is not turned the right way or looking where it should. This is what education has to deal with. — That seems likely.

Ode
Intimations of Immortality
from Recollections of Early Childhood

William Wordsworth
(1770-1850)

William Wordsworth is one of the greatest poets of the romantic period in England. During this era childhood and nature were idealized.

As a child, Wordsworth found it very difficult to think of his own eventual death. He also perceived a dream-like vividness and splendor in every experience. As he grew older, he began to lose "the visionary gleam—the glory and the dream" of his childhood. His poem below touches poignantly on this loss.

In Parts I-VIII of the poem, the writer raises questions about the loss of precious things—childhood, mystic experiences, a strong sense of the world of spirit in nature and in self. In parts IX-XI, he attempts an answer to this problem of loss, finding limited consolation in both the world of nature without as well as in the world of memory within.

The Child is Father of the Man;
And I could wish my days to be
Bound each to each by natural piety.

I

There was a time when meadow, grove, and stream,
The earth, and every common sight,
   To me did seem
  Appareled in celestial light,
The glory and the freshness of a dream.
It is not now as it hath been of yore—
   Turn wheresoe'er I may,
    By night or day,
The things which I have seen I now can see no more.

II

  The rainbow comes and goes,
  And lovely is the rose;
   The moon doth with delight
Look round her when the heavens are bare;

Waters on a starry night
Are beautiful and fair;
The sunshine is a glorious birth;
But yet I know, where'er I go,
That there hath passed away a glory from the earth.

III

Now, while the birds thus sing a joyous song
And while the young lambs bound
As to the tabor's sound,
To me alone there came a thought of grief:
A timely utterance gave that thought relief,
And I again am strong:
The cataracts blow their trumpets from the steep;
No more shall grief of mine the season wrong;
I hear the echoes through the mountains throng,
The winds come to me from the fields of sleep,
And all the earth is gay;
Land and sea
Give themselves up to jollity,
And with the heart of May
Doth every beast keep holiday—
Thou child of joy,
Shout round me, let me hear thy shouts, thou happy
shepherd-boy!

IV

Ye blessèd creatures, I have heard the call
Ye to each other make; I see
The heavens laugh with you in your jubilee;
My heart is at your festival,
My head hath its coronal,
The fulness of your bliss, I feel—I feel it all.
Oh evil day! if I were sullen
While earth herself is adorning,
This sweet May-morning,
And the children are culling
On every side,
In a thousand valleys far and wide,
Fresh flowers; while the sun shines warm,
And the babe leaps up on his mother's arm:
I hear, I hear, with joy I hear!

—But there's a tree, of many, one,
A single field which I have looked upon;
Both of them speak of something that is gone:
      The pansy at my feet
      Doth the same tale repeat:
Whither is fled the visionary gleam?
Where is it now, the glory and the dream?

V

Our birth is but a sleep and a forgetting:
The soul that rises with us, our life's star,
      Hath had elsewhere its setting,
        And cometh from afar:
      Not in entire forgetfulness,
      And not in utter nakedness,
But trailing clouds of glory do we come
      From God, who is our home.
Heaven lies about us in our infancy!
Shades of the prison-house begin to close
      Upon the growing boy,
But he beholds the light, and whence it flows;
  He sees it in his joy;
The youth, who daily farther from the east
      Must travel, still is Nature's priest,
      And by the vision splendid
      Is on his way attended;
At length the man perceives it die away
And fade into the light of common day.

VI

Earth fills her lap with pleasures of her own;
Yearnings she hath in her own natural kind.
And, even with something of a mother's mind
      And no unworthy aim,
      The homely nurse doth all she can
To make her foster-child, her inmate man,
      Forget the glories he hath known
And that imperial palace whence he came.

VII

Behold the child among his new-born blisses,
A six years' darling of a pigmy size!
See, where 'mid work of his own hand he lies,

114

Fretted by sallies of his mother's kisses,
With light upon him from his father's eyes!
See at his feet some little plan or chart,
Some fragment from his dream of human life,
Shaped by himself with newly learnèd art:
    A wedding or a festival,
    A mourning or a funeral,
      And this hath now his heart,
    And unto this he frames his song.
      Then will he fit his tongue
To dialogues of business, love, or strife;
    But it will not be long
    Ere this be thrown aside
    And with new joy and pride
The little actor cons another part,
Filling from time to time his "humorous stage"
With all the persons, down to palsied age,
That life brings with her in her equipage,
    As if his whole vocation
    Were endless imitation.

VIII

Thou whose exterior semblance doth belie
    Thy soul's immensity,
Thou best philosopher, who yet dost keep
Thy heritage, thou eye among the blind,
That, deaf and silent, read'st the eternal deep,
Haunted forever by the eternal mind—
    Mighty prophet! Seer blest!
    On whom those truths do rest
Which we are toiling all our lives to find,
In darkness lost, the darkness of the grave;
Thou over whom thy immortality
Broods like the day, a master o'er a slave,
A presence which is not to be put by;
Thou little child, yet glorious in the might
Of heaven-born freedom on thy being's height,
Why with such earnest pains dost thou provoke
The years to bring the inevitable yoke,
Thus blindly with thy blessedness at strife?
Full soon thy soul shall have her earthly freight
And custom lie upon thee with a weight
Heavy as frost, and deep almost as life!

Hirshhorn Museum and Sculpture Garden, Smithsonian Institution, Washington, D.C.

Woman and Little Girl in Front of the Sun *by Joan Miro (1893-   ).*
Spanish. Oil on canvas.

While Surrealists express ideas in personal and vivid ways, they often overturn our logical ideas about the world. The surrealist movement—whose ranks included poets and politicians, as well as artists—began in Europe as a revolt against the established politicians, artists and institutions associated with the chaos of World War I. Miro's paintings are usually marked by animation, humor and bright color which the viewer can appreciate, even though the shapes and lines may be puzzling. This work is not completely abstract like de Rivera's Construction no. 107 *(page 124). We can find sun, eyes and a little girl waving at us.*

IX

O joy! that in our embers
Is something that doth live
That nature yet remembers
What was so fugitive!
The thought of our past years in me doth breed
Perpetual benediction; not indeed
For that which is most worthy to be blest—
Delight and liberty, the simple creed
Of childhood, whether busy or at rest,
With new-fledged hope still fluttering in his breast—
Not for these I raise
The song of thanks and praise;
But for those obstinate questionings
Of sense and outward things,
Fallings from us, vanishings;
Blank misgivings of a creature
Moving about in worlds not realized,
High instincts before which our mortal nature
Did tremble like a guilty thing surprised:
But for those first affections,
Those shadowy recollections,
Which, be they what they may,
Are yet the fountain-like of all our day,
Are yet a master-light of all our seeing;
Uphold us, cherish, and have power to make
Our noisy years seem moments in the being
Of the eternal silence: truths that wake
To perish never:
Which neither listlessness, nor mad endeavor,
Nor man nor boy,
Nor all that is at enmity with joy,
Can utterly abolish or destroy!
Hence in a season of calm weather
Though inland far we be,
Our souls have sight of that immortal sea
Which brought us hither,
Can in a moment travel thither
And see the children sport upon the shore,
And hear the mighty waters rolling evermore.

X

Then sing, ye birds, sing, sing a joyous song!
  And let the young lambs bound
  As to the tabor's sound!
We in thought will join your throng!
  Ye that pipe and ye that play,
  Ye that through your hearts today
  Feel the gladness of the May!
What though the radiance which was once so bright
Be now for ever taken from my sight,
  Though nothing can bring back the hour
Of splendor in the grass, of glory in the flower;
  We will grieve not, rather find
  Strength in what remains behind;
  In the primal sympathy
  Which having been must ever be;
  In the soothing thoughts that spring
  Out of human suffering;
  In the faith that looks through death,
In years that bring the philosophic mind.

XI

And O, ye fountains, meadows, hills, and groves,
Forebode not any severing of our loves!
Yet in my heart of hearts I feel your might;
I only have relinquished one delight
To live beneath your more habitual sway.
I love the brooks which down their channels fret,
Even more than when I tripped lightly as they;
The innocent brightness of a new-born day
  Is lovely yet;
The clouds that gather round the setting sun
Do take a sober coloring from an eye
That hath kept watch o'er man's mortality;
Another race hath been, and other palms are won.
Thanks to the human heart by which we live,
Thanks to its tenderness, its joys, and fears,
To me the meanest flower that blows can give
Thoughts that do often lie too deep for tears.

Terra Incognita

D. H. Lawrence
(1885-1930)

D. H. Lawrence believed that the sense experience is closely related to the spiritual experience. In his writings, he consistently claims that there is an error in believing that the truths of the spiritual world can be analyzed and understood in rational, scientific terms. Rather, he writes, it is in moments when we touch and wonder that we open ourselves to the "vast realms of consciousness still undreamed of." His belief contrasts sharply with the philosophy that proclaims the inner world is experienced only through denial of the senses.

Lawrence always expressed the meaning of his poetry in vivid sense images such as the ones used in the poem below and the one already discussed in Session 2. This type of poetry requires the reader to look closely at the images in the poem in order to understand the meaning more clearly.

There are vast realms of consciousness still undreamed of
vast ranges of experience, like the humming of unseen harps
we know nothing of, within us.
Oh when man escaped from the barbed-wire entanglement
of his own ideas and his own mechanical devices
there is a marvellous rich world of contact and sheer fluid
  beauty
and fearless face-to-face awareness of now-naked life
and me, and you, and other men and women
and grapes, and ghouls, and ghosts and green moonlight
and ruddy-orange limbs stirring the limbo
of the unknown air, and eyes so soft
softer than the space between the stars.
And all things, and nothing, and being and not-being
alternately palpitant.
when at last we escape the barbed-wire enclosure
of *Know Thyself,* knowing we can never know,
we can but touch, and wonder, and ponder, and make our
  effort
and dangle in a last fastidious fine delight
as the fuchsia does, dangling her reckless drop
of purple after so much putting forth
and slow mounting marvel of a little tree.

Excerpt from

The Book of Job
Authorized (King James) Version

Written some time between the sixth and fourth centuries B.C., The Book of Job is considered by many to be one of the greatest literary masterpieces of all time. Its author is unknown. In the biblical story, Job was "perfect and upright, and one that feared God and eschewed evil," a man blessed with personal talents and prosperity. Yet for all this, he is visited by tragedy—the loss of his children, his possessions and his health—and finds it hard to understand why he is visited by such affliction. His friends believe his suffering is God's retribution for something he has done; Job cannot accept this explanation and asks for a response from God himself. In the following passage, God confronts Job. He does not tell Job why the burden of suffering has been laid on him but speaks of his own limitless knowledge and power. Job acknowledges the mystery of God's ways, regains his trust in him and accepts the fact that there is meaning in his life. Those who share Job's faith in the wisdom of an unseen God are sure there is meaning in all they experience and must be satisfied with that conviction without expecting a clear explanation.

Chapter 38

Then the Lord answered Job out of the whirlwind, and said,

2   Who is this that darkeneth counsel by words without knowledge?

3   Gird up now thy loins like a man: for I will demand of thee, and answer thou me.

4   Where wast thou when I laid the foundations of the earth? declare, if thou hast understanding.

5   Who hath laid the measures thereof, if thou knowest? or who hath stretched the line upon it?

6   Whereupon are the foundations thereof fastened? or who laid the corner stone thereof;

7   When the morning stars sang together, and all the sons of God shouted for joy?

8   Or who shut up the sea with doors, when it brake forth, as if it had issued out of the womb?

9   When I made the cloud the garment thereof, and thick darkness a swaddlingband for it,

10   And brake up for it my decreed place, and set bars and doors,

11   And said, Hitherto shalt thou come, but no further: and here shall thy proud waves be stayed?

12   Hast thou commanded the morning since thy days; and caused the dayspring to know his place;

13   That it might take hold of the ends of the earth, that the wicked might be shaken out of it?

14   It is turned as clay to the seal; and they stand as a garment.

15   And from the wicked their light is withholden, and the high arm shall be broken.

16   Hast thou entered into the springs of the sea? or hast thou walked in the search of the depth?

17   Have the gates of death been opened unto thee? or hast thou seen the doors of the shadow of death?

18   Hast thou perceived the breadth of the earth? declare if thou knowest it all.

19   Where is the way where light dwelleth? and as for darkness, where is the place thereof,

20   That thou shouldest take it to the bound thereof, and that thou shouldest know the paths to the house thereof?

21   Knowest thou it, because thou wast then born? or because the number of thy days is great?

22   Hast thou entered into the treasures of the snow? or hast thou seen the treasures of the hail,

23   Which I have reserved against the time of trouble, against the day of battle and war?

24   By what way is the light parted, which scattereth the east mind upon the earth?

25   Who hath divided a watercourse for the overflowing of waters, or a way for the lightning of thunder;

26   To cause it to rain on the earth, where no man is; on the wilderness, wherein there is no man;

27   To satisfy the desolate and waste ground; and to cause the bud of the tender herb to spring forth?

28   Hath the rain a father? or who hath begotten the drops of dew?

29   Out of whose womb came the ice? and the hoary frost of heaven, who hath gendered it?

30   The waters are hid as with a stone, and the face of the deep is frozen.

31   Canst thou bind the sweet influences of Pleiades* or loose the bands of Orion?*

32   Canst thou bring forth Mazzaroth* in his season? or canst thou guide Arcturus* with his sons?

33   Knowest thou the ordinances of heaven? canst thou set the dominion thereof in the earth?

34   Canst thou lift up thy voice to the clouds, that abundance of waters may cover thee?

35   Canst thou send lightnings, that they may go, and say unto thee, Here we are?

36   Who hath put wisdom in the inward parts? or who hath given understanding to the heart?

*Stars or planets

37   Who can number the clouds in wisdom? or who can stay the bottles of heaven,
38   When the dust groweth into hardness, and the clouds cleave fast together?
39   Wilt thou hunt the prey for the lion? or fill the appetite of the young lions,
40   When they couch in their dens, and abide in the covert to lie in wait?
41   Who provideth for the raven his food? when his young ones cry unto God, they wander for lack of meat.

· · · · ·

Chapter 40

Moreover the Lord answered Job, and said,
2   Shall he that contendeth with the Almighty instruct him? he that reproveth God, let him answer it.
3   Then Job answered the Lord, and said,
4   Behold, I am vile;** what shall I answer thee? I will lay mine hand upon my mouth.
5   Once have I spoken; but I will not answer: yea, twice; but I will proceed no further.

**A better translation of the Hebrew is "of small account."

Yin-Yang symbol

Symbols express realities that cannot be seen. Poetry is a symbol. So, in fact, are music and art. The ancient Chinese symbol pictured here represents the dual forces in nature: Yang is male, light, hot, active; yin is female, dark, cold, passive. They are complementary and balancing. The greater one grows, the sooner it yields to the other, in the same fashion that the tide at its lowest ebb begins to give way to high tide. Consider how the shape of this symbol depicts the intertwining relationships and rhythms of nature.

Poems

Emily Dickinson
(1830-1886)

Emily Dickinson is considered one of the most distinguished American poets. She lived a secluded life in her father's home in Massachusetts, devoting herself to her garden and a few friends. In spite of the narrowness of her activities, she lived an intense inner life, and her poetry reveals a witty, rebellious, original woman. She continually questioned the meaning of life and would accept no easy answers. In her poetry Dickinson describes times of doubt as well as times of ecstasy and never acknowledges one or the other as absolute.

The brevity of Emily Dickinson's poems makes them difficult reading for some, because there is no story, only short, quick impulses of intense feeling. She strove constantly to perfect her ability in the craft of poetry. The elements of this craft came from the world in which she lived: The language is a mingling of the lofty speech of religion with the common speech of the kitchen and garden; the rhythms are similar to the stark hymn-book measures with which she was familiar and which she adapted to suit her needs.

I

This World is not Conclusion.
A Species stands beyond -
Invisible, as Music -
But positive, as Sound -
It beckons, and it baffles -
Philosophy - don't know -
And through a Riddle, at the last -
Sagacity, must go -
To guess it, puzzles scholars -
To gain it, Men have borne
Contempt of Generations
And Crucifixion, shown -

Faith slips - and laughs, and rallies -
Blushes if any see -
Plucks at a twig of Evidence -
And asks a Vane, the way -
Much Gesture, from the Pulpit -
Strong Hallelujahs roll -
Narcotics cannot still the Tooth
That nibbles at the soul -

II

We grow accustomed to the Dark -
When Light is put away -
As when the Neighbor holds the Lamp
To witness her Goodbye -

A Moment - We uncertain step
For newness of the night -
Then - fit our Vision to the Dark -
And meet the Road - erect -

And so of larger - Darknesses -
Those Evenings of the Brain -
When not a Moon disclose a sign -
Or Star - come out - within -

The Bravest - grope a little -
And sometimes hit a Tree
Directly in the Forehead -
But as they learn to see -

Either the Darkness alters -
Or something in the sight
Adjusts itself to Midnight -
And Life steps almost straight.

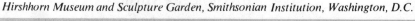

Hirshhorn Museum and Sculpture Garden, Smithsonian Institution, Washington, D.C.

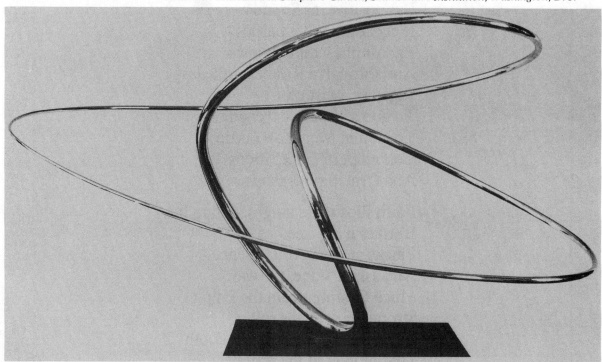

Further Readings

Berger, Peter. *A Rumor of Angels: Modern Society and the Rediscovery of the Supernatural.* 1969. A philosophical discussion of the rediscovery of the supernatural as a possibility for theological thought in our time.

Hammarskjöld, Dag. *Markings.* 1964. A personal spiritual journal that reveals the inner life of a man whose public image as Secretary General of the United Nations was universally known and admired.

Jung, C.G. *Man and His Symbols.* 1964. Mysterious world of dreams and the symbols they evoke. Profusely illustrated introduction to Jung's ideas about the collective unconscious.

Lao-tzu. *Tao Te Ching.* An ancient Chinese text from which arose one of China's three major schools of thought. Through a beguiling series of metaphors and epigrams, the book tries to capture the essence of the unchanging principle unifying the natural world.

Singer, Isaac Bashevis. *Little Boy in Search of God: Mysticism in a Personal Light.* 1976. Memoirs on the evolution of Singer's mysticism and beliefs. Son of a rabbi, he studied the traditional Jewish writings but went on to study the philosophers and psychics. His search for God blends with his youthful search for love and sex.

Smart, Ninian. *The Long Search.* 1977. A survey of the world's living religions comparing the ways people express their belief in an Ultimate Being. Enlightening and accessible.

Construction no. 107 by José de Rivera (1904-   ). Sculpture, stainless steel forged rod.

The beauty of abstract art is found in its form, its color and its texture, and not in its representation of an object that is readily recognizable. The lively spirit and curves of the work pictured here may surprise some viewers who associate steel with rigid building units. This type of sculpture contrasts with earlier abstract metal sculptures which were usually welded and angular. In this piece, as in Henry Moore's sculpture (Session 2), the open spaces are an important part of the total conception.

Section 6
ACCEPTING THE INEVITABLE

The last section dealt with a deeply rooted and persistent attitude toward the human need for meaning—the belief that meaning can be found only in a realm beyond the world of our experience. In this session we consider a markedly different point of view; namely, that it is pointless to concern ourselves with an eternal or supernatural world. We should accept the world as it is and change our inward attitude toward events, learning to live in peace and confidence. Rather than imagining some God who offers the possibility of altering circumstances to fit our wishes, we should recognize the reality of things as they are and avoid the unnecessary pain and anguish that come from wishing them to be different. We discover meaning, in this view, when we recognize that there is no explanation for our experiences and adapt ourselves to this fact. We achieve freedom from anxiety when we realize that neither God nor we have the freedom to alter the outcome of things—only the freedom not to fear them.

The power of such an approach to life is dramatically illuminated in the selection by Viktor Frankl. He describes the way in which he and some others triumphed over the horrors of a concentration camp when all hope of deliverance was lost. In "an existence restricted by external forces" and denied fulfillment in beauty, art or nature, these people found a spiritual freedom in suffering that made life purposeful.

Frankl's response to the world is not new. Indeed, it is as ancient as the confidence in a transcendent truth to be discovered in the unseen. Stoicism, as this response is called, was the prevailing view of the ancient Roman world. One of the best known exponents of the philosophy was the

Lit by night lights, the railroad tracks go their way and—if we let them—act as symbols of our own destinies.

noted Roman emperor Marcus Aurelius. In the excerpt from his work included in this session, he argues that we cannot control the external events affecting us, but we have the ability to control our responses to them. Tranquillity is always possible for the inner self, or mind, and we should avoid involvement so that personal tragedy and even death itself do not cause us distress. Aurelius speaks of God and prayer; but God, for him, is the course of nature, and prayer is seeking a proper attitude of detachment rather than a change in one's situation.

Each of us has some stoical elements in our make-up, but truly stoical people are remarkable. You may know such individuals. What aspects of the stoical character are appealing? If you personally find the stoic solution to the problem of meaning inadequate, how would you describe what is missing?

One possible weakness in Stoicism (though obviously not a weakness from the stoic's point of view) is illustrated by the reading from Tolstoy's *War and Peace*. Platon Karataev is a remarkable character who, despite poverty and severe misfortune, comes to terms with his life and accepts the inevitable with courage and patience. But it may be significant that Pierre feels that "in spite of Karataev's affectionate tenderness for him . . . [Karataev] would not have grieved for a moment at parting from him." This distancing of oneself from others, this avoidance of emotional ties because they cause pain, is a difficult and unappealing posture for many people. Is it desirable for us to strive "to be always the same . . . on the occasion of the loss of a child," in the words of Marcus Aurelius, and to consider life of no value? Can the stoic solution to life's problems result in unconcern for the life of others? Are there not things and people about whom we *should* feel passionately—an emotional stance the stoic always tries to avoid? Auden's poem, *"Musée des Beaux Arts,"* hints at the danger that the other face of Stoicism may be indifference or irresponsibility.

One inevitable experience is death, and a stoical ability to be "neither careless nor impatient nor contemptuous" (Aurelius) about it is reflected in Anne Sexton's "Courage" and Emerson's "Terminus." To what extent does their poetry reflect your own attitude toward death, and to what extent does it help to clarify and strengthen your thinking?

Although Stoicism was originally opposed to any conception of a supernatural God, it has had a considerable influence on our religious traditions. But in Jewish and Christian life one believes in providence rather than fate and submits to the will of God rather than impersonal nature. Providence is directed to a goal, however obscure to us, whereas fate is mere purposeless happening. According to the sonnet "On His Blindness," John Milton accepts the "mild yoke" laid on him by God; he does not see his affliction as an arbitrary tragedy due to natural causes. Many Negro spirituals also reflect an acceptance of injustice as God's mysterious will, but at the same time they exhibit confidence in the ultimate triumph of justice and truth. In your experience, are those who bear pain and disappointment courageously inspired by religious confidence or by the rational acceptance of brute facts taught by Marcus Aurelius?

Excerpt from

Man's Search for Meaning
Viktor Frankl
(1905-   )

Viktor Frankl, Austrian-born psychiatrist and author, spent three years in Auschwitz and other Nazi concentration camps. On his release, he learned that most of his family had been killed. Out of this tragic experience he developed a profound understanding of the human situation described in his popular book, Man's Search for Meaning.

Frankl theorizes that acceptance of the inevitable—whether suffering or some other fate—is not only possible but can be a way to maintain one's dignity and to experience an inner freedom. Though we may not have control over the external forces of our lives, he argues, we have a multitude of choices on how we will react to them. Frankl's experiences and views led him to develop a new approach to psychiatry, which he terms logotherapy *(literally, "meaning-therapy"). It challenges the patient to accept his present situation and direct his future toward the accomplishment of a specific goal that will give meaning to his life.*

We who lived in concentration camps can remember the men who walked through the huts comforting others, giving away their last piece of bread. They may have been few in number, but they offer sufficient proof that everything can be taken from a man but one thing: the last of the human freedoms—to choose one's attitude in any given set of circumstances, to choose one's own way.

And there were always choices to make. Every day, every hour, offered the opportunity to make a decision, a decision which determined whether you would or would not submit to those powers which threatened to rob you of your very self, your inner freedom; which determined whether or not you would become the plaything of circumstance, renouncing freedom and dignity to become molded into the form of the typical inmate.

Seen from this point of view, the mental reactions of the inmates of a concentration camp must seem more to us than the mere expression of certain physical and sociological conditions. Even though conditions such as lack of sleep, insufficient food and various mental stresses may suggest that the inmates were bound to react in certain ways, in the final analysis it becomes clear that the sort of person the prisoner became was the result of an inner decision, and not the result of camp influences alone. Fundamentally, therefore, any man can, even under such circumstances, decide what shall become of him—mentally and spiritually. He may retain his human dignity even in a concentration camp.

Dostoevski said once, "There is only one thing I dread: not to be worthy of my sufferings." These words frequently came to my mind after I became acquainted with those martyrs whose behavior in camp, whose suffering and death, bore witness to the fact that the last inner freedom cannot be lost. It can be said that they were worthy of their sufferings; the way they bore their suffering was a genuine inner achievement. It is this spiritual freedom—which cannot be taken away—that makes life meaningful and purposeful.

An active life serves the purpose of giving man the opportunity to realize values in creative work, while a passive life of enjoyment affords him the opportunity to obtain fulfillment in experiencing beauty, art, or nature. But there is also purpose in that life which is almost barren of both creation and enjoyment and which admits of but one possibility of behavior: namely, in man's attitude to his existence, an existence restricted by external forces. A creative life and a life of enjoyment are banned to him. But not only creativeness and enjoyment are meaningful. If there is a meaning in life at all, then there must be a meaning in suffering. Suffering is an ineradicable part of life, even as fate and death. Without suffering and death human life cannot be complete.

The way in which a man accepts his fate and all the suffering it entails, the way in which he takes up his cross, gives him ample opportunity—even under the most difficult circumstances—to add a deeper meaning to his life. It may remain brave, dignified and unselfish. Or in the bitter fight for self-preservation he may forget his human dignity and become no more than an animal. Here lies the chance for a man either to make use of or to forego the opportunities of attaining the values that a difficult situation may afford him. And this decides whether he is worthy of his sufferings or not.

Do not think that these considerations are unworldly and too far removed from real life. It is true that only a few people are capable of reaching such high standards. Of the prisoners only a few kept their full inner liberty and obtained those values which their suffering afforded, but even one such example is sufficient proof that man's inner strength may raise him above his outward fate. Such men are not only in concentration camps. Everywhere man is confronted with fate, with the chance of achieving something through his own suffering.

Excerpt from

The Meditations of Marcus Aurelius

Marcus Aurelius Antoninus
(121-180 A.D.)

From his youth, Marcus Aurelius was a serious student of Stoicism, the philosophy that teaches one to accept the unalterable destiny of life without passion, manifesting neither joy nor grief. He believed that acceptance of the inevitable leads to tranquillity of the inner being. His Meditations, *originally entitled* Marcus Aurelius to Himself, *is a series of miscellaneous jottings and reflections. The volume was little known until the 16th century but has since been recognized as an outstanding statement of Stoic thought.*

Named Roman emperor in 169 A.D., Marcus Aurelius was noted for his virtue and fairness. Unlike his predecessors, he exhibited a humanitarian attitude toward his people: He was concerned for the poor, generous to political opponents and disgusted by the brutality of the gladiatorial shows. He was responsible for persecuting Christians, however, because he perceived them to be a threat to the unity of the state.

I.8 From Apollonius I learned freedom of will and undeviating steadiness of purpose; and to look to nothing else, not even for a moment, except to reason; and to be always the same, in sharp pains, on the occasion of the loss of a child, and in long illness. . . .

I.15 From Maximus I learned self-government, and not to be led aside by anything; and cheerfulness in all circumstances, as well as in illness; and a just admixture in the moral character of sweetness and dignity, and to do what was set before me without complaining.

IV. 3 Men seek retreats for themselves, houses in the country, seashores, and mountains; and thou too art wont to desire such things very much. But this is altogether a mark of the most common sort of man, for it is in thy power whenever thou shalt choose to retire into thyself. For nowhere either with more quiet or more freedom from trouble does a man retire than into his own soul, particularly when he has within him such thoughts that by looking into them he is immediately in perfect tranquility; and I affirm that tranquility is nothing else than the good ordering of the mind.

IV.48 . . . always observe how ephemeral and worthless human things are, and what was yesterday a little mucus tomorrow will be a mummy or ashes. Pass then through this little space of time conformably to nature, and end thy journey in content, just as an olive falls off when it is ripe, blessing nature who produced it, and thanking the tree

Despair *by Hugo Robus (1885-1964). Sculpture, bronze.*

The lines and volumes of the sculpture have been exaggerated and simplified by the artist in order to convey the forceful emotional impact of the theme.

on which it grew.

IV.50 Do not then consider life a thing of any value. For look to the immensity of time behind thee, and to the time which is before thee, another boundless space. In this infinity then what is the difference between him who lives three days and him who lives three generations?

V.8 Let the perfecting and accomplishment of the things, which the common nature judges to be good, be judged by thee to be of the same kind as thy health. And so accept everything which happens, even if it seems disagreeable, because it leads to this, to the health of the universe and to the prosperity and felicity of God (Zeus). For he would not have brought on any man what he has brought, if it were not useful for the whole. Neither does the nature of anything, whatever it may be, cause anything which is not suitable to that which is directed by it. For two reasons then it is right to be content with that which happens to thee; the one, because it was done for thee and prescribed for thee, and in a manner had reference to thee, originally from the most ancient causes spun with thy destiny; and the other, because even that which comes severally to every man is to the power which administers the universe a cause of felicity and perfection, nay even of its very continuance.

For the integrity of the whole is multilated, if thou cuttest off anything whatever from the conjunction and continuity either of the parts or of the causes. And thou dost cut off, as far as it is in thy power, when thou art dissatisfied, and in a manner triest to put anything out of the way.

VII.52 It is in our power to have no opinion about a thing, and not to be disturbed in our soul; for things themselves have no natural power to form our judgments.

VII. 68 It is in thy power to live free from all compulsion in the greatest tranquility of mind, even if all the world cry out against thee as much as they choose, and even if wild beasts tear in pieces the members of this kneaded matter which has grown around thee. For what hinders the mind in the midst of all this from maintaining itself in tranquility and in a just judgment of all surrounding things and in a ready use of the objects which are presented to it?

VIII.28 Pain is either an evil to the body—then let the body say what it thinks of it—or to the soul; but it is in the power of the soul to maintain its own serenity and tranquility, and not to think that pain is an evil. For every judgment and movement and desire and aversion is within, and no evil ascends so high.

Excerpt from
War and Peace
Leo Tolstoy
(1828-1910)

Count Leo Tolstoy, a member of the Russian nobility, is acclaimed as one of the world's finest writers. His masterpiece War and Peace *traces the lives of the Russian aristocracy when Napoleon was invading their country in 1812. It illustrates Tolstoy's theory that history is not made by heroic figures; rather, events proceed toward an unalterable end, with the result that leaders like Napoleon become mere pawns in the course of history.*

Tolstoy's acceptance of the inevitable is reflected in many of the characters of his novels. The background of the following excerpt from War and Peace *is: Pierre Bezukhov, believing himself destined to kill Napoleon, has refused to leave Moscow after the French occupation and is taken into custody by the invaders. In prison, and later during the French retreat from Moscow, he comes to know Platon Karataev who teaches him to live for each moment. Even in severe deprivation, Karataev finds pleasure in the people around him and the activities he is allowed to pursue, never becoming irrevocably attached to any of them.*

Book XII, Chapter XIII

Twenty-three soldiers, three officers, and two officials, were confined in the shed in which Pierre had been placed and where he remained for four weeks.

When Pierre remembered them afterwards they all seemed misty figures to him except Platon Karataev, who always remained in his mind a most vivid and precious memory and the personification of everything Russian, kindly, and round. When Pierre saw his neighbour next morning at dawn, the first impression of him, as of something round, was fully confirmed: Platon's whole figure—in a French overcoat girdled with a cord, a soldier's cap, and bast shoes—was round. His head was quite round, his back, chest, shoulders, and even his arms, which he held as if ever ready to embrace something, were rounded, his pleasant smile and his large gentle brown eyes were also round.

Platon Karataev must have been fifty judging by his stories of campaigns he had been in, told as by an old soldier. He did not himself know his age and was quite unable to determine it. But his brilliantly white, strong teeth, which showed in two unbroken semicircles when he laughed—as he often did—were all sound and good, there was not a grey hair in his beard or on his head, and his whole body gave an impression of suppleness and especially of firmness and endurance.

His face, despite its fine, rounded wrinkles, had an expression of innocence and youth, his voice was pleasant and musical. But the chief peculiarity of his speech was its directness and appositeness. It was evident that he never considered what he had said or was going to say, and consequently the rapidity and justice of his intonation had an irresistible persuasiveness.

His physical strength and agility during the first days of his imprisonment were such that he seemed not to know what fatigue and sickness meant. Every night, before lying down, he said: "Lord, lay me down as a stone and raise me up as a loaf!" and every morning on getting up he said: "I lay down and curled up, I get up and shake myself." And indeed he only had to lie down, to fall asleep like a stone, and he only had to shake himself, to be ready without a moment's delay for some work, just as children are ready for play directly they awake. He could do everything, not very well but not badly. He baked, cooked, sewed, planed, and mended boots. He was always busy, and only at night allowed himself conversation—of which he was fond—and songs. He did not sing like a trained singer who knows he is listened to, but like the birds, evidently giving vent to the sounds in the same way that one stretches oneself, or walks about to get rid of stiffness, and the sounds were always high-pitched, mournful, delicate, and almost feminine, and his face at such times was very serious.

Having been taken prisoner and allowed his beard to grow, he seemed to have thrown off all that had been forced upon him—everything military and alien to himself—and had returned to his former peasant habits. . . .

He did not like talking about his life as a soldier, though he did not complain, and often mentioned that he had not been flogged once during the whole of his army service. When he related anything it was generally some old and evidently precious memory of his "Christian" life, as he called his peasant existence. The proverbs, of which his talk was full, were for the most part not the coarse and indecent saws soldiers employ, but those folk-sayings which taken without a context seem so insignificant, but when used appositely suddenly acquire a significance of profound wisdom.

He would often say the exact opposite of what he had said on a previous occasion, yet both would be right. He liked to talk and he talked well, adorning his speech with terms of endearment and with folk-sayings which Pierre thought he invented himself, but the chief charm of his talk lay in the fact that the commonest events—sometimes just such as Pierre had witnessed without taking notice of them—assumed in Karataev's speech a character of solemn fitness. He liked to hear the folk-tales one of the soldiers used to tell of an evening (they were always the same), but most of all he liked to hear stories of real life. He would smile joyfully when listening to such stories, now and then putting in a word or asking a question to make the moral beauty of what was told clear to himself. Karataev had no attachments, friendships, or love, as Pierre understood them, but loved and lived affectionately with everything life brought him in contact with, particularly with man—not any particular man, but those with whom he happened to be. He loved his dog, his comrades, the French, and Pierre who was his neighbour, but Pierre felt that in spite of Karataev's affectionate tenderness for him (by which he unconsciously gave Pierre's spiritual life its due) he would not have grieved for a moment at parting from him. And Pierre began to feel in the same way towards Karataev.

To all the other prisoners Platon Karataev seemed a most ordinary soldier. They called him "little falcon" or "Platosh," chaffed him good-naturedly, and sent him on errands. But to Pierre he always remained what he had seemed that first night: an unfathomable, rounded, eternal personification of the spirit of simplicity and truth.

Platon Karataev knew nothing by heart, except his prayers. When he began to speak he seemed not to know how he would conclude.

Sometimes Pierre, struck by the meaning of his words, would ask him to repeat them, but Platon could never recall what he had said a moment before, just as he never could repeat to Pierre the words of his favourite song: *Native* and *birch-tree* and *my heart is sick* occurred in it, but when spoken and not sung no meaning could be got out of it. He did not, and could not, understand the meaning of words apart from their context. Every word and action of his was the manifestation of an activity unknown to him, which was his life. But his life, as he regarded it, had no meaning as a separate thing. It had meaning only as part of a whole of which he was always conscious. His words and ac-

tions flowed from him as evenly, inevitably, and spontaneously, as fragrance exhales from a flower. He could not understand the value or significance of any word or deed taken separately.

. . . . .

Book XIV, Chapter XII

While imprisoned in the shed Pierre had learned not with his intellect but with his whole being, by life itself, that man is created for happiness, that happiness is within him, in the satisfaction of simple human needs, and that all unhappiness arises not from privation but from superfluity. And now during these last three weeks of the march he had learned still another new, consolatory truth—that there is nothing in the world that is terrible. He had learned that, as there is no condition in which man can be happy and entirely free, so there is no condition in which he need be unhappy and not free. He learned that suffering and freedom have their limits, and that those limits are very near together; that the person in a bed of roses with one crumpled petal suffered as keenly as he now, sleeping on the bare damp earth with one side growing chilled while the other was warming; and that when he had put on tight dancing shoes he had suffered just as he did now when he walked with bare feet that were covered with sores—his footgear having long since fallen to pieces. He discovered that when he had married his wife—of his own free will as it had seemed to him—he had been no more free than now when they locked him up at night in a stable. Of all that he himself subsequently termed his sufferings, but which at the time he scarcely felt, the worst was the state of his bare, rubbed, and scab-covered feet. (The horseflesh was appetising and nourishing, the saltpetre flavour of the gunpowder they used instead of salt was even pleasant; there was no great cold, it was always warm walking in the daytime, and at night there were the camp fires; the lice that devoured him warmed his body.) The one thing that was at first hard to bear was his feet.

After the second day's march Pierre, having examined his feet by the camp fire, thought it would be impossible to walk on them; but when everybody got up, he went along, limping, and when he had warmed up, walked without feeling the pain, though at night his feet were more terrible to look at than before. But he did not look at them and thought of other things.

Only now did Pierre realize the full strength of life in man, and the saving power he has of transferring his attention from one thing to another, which is like the safety valve of a boiler that allows superfluous steam to blow off when the pressure exceeds a certain limit.

He did not see and did not hear how they shot the prisoners who lagged behind, though more than a hundred had perished in that way. He did not think of Karataev, who grew weaker every day and evidently would soon have to share that fate. Still less did Pierre think about himself. The harder his position became and the more terrible

the future, the more independent of that position in which he found himself were the joyful and comforting thoughts, memories, and imaginings, that came to him.

Book XIV, Chapter XIII

At mid-day on the 22nd of October Pierre was going uphill along the muddy, slippery road, looking at his feet and at the roughness of the way. . . .

Pierre walked along, looking from side to side, counting his steps in threes, and reckoning them off on his fingers. Mentally addressing the rain, he repeated: "Now then, now then, go on! Pelt harder!"

It seemed to him that he was thinking of nothing, but far down and deep within him his soul was occupied with something important and comforting. This something was a most subtle spiritual deduction from a conversation with Karataev the day before.

At their yesterday's halting-place, feeling chilly by a dying camp fire, Pierre had got up and gone to the new one, which was burning better. There Platon Karataev was sitting, covered up—head and all—with his greatcoat as if it were a vestment, telling the soldiers in his effective and pleasant though now feeble voice a story Pierre knew. It was already past midnight, the hour when Karataev was usually free of his fever and particularly lively. When Pierre reached the fire and heard Planton's voice enfeebled by illness, and saw his pathetic face brightly lit up by the blaze, he felt a painful prick at his heart. His feeling of pity for this man frightened him and he wished to go away, but there was no other fire and Pierre sat down, trying not to look at Platon.

"Well, how are you?" he asked.

"How am I? If we grumble at sickness, God won't grant us death," replied Platon, and at once resumed the story he had begun.

"And so, brother," he continued, with a smile on his pale, emaciated face and a particularly happy light in his eyes, "you see, brother . . ."

Pierre had long been familiar with that story. Karataev had told it to him alone some half dozen times and always with a specially joyful emotion. But well as he knew it Pierre now listened to that tale as to something new, and the quiet rapture Karataev evidently felt as he told it communicated itself also to Pierre. The story was of an old merchant who lived a good and God-fearing life with his family, and who went once to the Nizhni fair with a companion—a rich merchant.

Having put up at an inn they both went to sleep, and next morning his companion was found robbed and with his throat cut. A blood-stained knife was found under the old merchant's pillow. He was tried, knouted, and his nostrils having been torn off, "all in due order" as Karataev put it, he was sent to hard labour in Siberia.

"And so, brother" (it was at this point that Pierre came up), "ten years or more passed by. The old man was living as a convict, submitting as he should, and doing no wrong. Only he prayed to God for death. Well one night the convicts were gathered, just as we are, with the old man among them. And

they began telling what each was suffering for, and how they had sinned against God. One told how he had taken a life, another had taken two, a third had set a house on fire, while another had simply been a vagrant and had done nothing. So they asked the old man: 'What are you being punished for, Daddy?'—'I, my dear brothers,' he said, 'am being punished for my own and other men's sins. But I have not killed any one, or taken anything that was not mine, but have only helped my poorer brothers. I was a merchant, my dear brothers, and had much property.' And he went on to tell them all about it in due order. 'I don't grieve for myself,' he says, 'God it seems has chastened me. Only I am sorry for my old wife and the children,' and the old man began to weep. Now it happened that among the group was the very man who had killed the other merchant. 'Where did it happen, Daddy?' he said. 'When, and in what month?' He asked all about it and his heart began to ache. So he comes up to the old man like this, and falls down at his feet! 'You are perishing because of me, Daddy,' he says. 'It is quite true, lads, that this man,' he says, 'is being tortured innocently and for nothing! I,' he says, 'did that deed, and I put the knife under your head while you were asleep. Forgive me, Daddy,' he says, 'for Christ's sake!' "

Karataev paused, smiling joyously as he gazed into the fire, and he drew the logs together.

"And the old man said, 'God will forgive you, we are all sinners in His sight. I suffer for my own sins,' and he wept bitter tears. Well and what do you

139

think, dear friends?" Karataev continued, his face brightening more and more with a rapturous smile, as if what he now had to tell contained the chief charm and the whole meaning of his story: "What do you think, dear fellow? That murderer confessed to the authorities. 'I have taken six lives,' he says (he was a great sinner) 'but what I am most sorry for is this old man. Don't let him suffer because of me.' So he confessed, and it was all written down and the papers sent off in due order. The place was a long way off, and while they were judging, with one thing and another, filling in the papers all in due order—the authorities I mean—time passed. The affair reached the Tsar. After a while the Tsar's decree came to

set the merchant free and give him a compensation that had been awarded. The paper arrived and they began to look for the old man. 'Where is the old man who has been suffering innocently and in vain? A paper has come from the Tsar!' So they began looking for him," here Karataev's lower jaw trembled, "but God had already forgiven him—he was dead! That's how it was, dear fellow!" Karataev concluded, and sat for a long time silent gazing before him with a smile.

And Pierre's soul was dimly but joyfully filled not by the story itself but by its mysterious significance: by the rapturous joy that lit up Karataev's face as he told it, and the mystic significance of that joy.

Musées Royaux des Beaux-Arts, Brussels, Belgium

The Fall of Icarus *by Pieter Brueghel the Elder (1525-1569). Flemish. Oil.*

Musée des Beaux Arts

W. H. Auden
(1907-1973)

W. H. Auden, born in England, emigrated to the United States in 1930 and became a citizen in 1946. He received the Pulitzer Prize for his poetry in 1948. Auden's poetry reflects his continual search for order and peace: Order in the external world of ideas and events, peace in his own heart.

In "Musée des Beaux Arts," the poet ponders to himself as he tours a museum of fine arts. He mentions details from exhibited paintings, focusing particularly on "The Fall of Icarus," a famous painting by Brueghel, the Flemish artist. Indirectly, the paintings he views raise serious questions about the ultimate meaning of human suffering: It is portrayed as neither noble nor redemptive but only as a brief, apparently meaningless episode in the midst of ordinary events, stoically accepted as such, while life goes on its usual way.

About suffering they were never wrong,
The Old Masters: how well they understood
Its human position; how it takes place
While someone else is eating or opening a window or just walking dully
    along;
How, when the aged are reverently, passionately waiting
For the miraculous birth, there always must be
Children who did not specially want it to happen, skating
On a pond at the edge of the wood:
They never forgot
That even the dreadful martyrdom must run its course
Anyhow in a corner, some untidy spot
Where the dogs go on with their doggy life and the torturer's horse
Scratches its innocent behind on a tree.
In Brueghel's Icarus, for instance: how everything turns away
Quite leisurely from the disaster; the ploughman may
Have heard the splash, the forsaken cry,
But for him it was not an important failure; the sun shone
As it had to on the white legs disappearing into the green
Water; and the expensive delicate ship that must have seen
Something amazing, a boy falling out of the sky,
Had somewhere to get to and sailed calmly on.

Museum of Modern Art, New York, New York

Christina's World (1948) *By Andrew Wyeth (1917-   ). Tempera on gesso panel.*

Andrew Wyeth usually paints in egg tempera, a medium popular in the 14th and 15th centuries. The medium is effective in showing delicate details like leaves of grass, hair and weathered wood. He never joined the abstract or "pop" art schools which were dominant during his career. Wyeth's subjects are often neighbors or friends from Pennsylvania or Maine. Christina Olson was crippled by infantile paralysis and unable to travel freely around her farm. This painting shows her looking at her "world" from the spot where she has crawled.

Courage

Anne Sexton
(1928-1974)

Anne Sexton is a contemporary American poet who writes about inner emotions and conflicts. Her themes usually deal with home life and the cycles of human life and relationships, and she is at different times tender, questioning, depressed or ecstatic. She often suffered from depression and mental breakdowns. Like other "confessional" poets, she used her writing to reveal her private, inner struggles. Sexton taught creative writing for some years at Boston University before her death and is considered one of the finest poets of our time.

It is in the small things we see it.
The child's first step,
as awesome as an earthquake.
The first time you rode a bike,
wallowing up the sidewalk.
The first spanking when your heart
went on a journey all alone.
When they called you crybaby
or poor or fatty or crazy
and made you into an alien,
you drank their acid
and concealed it.

Later,
if you faced the death of bombs and bullets
you did not do it with a banner,
you did it with only a hat to
cover your heart.
You did not fondle the weakness inside you
though it was there.
Your courage was a small coal
that you kept swallowing.
If your buddy saved you
and died himself in so doing,
then his courage was not courage,
it was love; love as simple as shaving soap.
Later,
if you have endured a great despair,

143

then you did it alone,
getting a transfusion from the fire,
picking the scabs off your heart,
then wringing it out like a sock.
Next, my kinsman, you powdered your sorrow,
you gave it a back rub
and then you covered it with a blanket
and after it had slept a while
it woke to the wings of the roses
and was transformed.

Later,
when you face old age and its natural conclusion
your courage will still be shown in the little ways,
each spring will be a sword you'll sharpen,
those you love will live in a fever of love,
and you'll bargain with the calendar
and at the last moment
when death opens the back door
you'll put on your carpet slippers
and stride out.

Terminus

Ralph Waldo Emerson
(1803-1882)

Ralph Waldo Emerson, a renowned American writer and thinker of the 19th century, believed that the poet is like a prophet and priest, interpreting truth and beauty to others. Fiercely individualistic, he was convinced that a unifying spirit exists in and over all. Perfection for him consisted in yielding oneself to the perfect whole without losing one's own uniqueness.

Emerson is probably best known in popular circles for his essays and journals. His essays, "Nature," "Self-Reliance" and "The American Scholar," are among the most famous.

In the poem selected here, the poet feels called by the Roman god of boundaries, Terminus, to accept the growing limitations of age and to adapt himself to the storm of time. The images in the poem are drawn from Emerson's personal familiarity with the New England seacoast and with generations of seamen.

It is time to be old,
To take in sail:—
The god of bounds,
Who sets to seas a shore,
Came to me in his fatal rounds,
And said: "No more!
No farther shoot
Thy broad ambitious branches, and thy root.
Fancy departs: no more invent;
Contract thy firmament
To compass of a tent.
There's not enough for this and that,
Make thy option which of two;
Economize the failing river,
Not the less revere the Giver,
Leave the many and hold the few.
Timely wise accept the terms,
Soften the fall with wary foot;
A little while
Still plan and smile,
And,—fault of novel germs,—
Mature the unfallen fruit.

Curse, if thou wilt, thy sires,
Bad husbands of their fires,
Who, when they gave thee breath,
Failed to bequeath
The needful sinew stark as once,
The Baresark marrow to thy bones,
But left a legacy of ebbing veins,
Inconstant heat and nerveless reins,—
Amid the Muses, left thee deaf and dumb,
Amid the gladiators, halt and numb."

As the bird trims her to the gale,
I trim myself to the storm of time,
I man the rudder, reef the sail,
Obey the voice at eve obeyed at prime:
"Lowly faithful, banish fear,
Right onward drive unharmed;
The port, well worth the cruise, is near,
And every wave is charmed."

Facing page, The Blind Botanist *by Ben Shahn (1898-1970). Tempera on masonite.*

Shahn's work is part of the "social realism" art movement which developed during America's Great Depression years. Artists in the movement focused on social and economic issues which affected the ordinary person. This more recent painting (1954) has been called an allegory on man's limited ability to understand the world around him.

On His Blindness

John Milton
(1608-1674)

*John Milton is considered the most distinguished poet of the Renaissance in Eng-
land. His sonnets, including the one selected here, are among the finest ever written.
Milton's sight was weak from childhood, and, when he became blind in his early thir-
ties, he felt as if the greatest gift God had given him—that of being a writer—was lost
to him forever. In this poem he asks himself "fondly" (foolishly) whether God will
expect as much from him when blind as when he could see.*

*Despite initial despondency over his blindness, Milton went on to write some of
his greatest works later in life, including* Paradise Lost, *a monumental epic poem
based on the story of Genesis. Milton's intense creative activity after his blindness
gives new meaning to his famous line, "They also serve who only stand and wait."*

When I consider how my light is spent
Ere half my days in this dark world and wide,
And that one talent which is death to hide
Lodged with me useless, though my soul more bent
To serve therewith my Maker and present
My true account, less He returning chide,
"Doth God exact day-labor, light denied?"
I fondly ask. But Patience, to prevent
That murmur, soon replies, "God doth not need
Either man's work or his own gifts. Who best
Bear his mild yoke, they serve him best. His state
Is kingly: thousands at his bidding speed
And post o'er land and ocean without rest;
They also serve who only stand and wait."

Further Readings

Greenfeld, Josh. *A Child Called Noah*. 1972. The diary of a family who copes with their autistic child, refusing to succumb to despair.

Lee, Laurel. *Walking through the Fire*. 1977. Hospital journal of a 31-year-old woman, pregnant with her third child, who contracts Hodgkins disease. The book is filled with courage, humor and a steadfast faith in God.

Olsen, Tillie. *Tell Me a Riddle*. 1971. The title story of this collection of short stories tells of the slow dying of a strong woman and of the quarrel she has with her husband of 47 years about how they are to live out their remaining time. Their conflict and the story are filled with sadness and humor.

Schwerin, Doris. *Diary of a Pigeon Watcher*. 1976. Recovering from a traumatic mastectomy, the author tells her story of survival of the spirit.

Section 7

LIFE AFTER DEATH

Belief in some kind of existence after death is widespread, if not universal, throughout human history. In the acceptance of the inevitable discussed in the last section, the ability to understand suffering as part of God's will frequently depends on belief in a happier condition after death. Many believe life on earth has meaning because it prepares us for eternal union with God.

We saw that Plato attributed to the soul a memory of the spiritual realm from which it comes at birth and to which it returns at death. Belief in the immortality of the soul and its ultimate independence from the body is basic to many of the great religions. The first reading is taken from the Hindu scripture, *The Bhagavad Gītā* or "Song of the Blessed Lord," which declares the soul to be indestructible and eternal, passing through a series of lives until it is sufficiently purified from worldly attachments to attain eternal fellowship with God. Death is of no importance. What matters is the living of one's life in loving obedience to God. Meaning is found in preparing for a richer existence beyond the present one.

Hope of life after death was not a reality throughout most of the period covered by the Old Testament, nor is it emphasized in Reform Judaism today. In ancient Israel, while there was an idea of a shadowy but unattractive existence in the underworld after death, hope and meaning for the Israelites centered on membership in the ongoing nation. A kind of immortality was attained if one had children—an idea still reflected in Jewish life in the importance attached to the family and its continuance. Some may feel that their physical descendants represent a sufficient kind of life after death. Others may agree with the view of Dr. Zhivago in the

---

Large redwoods in Del Norte State Park, California.

151

second selection; namely, that the memory other people have of us constitutes our continued life. Any written or visual traces we leave may also allow us to live in the minds of people for many generations. In Sonnet 65, Shakespeare expresses the hope that his writing will help him achieve immortality.

When Judaism and Christianity came to a faith in life after death, they spoke of the hope of "resurrection"—not merely the survival of an inner spiritual "soul" but the raising from the dead of the whole person to participate in the kingdom of God. According to this interpretation, at the end of time, the world's evils and distortions will be eliminated and a condition of perfect bliss established for God's people. The whole person— body, mind and spirit—will be brought to fullness of life and human potentialities realized by the power of God. A classical description of this hope is found in the selection from The Book of Revelation by John. The historical identification of the details in John's picture of a future free from pain, sorrow, death and sin are not important for our purposes. The author's symbolic language should be appreciated as the great literature it is, even though it may be debated whether such imagery is as meaningful for us as it was for its first readers 1900 years ago.

Other selections in this section reflect, from later ages, the same confidence as that expressed in The Book of Revelation. In "Death Be Not Proud," John Donne proclaims that despite its apparent power, death is not eternal. In a contemporary context, James Agee's Death in the Family tells how a family responds with faith to the totally unexpected death of a beloved father and husband. The sense of the dead man's presence, described in the second passage, is so strong that some members of his family are convinced his continued concern for them has caused his spirit to return. Do you agree that a condition of restlessness may exist in departed souls or spirits until they are set free from earthly attachments? How do you react to Andrew's scepticism in the story?

Much attention has been given lately to the experiences of persons who have been very close to, or apparently over, the brink of death and then revived by modern medical techniques. Raymond A. Moody has engaged in a careful study of such experiences; our final reading summarizes and illustrates his findings. You may have had such an experience yourself or known others who have. To what extent do accounts such as these offer objective evidence of life after life? To what extent do they seem to you to contribute to a solution of the search for meaning?

The Bhagavad Gītā

The Bhagavad Gītā was written about 200 B.C. and is the most widely read and prized of all Hindu sacred writings. In it a famous warrior, disturbed by having to fight in a battle with some of his relatives, is shown that killing or being killed does not affect the real self because the soul is immortal.

Earlier Hindu thought had held that the soul had to pass through a long tedious series of births and deaths before having the opportunity to enjoy union with God. The Bhagavad Gītā brought new hope to people of all castes and conditions by proclaiming that the soul that truly serves and loves God goes immediately to him at death.

Chapter II

11.   The Blessed One said:
        Thou hast mourned those who should not be mourned,
           And (yet) thou speakest words about wisdom!
        Dead and living men
           The (truly) learned do not mourn.

. . . . .

13.   As to the embodied (soul) in this body
           Come childhood, youth, old age,
        So the coming to another body;
           The wise man is not confused herein.

14.   But contacts with matter, son of Kuntī,
           Cause cold and heat, pleasure and pain;
        They come and go, and are impermanent;
           Put up with them, son of Bharata!

15.   For whom these (contacts) do not cause to waver,
           The man, O bull of men,
         To whom pain and pleasure are alike, the wise,
           He is fit for immortality.

16.   Of what is not, no coming to be occurs;
           No coming not to be occurs of what is;
         But the dividing-line of both is seen,
           Of these two, by those who see the truth.

17. But know that that is indestructible,
        By which this all is pervaded;
      Destruction of this imperishable one
        No one can cause.

            . . . . .

20. He is not born, nor does he ever die;
        Nor, having come to be, will he ever more come not to be.
      Unborn, eternal, everlasting, this ancient one
        Is not slain when the body is slain.

21. Who knows as indestructible and eternal
        This unborn, imperishable one,
      That man, son of Pṛthā, how
        Can he slay or cause to slay—whom?

22. As leaving aside worn-out garments,
        A man takes other, new ones,
      So leaving aside worn-out bodies
        To other, new ones goes the embodied (soul).

23. Swords cut him not,
        Fire burns him not,
      Water wets him not,
        Wind dries him not.

            . . . . .

27. For to one that is born death is certain,
        And birth is certain for one that has died;
      Therefore, the thing being unavoidable,
        Thou shouldst not mourn.

            . . . . .

30. This embodied (soul) is eternally unslayable
        In the body of everyone, son of Bharata;
      Therefore all beings
        Thou shouldst not mourn.

Excerpt from

Doctor Zhivago

Boris Pasternak
(1890-1960)

In his famous novel, Doctor Zhivago, *Boris Pasternak suggests one way of viewing life after death. In the following conversation with Anna Ivanovna Gromeko, the mother of his future wife, Yura Zhivago tries to respond to her fears about dying: "You in others—this is your soul." He believes that we become immortal as we exist in the memory of the people who have known us. At the conclusion of the novel, Zhivago's own life is perceived as richer after death because of his poetry.*

Born in Russia of Jewish parents, Pasternak became a (Russian Orthodox) Christian, though he always regarded himself as a seeker rather than a finder of spiritual truth. Doctor Zhivago, *acclaimed as a masterpiece of contemporary fiction, has never been published in Russia because the hero, like the author, did not conform to the Soviet Union's official political views.*

One night at the end of November Yura came home late from the university; he was exhausted and had eaten nothing all day. He was told that there had been a terrible alarm that afternoon. Anna Ivanovna had had convulsions. Several doctors had seen her; at one time they had advised Alexander Alexandrovich to send for the priest, but later they had changed their minds. Now she was feeling better; she was fully conscious and had asked for Yura to be sent to her the moment he got back.

Yura went up at once.

The room showed traces of the recent commotion. A nurse, moving noiselessly, was rearranging something on the night table. Towels that had been used for compresses were lying about, damp and crumpled. The water in the slop basin was pinkish with expectorated blood, and broken ampoules and swollen tufts of cotton wool floated on its surface.

Anna Ivanovna lay drenched in sweat, with parched lips. Her face had become haggard since morning.

"Can the diagnosis be wrong?" Yura wondered. "She has all the symptoms of lobar pneumonia. It looks like the crisis." After greeting her and saying the encouraging, meaningless things that are always said on such occasions, he sent the nurse out of the room, took Anna Ivanovna's wrist to feel her pulse, and reached into his coat pocket for his stethoscope. She moved her head to indicate that this was unnecessary. He realized that she wanted him for some other reason. She spoke with effort.

"They wanted to give me the last sacraments. . . . Death is hanging over me. . . . It may come any moment. . . . When you go to have a tooth out you're frightened, it'll hurt, you prepare yourself. . . . But this isn't a tooth, it's everything, the whole of you, your whole life . . . being pulled out. . . . And what is it? Nobody knows. . . . And I am sick at heart and terrified."

She fell silent. Tears were streaming down her cheeks. Yura said nothing. A moment later Anna Ivanovna went on.

"You're clever, talented. . . . That makes you different. . . . You surely know something. . . . Comfort me."

"Well, what is there for me to say?" replied Yura. He fidgeted on his chair, got up, paced the room, and sat down again. "In the first place, you'll feel better tomorrow. There are clear indications—I'd stake my life on it—that you've passed the crisis. And then—death, the survival of consciousness, faith in resurrection. . . . You want to know my opinion as a scientist? Perhaps some other time? No? Right now? Well, as you wish. But it's difficult like that, all of a sudden." And there and then he delivered a whole impromptu lecture, astonished that he could do it.

"Resurrection. In the crude form in which it is preached to console the weak, it is alien to me. I have always understood Christ's words about the living and the dead in a different sense. Where could you find room for all these hordes of people accumulated over thousands of years? The universe isn't big enough for them; God, the good, and meaningful purpose would be crowded out. They'd be crushed by these throngs greedy merely for the animal life.

"But all the time, life, one, immense, identical throughout its innumerable combinations and transformations, fills the universe and is continually reborn.

You are anxious about whether you will rise from the dead or not, but you rose from the dead when you were born and you didn't notice it.

"Will you feel pain? Do the tissues feel their disintegration? In other words, what will happen to your consciousness? But what is consciousness? Let's see. A conscious attempt to fall asleep is sure to produce insomnia, to try to be conscious of one's own digestion is a sure way to upset the stomach. Consciousness is a poison when we apply it to ourselves. Consciousness is a light directed outward, it lights up the way ahead of us so that we don't stumble. It's like the headlights on a locomotive—turn them inward and you'd have a crash.

"So what will happen to your consciousness? *Your* consciousness, yours, not anyone else's. Well, what are *you*? There's the point. Let's try to find out. What is it about you that you have always known as yourself? What are you conscious of in yourself? Your kidneys? Your liver? Your blood vessels? No. However far back you go in your memory, it is always in some external, active manifestation of yourself that you come across your identity—in the work of your hands, in your family, in other people. And now listen carefully. You in others—this is your soul. This is what you are. This is what your consciousness has breathed and lived on and enjoyed throughout your life—your soul, your immortality, your life in others. And what now? You have always been in others and you will remain in others. And what does it matter to you if later on that is called your memory? This will be you—the you that enters the future and becomes a part of it.

"And now one last point. There is nothing to fear. There is no such thing as death. Death has nothing to do with us. But you said something about being talented—that it makes one different. Now, that does have something to do with us. And talent in the highest and broadest sense means talent for life.

"There will be no death, says St. John. His reasoning is quite simple. There will be no death because the past is over; that's almost like saying there will be no death because it is already done with, it's old and we are bored with it. What we need is something new, and that new thing is life eternal."

He was pacing up and down the room as he was talking. Now he walked up to Anna Ivanovna's bed and putting his hand on her forehead said, "Go to sleep." After a few moments she began to fall asleep.

Yura quietly left the room and told Egorovna to send in the nurse. "What's come over me?" he thought. "I'm becoming a regular quack—muttering incantations, laying on the hands. . . ."

Next day Anna Ivanovna was better.

John R. Griffin plays while his brother Arthur "beats the straws"!

". . . in the work of your hands, in your family, in other people . . . You in others—this is your soul. This is what you are."

―*from* Doctor Zhivago

Sonnet 65

William Shakespeare
(1564-1616)

William Shakespeare is recognized throughout the world as a playwright and poet without peer. Little is known of his personal life: He was married, had children and made his living as a playwright and actor in London. The details of his life remain a mystery.

Shakespeare's 154 sonnets are the most personal of his writings. They tell us of his struggles to find meaning in life, particularly when confronted by the passing of time and its decaying effects on beauty and love.

The form of Sonnet 65 is that of the classic Shakespearean sonnet, in which a problem is presented and defined in the first 12 lines, and then an answer or resolution given in the final couplet. The last lines have given comfort and consolation to writers through the ages.

Since brass, nor stone, nor earth, nor boundless sea,
But sad mortality o'ersways their power,
How with this rage shall beauty hold a plea,
Whose action* is no stronger than a flower?
O, how shall summer's honey breath hold out
Against the wrackful† siege of batt'ring days,
When rocks impregnable are not so stout,
Nor gates of steel so strong, but Time decays?
O fearful meditation! Where, alack,
Shall Time's best jewel from Time's chest lie hid?
Or what strong hand can hold his swift foot back?
Or who his spoil of beauty can forbid††?
O, none! unless this miracle have might,
That in black ink my love may still shine bright.

---

*vigor
†destructive
††prevent

Excerpt from

The Book of Revelation
Authorized (King James) Version

The Book of Revelation, or the Apocalypse as it is sometimes called, is the last book of The Bible. *It was written c. 95 A.D. by a man called John, who had been exiled to the island of Patmos off the coast of what is now Turkey. He writes to offer encouragement and strength to other Christians facing the threat of persecution and death for their faith.*

Chapter 20 speaks of the long period of time (symbolically, the "thousand years") between Christ's victory over death and the end of time. During this era those who bear witness to God's word share in his glorious reign. The remainder of the excerpt (Rv 21:1—22:5) provides a series of striking visions depicting the heavenly kingdom under symbols of a new heaven and a new earth.

Chapter 20

And I saw an angel come down from heaven, having the key of the bottomless pit and a great chain in his hand.

2   And he laid hold on the dragon, that old serpent, which is the Devil, and Satan, and bound him a thousand years,

3   And cast him into the bottomless pit, and shut him up, and set a seal upon him, that he should deceive the nations no more, till the thousand years should be fulfilled: and after that he must be loosed a little season.

4   And I saw thrones, and they sat upon them, and judgment was given unto them: and I saw the souls of them that were beheaded for the witness of Jesus, and for the word of God, and which had not worshipped the beast, neither his image, neither had received his mark upon their foreheads, or in their hands; and they lived and reigned with Christ a thousand years.

5   But the rest of the dead lived not again until the thousand years were finished. This is the first resurrection.

. . . . .

Chapter 21

And I saw a new heaven and a new earth: for the first heaven and the first earth were passed away; and there was no more sea.

2   And I John saw the holy city, new Jerusalem, coming down from God out of heaven, prepared as a bride adorned for her husband.

3   And I heard a great voice out of heaven saying, Behold, the tabernacle of God is with men, and he will dwell with them, and they shall be his people and God himself shall be with them, and be their God.

4   And God shall wipe away all tears from their eyes; and there shall be no more death, neither sorrow, nor crying, neither shall there be any more pain: for the former things are passed away.

5   And he that sat upon the throne said, Behold, I make all things new. And he said unto me, Write: for these words are true and faithful.

6   And he said unto me, It is done. I am Alpha and Omega, the beginning and the end. I will give unto him that is athirst of the fountain of the water of life freely.

7   He that overcometh shall inherit all things; and I will be his God, and he shall be my son.

8   But the fearful, and unbelieving, and the abominable, and murderers, and whoremongers, and sorcerers, and idolaters, and all liars, shall have their part in the lake which burneth with fire and brimstone: which is the second death.

9   And there came unto me one of the seven angels which had the seven vials full of the seven last plagues, and talked with me, saying, Come hither, I will shew thee the bride, the Lamb's wife.

10   And he carried me away in the spirit to a great and high mountain, and shewed me that great city, the holy Jerusalem, descending out of heaven from God,

11   Having the glory of God: and her light was like unto a stone most precious, even like a jasper stone, clear as crystal;

12   And had a wall great and high, and had twelve gates, and at the gates twelve angels, and names written thereon, which are the names of the twelve tribes of the children of Israel:

13   On the east three gates; on the north three gates; on the south three gates; and on the west three gates.

14   And the wall of the city had twelve foundations, and in them the names of the twelve apostles of the Lamb.

15   And he that talked with me had a golden reed to measure the city, and the gates thereof, and the wall thereof.

16   And the city lieth foursquare, and the length is as large as the breadth: and he measured the city with the reed, twelve thousand furlongs. The length and the breadth and the height of it are equal.

17   And he measured the wall thereof, an hundred and forty and four cubits, according to the measure of a man, that is, of the angel.

18   And the building of the wall of it was of jasper: and the city was pure gold, like unto clear glass.

19   And the foundations of the wall of the city were garnished with all manner of precious stones. The first foundation was jasper; the second, sapphire; the third, a chalcedony; the fourth, an emerald;

20   The fifth, sardonyx; the sixth, sardius; the seventh, chrysolyte; the eighth, beryl; the ninth, a topaz; the tenth, a chrysoprasus; the eleventh, a jacinth; the twelfth, an amethyst.

21   And the twelve gates were twelve pearls; every several gate was of one pearl:

and the street of the city was pure gold, as it were transparent glass.

22 And I saw no temple therein: for the Lord God Almighty and the Lamb are the temple of it.

23 And the city had no need of the sun, neither of the moon, to shine in it: for the glory of God did lighten it, and the Lamb is the light thereof.

24 And the nations of them which are saved shall walk in the light of it: and the kings of the earth do bring their glory and honour into it.

25 And the gates of it shall not be shut at all by day: for there shall be no night there.

26 And they shall bring the glory and honour of the nations into it.

27 And there shall in no wise enter into it any thing that defileth, neither whatsoever worketh abomination, or maketh a lie: but they which are written in the Lamb's book of life.

Chapter 22

And he shewed me a pure river of water of life, clear as crystal, proceeding out of the throne of God and of the Lamb.

2 In the midst of the street of it, and on either side of the river, was there the tree of life, which bare twelve manner of fruits, and yielded her fruit every month: and the leaves of the tree were for the healing of the nations.

3 And there shall be no more curse: but the throne of God and of the Lamb shall be in it; and his servants shall serve him:

4 And they shall see his face; and his name shall be in their foreheads.

5 And there shall be no night there; and they need no candle, neither light of the sun; for the Lord God giveth them light: and they shall reign for ever and ever.

Death, Be Not Proud

John Donne
(1572-1631)

Two themes, death and resurrection, pervade the religious poems of John Donne. As an ordained minister, he was a practical moralist, and in his later years he was burdened by the consciousness of his sins and his need for God's mercy.

Donne's religious poetry affirms orthodox Christian beliefs—but never as mere abstract theological doctrines. For him these tenets are an integral part of the believing Christian's everyday life. "Death, Be Not Proud" affirms the Christian faith in a life after this life—the ultimate means by which death itself is destroyed.

Death, be not proud, though some have called thee
Mighty and dreadful, for thou art not so;
For those whom thou think'st thou dost overthrow
Die not, poor Death, nor yet canst thou kill me.

From rest and sleep, which but thy pictures be,
Much pleasure, then from thee much more must flow,
And soonest our best men with thee do go,
Rest of their bones, and souls' delivery.
Thou art slave to fate, chance, kings, and desperate
    men,
And dost with poison, war, and sickness dwell,
And poppy or charms can make us sleep as well
And better than thy stroke; why swell'st thou then?
One short sleep past, we wake eternally,
And Death shall be no more; Death, thou shalt die.

Excerpts from

A Death in the Family

James Agee
(1909-1955)

Two excerpts from the novel, A Death in the Family, *follow. In the first, we meet Rufus once again—the child (in the selection from Session 2) who knew a deep and loving relationship with his father. Two days have elapsed since the scene of their walk together. Jay, the father, has been killed in a car accident the night before. Rufus and his sister are eating breakfast with Aunt Hannah, who tries to explain their father's death in a way the children will understand, a way in keeping with her own faith in life after death.*

The second scene focuses on other members of the family as they sense, in various ways, the presence of Jay's spirit in their midst. The scenes portray two human situations often experienced after a family member dies.

Catherine did not like being buttoned up by Rufus or bossed around by him, and breakfast wasn't like breakfast either. Aunt Hannah didn't say anything and neither did Rufus and neither did she, and she felt that even if she wanted to say anything she oughtn't. Everything was queer, it was so still and it seemed dark. Aunt Hannah sliced the banana so thin on the Post Toasties it looked cold and wet and slimy. She gave each of them a little bit of coffee in their milk and she made Rufus' a little bit darker than hers. She didn't say, "Eat"; "Eat your breakfast, Catherine"; "Don't dawdle," like Catherine's mother; she didn't say anything. Catherine did not feel hungry, but she felt mildly curious because things tasted so different, and she ate slowly ahead, tasting each mouthful. Everything was so still that it made Catherine feel uneasy and sad. There were little noises when a fork or spoon touched a dish; the only other noise was the very thin dry toast Aunt Hannah kept slowly crunching and the fluttering sipping of the steamy coffee with which she wet each mouthful of dry crumbs enough to swallow it. When Catherine tried to make a similar noise sipping her milk, her Aunt Hannah glanced to her sharply as if she wondered if Catherine was trying to be a smart aleck but she did not say anything. Catherine was not trying to be a smart aleck but she felt she had better not make that noise again. The fried eggs had hardly any pepper and they were so soft the yellow ran out over the white and the white plate and looked so nasty she didn't want to eat it but she ate it because she didn't want to be told to and because she felt there was some special reason, still, why she ought to be a good girl. She felt very uneasy, but there was nothing to do but eat, so she always took care to get a good hold on her tumbler and did not take too much on her spoon, and hardly spilled at all, and when she became aware of how little she was spilling it made her feel like a big girl and yet she did not feel any less uneasy, because she knew there was something wrong. She was not as much interested in eating as she was in the way things were, and listening carefully, looking mostly at her plate, every sound she heard and the whole quietness which was so much stronger than the sounds, meant that things were not good. What it was was that he wasn't here. Her mother wasn't either, but she was upstairs. He wasn't even upstairs. He was coming home last night but he didn't come home. . . . Her mother said he wasn't coming home ever any more. That was what she said, but why wasn't he home eating breakfast right this minute? Because he was not with them eating breakfast it wasn't fun and everything was so queer. Now maybe in just a minute he would walk right in and grin at her and say, "Good morning, merry sunshine," because her lip was sticking out, and even bend down and rub her cheek with his whiskers and then sit down and eat a big breakfast and then it would be all fun again and she would watch from the window when he went to work and just before he went out of sight he would turn around and she would wave but why wasn't he right here now where she wanted him to be and why didn't he come home? Ever any more. He won't come home again ever any more. Won't come home again ever. But he will, though, because it's home. But why's he not here? He's up seeing Grampa Follet. Grampa Follet is very, very sick. But Mama didn't feel awful then, she feels awful now. But

why didn't he come back when she said he would? He went to heaven and now Catherine could remember about heaven, that's where God lives, way up in the sky. Why'd he do that? God took him there. But why'd he go there and not come home like Mama said? Last night Mama said he was coming home last night. We could even wait up a while and when he didn't and we had to go to bed she *promised* he would come if we went to sleep and she promised he'd be here at breakfast time and now it's breakfast time and she says he won't come home ever any more. Now her Aunt Hannah folded her napkin, and folded it again more narrowly, and again still more narrowly, and pressed the butt end of it against her mouth, and laid it beside her plate, where it slowly and slightly unfolded, and, looking first at Rufus and then at Catherine and then back at Rufus, said quietly, "I think you ought to know about your father. Whatever I can tell you. Because your mother's not feeling well."

Now I'll know when he *is* coming home, Catherine thought. All through breakfast, Rufus had wanted to ask questions, but now he felt so shy and uneasy that he could hardly speak. "Who hurt him?" he finally asked.

"Why nobody hurt him, Rufus," she said, and she looked shocked. "What on earth made you think so?"

Mama said so, Catherine thought.

"Mama said he got hurt so bad God put him to sleep," Rufus said.

Like the kitties, Catherine thought; she saw a dim, gigantic old man in white take her tiny father by the skin of the neck and put him in a huge slop jar full of water and sit on the lid, and she heard the tiny scratching and the stifled mewing.

"That's true he was hurt, but nobody hurt him," her Aunt Hannah was saying. How could that be, Catherine wondered. "He was driving home by himself. That's all, all by himself, in the auto last night, and he had an accident."

Rufus felt his face get warm and he looked warningly at his sister. He knew it could not be that, not with his father, a grown man, besides, God wouldn't put you to sleep for *that,* and it didn't hurt, anyhow. But Catherine might think so. Sure enough, she was looking at her aunt with astonishment and disbelief that she could say such a thing about her father. Not in his *pants,* you dern fool, Rufus wanted to tell her, but his Aunt Hannah continued: "A *fatal* accident"; and by her voice, as she spoke the strange word, "fatal," they knew she meant something very bad. "That means that, just as your mother told you, that he was hurt so badly that God put him to sleep right away."

Like the rabbits, Rufus remembered, all torn white bloody fur and red insides. He could not imagine his father like that. Poor little things, he remembered his mother's voice comforting his crying, hurt so terribly that God just let them go to sleep.

If it was in the auto, Catherine thought, then he wouldn't be in the slop jar.

They couldn't be happy any more if He hadn't, his mother had said. They could never get well.

Hannah wondered whether they could comprehend it at all and whether she should try to tell them. She doubted it. Deeply uncertain, she tried again.

"He was driving home last night," she said, "about nine, and apparently something was already wrong with the steering mech—with the wheel you guide the machine with. But your father didn't know it. Because there wasn't any way he could know until something went wrong and then it was too late. But one of the wheels struck a loose stone in the road and the wheel turned aside very suddenly, and when . . ." She paused and went on more quietly and slowly: "You see, when your father tried to make the auto go where it should, stay on the road, he found he couldn't, he didn't have any control. Because something was wrong with the steering gear. So, instead of doing as he tried to make it, the auto twisted aside because of the loose stone and ran off the road into a deep ditch." She paused again. "Do you understand?"

They kept looking at her.

"Your father was thrown from the auto," she said. "Then the auto went on without him up the other side of the ditch. It went up an eight-foot embankment and then it fell down backward, turned over and landed just beside him.

"They're pretty sure he was dead even before he was thrown out. Because the only mark on his whole body," and now they began to hear in her voice a troubling intensity and resentment, "was right—here!" She pressed the front of her forefinger to the point of her chin, and looked at them almost as if she were accusing them.

They said nothing.

I suppose I've got to finish, Hannah thought; I've gone this far.

"They're pretty sure how it happened," she said. "The auto gave such a sudden terrible *jerk*"—she jerked so violently that both children jumped, and startled her; she demonstrated what she saw next more gently: "that your father was thrown forward and struck his chin, very hard, against the wheel, the steering wheel, and from that instant he never knew anything more."

She looked at Rufus, at Catherine, and again at Rufus. "Do you understand?" They looked at her.

After a while Catherine said, "He hurt his chin."

"Yes, Catherine. He did," she replied. "They believe he was *instantly killed,* with that one single blow, because it happened to strike just exactly where it did. Because if you're struck very hard in just that place, it jars your whole head, your brain so hard that—sometimes people die in that very instant." She drew a deep breath and let it out long and shaky. "Concussion of the brain, that is called," she said with most careful distinctness, and bowed her head for a moment; they saw her thumb make a small cross on her chest.

She looked up. "Now do you understand, children?" she asked earnestly. "I know it's very hard to understand. You please tell me if there's anything you want to know and I'll do my best to expl—tell you better."

Rufus and Catherine looked at each other and looked away. After a while Rufus said, "Did it hurt him bad?"

"He could never have felt it. That's the one great mercy" (or *is* it she wondered); "the doctor is sure of that."

Catherine wondered whether she could ask one question. She thought she'd better not.

"What's an eight foot embackmut?" asked Rufus.

"Em-bank-ment," she replied. "Just a bank. A steep little hill, eight feet high. Bout's high's the ceiling."

He and Catherine saw the auto climb it and fall backward rolling and come to rest beside their father. Umbackmut, Catherine thought; em-*bank*-ment, Rufus said to himself.

"What's instintly?"

"Instantly is—quick's that"; she snapped her fingers, more loudly than she had expected to; Catherine flinched and kept her eyes on the fingers. "Like snapping off an electric light," Rufus nodded. "So you can be very sure, both of you, he never felt a moment's pain. Not one moment.

"When's . . ." Catherine began.

"What's . . ." Rufus began at the same moment; they glared at each other.

"What is it, Catherine?"

"When's Daddy coming home?"

"Why *good golly,* Catherine," Rufus began. "Hold your tongue!" his Aunt Hannah said fiercely, and he listened, scared, and ashamed of himself.

"Catherine, he *can't* come home," she said very kindly. "That's just what all this means, child." She put her hand over Catherine's hand and Rufus could see that her chin was trembling. "He died, Catherine," she said. "That's what your mother means. God put him to sleep and took him, took his soul away with Him. So he can't come home . . ."

She stopped, and began again. "We'll see him once more," she said, "tomorrow or day after; that I promise you," she said, wishing she was sure of Mary's views about this. "But he'll be asleep then. And after that we won't see him any more in this world. Not until God takes us away too.

"Do you see, child?" Catherine was looking at her very seriously. "Of course you don't, God bless you"; she squeezed her hand. "Don't ever try too hard to understand, child. Just try to understand it's so. He'd come if he could but he simply can't because God wants him with Him. That's all." She kept her hand over Catherine's a little while more, while Rufus realized much more clearly than before that he really could not and would not come home again: because of God.

"He would if he could but he can't," Catherine finally said, remembering a joking phrase of her mother's.

Hannah, who knew the joking phrase too, was startled, but quickly realized that the child meant it in earnest, "That's it," she said gratefully.

But he'll come once more, anyway, Rufus realized, looking forward to it. Even if he *is* asleep.

"What was it you wanted to ask, Rufus?" he heard his aunt say.

He tried to remember and remembered. "What's kuh, kuh-kush, kuh . . . ?"

"Con-*cus*-sion, Rufus. Concus-sion of the brain. That's the doctor's name for what happened. It means, it's as if the brain were hit very hard and suddenly, and joggled loose. The instant

that happens, your father was—he . . . ."

"Instantly killed."

She nodded.

"Then it was that, that put him to sleep."

"Hyess."

"*Not* God."

Catherine looked at him, bewildered.

★ ★ ★

The following scene involves Mary, the children's mother, and her family: Parents, brother and aunt. It presents a short period of time in which the family members experience an overwhelming feeling that the spirit of the person who has died returns among them.

And she thought with such exactness and with such love of her husband's face, and of his voice, and of his hands, and of his way of smiling too warmly even though his eyes almost never lost their sadness. . . .

"Hark!" Hannah whispered.

"What *is* it?"

"*Ssh!* Listen."

"What's up?" Joel asked.

"Be quite, Joel *please*. There's something."

They listened most intently.

"I can't hear anything," Andrew whispered.

"Well *I* do," Hannah said, in a low voice. "Hear it or feel it. There's *something*."

And again in silence they listened.

It began to seem to Mary, as to Hannah, that there was someone in the house other than themselves. She thought of the children; they might have waked up. Yet listening as intently as she could, she was not at all sure that there was any sound; and whoever or whatever it might be, she became sure that it was no child, for she felt in it a terrible forcefulness, and concern, and restiveness, which were no part of any child.

"There *is* something," Andrew whispered.

Whatever it might be, it was never for an instant at rest in one place. It was in the next room; it was in the kitchen; it was in the dining room.

"I'm going out to see," Andrew said; he got up.

"Wait, Andrew, don't, not yet," Mary whispered. "No; no"; now it's going upstairs, she thought; it's along the—it's in the children's room. It's in *our* room.

"Has somebody come into the house?" Catherine inquired in her clear voice.

Andrew felt the flesh go cold along his spine. He bent near her. "What made you think so, Mama?" he asked quietly.

"It's right here in the room with us," Mary said in a cold voice.

"Why, how very stupid of me, I *thought I heard.* Footsteps." She gave her short, tinkling laugh. "I must be getting old and dippy." She laughed again. *"Sshh!"*

"It's Jay," Mary whispered. "I know it now. I was so wrapped up in wondering *what* on earth . . . Jay. Darling. Dear heart, can you hear me?

"Can you tell me if you hear me, dearest?

"Can you?

"Can't you?

"Oh try your best, my dear. Try your *very* hardest to let me know.

"You can't, can you? You can't, no matter *how* hard.

"But O, do hear me, Jay. I do pray God with all my heart you can hear me, I want so to assure you.

"Don't be troubled, dear one. Don't you worry. Stay near us if you can. *All* you can. But let not your heart be troubled. They're all right, my sweetheart, my husband. I'm going to be all right. Don't you worry. We'll make out. Rest, my dear. Just rest, just rest, my heart. Don't ever be troubled again. Never again, darling. Never never again."

"May the souls of the faithful through the mercy of God rest in peace." Hannah whispered. "Blessed are the dead."

"Mary!" her brother whispered. He was crying.

"He's not here any more now," she said. "We can talk."

"Mary, in God's name what was it?"

"It was Jay, Andrew."

"It was *something.* I haven't any doubt of that, but—good God, Mary."

"It was Jay, all right. I *know!* Who else would be coming here tonight, so terribly worried, so terribly concerned for us, and restless! Besides, Andrew, it—it simply *felt* like Jay."

"You mean . . ."

"I just mean it felt like his *presence.*"

"To me, too," Hannah said.

. . . . .

. . . they sat quietly and in the silence they began to listen again. At first there was nothing, but after a few minutes Hannah whispered, "He's there," and Andrew whispered, "Where?" and Mary said quietly, "With the children," and quietly and quickly left the room.

When she came through the door of the children's room she could feel his presence as strongly throughout the room as if she had opened a furnace door: the presence of his strength, of virility, of helplessness, and of pure calm. She fell down on her knees in the middle of the floor and whispered, "Jay. My dear. My dear one. You're all right now, darling. You're not troubled any more, are you, my darling? Not any more. Not ever any more, dearest. I can feel how it is with you. I know, my dearest. It's terrible to go. You don't want to. Of *course* you don't. But you've got to. And you know they're going to be all right. Everything is going to be all right, my darling. God take you. God keep you, my own beloved. God make His light shine upon you." And even while she whispered, his presence became faint, and in a moment of terrible dread she cried out "Jay!" and hurried to her daughter's crib. "Stay with me one minute," she whispered, "just one minute, my dearest"; and in some force he did return; she felt him with her, watching his child. Catherine was sleeping with all her might and her thumb was deep in her mouth; she was scowling fiercely. "Mercy, child," Mary whispered, smiling, and touched her hot forehead to smooth it, and she growled.

"God bless you, God keep you," her mother whispered, and came silently to her son's bed. There was the cap in its tissue paper, beside him on the floor; he slept less deeply than his sister, with his chin lifted, and his forehead flung back; he looked grave, serene and expectant.

"Be with us all you can," she whispered. "This is good-bye." And again she went to her knees. Good-bye, she said again, within herself; but she was unable to feel much of anything. "God help me to *realize* it," she whispered, and clasped her hands before her face: but she could realize only that he was fading, and that it was indeed good-bye, and that she was at that moment unable to be particularly sensitive to the fact.

And now he was gone entirely from the room, from the house, and from this world.

"Soon, Jay. Soon, dear," she whispered; but she knew that it would not be soon. She knew that a long life lay ahead of her, for the children were to be brought up, and God alone could know what change and chance might work upon them all, before they met once more. She felt at once calm and annihilating emptiness, and a cold and overwhelming fullness.

"God help us all," she whispered. "May God in His loving mercy keep us all."

She signed herself with the Cross and left the room.

Excerpt from

Life After Life

Raymond A. Moody, Jr.
(1944-   )

Raymond A. Moody, a psychiatrist and former teacher of philosophy, studied the experiences of more than 100 people who had been declared "clinically dead," but who later revived, and found a striking similarity in their accounts. Typically, Dr. Moody reports, a dying person suddenly finds himself out of his physical body and watching the attempts at his revival from a distance. The spirits of relatives and friends already dead meet him and a mysterious "being of light" appears, who helps him to evaluate his past life. He approaches a border between earthly life and the next life but is unable to cross that barrier (though he wishes to), because the time for his death has not yet come. The following passage illustrates the central experience of meeting a personal, comforting and loving presence.

What is perhaps the most incredible common element in the accounts I have studied, and is certainly the element which has the most profound effect upon the individual, is the encounter with a very bright light. Typically, at its first appearance this light is dim, but it rapidly gets brighter until it reaches an unearthly brilliance. Yet, even though this light (usually said to be white or "clear") is of an indescribable brilliance, many make the specific point that it does not in any way hurt their eyes, or dazzle them, or keep them from seeing other things around them (perhaps because at this point they don't have physical "eyes" to be dazzled).

Despite the light's unusual manifestation, however, not one person has expressed any doubt whatsoever that it was a being, a being of light. Not only that, it is a personal being. It has a very definite personality. The love and the warmth which emanate from this being to the dying person are utterly beyond words, and he feels completely surrounded by it and taken up in it, completely at ease and accepted in the presence of this being. He senses an irresistible magnetic attraction to this light. He is ineluctably drawn to it.

Interestingly, while the above description of the being of light is utterly invariable, the identification of the being varies from individual to individual and seems to be largely a function of the religious background, training, or beliefs of the person involved. Thus, most of those who are Christians in training or belief identify the light as Christ and sometimes draw Biblical parallels in support of their interpretation. A Jewish man and woman identified the light as an "angel." It was clear, though, in both cases, that the subjects did not mean to imply that the being had wings, played a harp, or even had a human shape or appearance. There was only the light. What each was trying to get across was that they took the being to be an emissary, or a guide. A man who had had no religious beliefs or training at all prior to his experience simply identified what he saw as "a being of light." The same label was used by one lady of the Christian faith, who apparently did not feel any compulsion at all to call the light "Christ."

Shortly after its appearance, the being begins to communicate with the person who is passing over. Notably, this communication is of the same direct kind which we encountered earlier in the description of how a person in the spiritual body may "pick up the thoughts" of those around him. For, here again, people claim that they did not hear any physical voice or sounds coming from the being, nor did they respond to the being through audible sounds. Rather, it is reported that direct, unimpeded transfer of thoughts takes place, and in such a clear way that there is no possibility whatsoever either of misunderstanding or of lying to the light.

Furthermore, this unimpeded exchange does not even take place in the native language of the person. Yet, he understands perfectly and is instantaneously aware. He cannot even translate the thoughts and exchanges which took place while he was near death into the human language which he must speak now, after his resuscitation.

The next step of the experience clearly illustrates the difficulty of translating from this unspoken language. The being almost im-

mediately directs a certain thought to the person into whose presence it has come so dramatically. Usually the persons with whom I have talked try to formulate the thought into a question. Among the translations I have heard are: "Are you prepared to die?", "Are you ready to die?", "What have you done with your life to show me?", and "What have you done with your life that is sufficient?" The first two formulations which stress "preparation," might at first seem to have a different sense from the second pair, which emphasize "accomplishment." However, some support for my own feeling that everyone is trying to express the same thought comes from the narrative of one woman who put it this way:

> The first thing he said to me was, that he kind of asked me if I was ready to die, or what I had done with my life that I wanted to show him.

Furthermore, even in the case of more unusual ways of phrasing the "question," it turns out, upon elucidation, to have much the same force. For example, one man told me that during his "death,"

> The voice asked me a question: "Is it worth it?" And what it meant was, did the kind of life I had been leading up to that point seem worthwhile to me then, knowing what I then knew.

Incidentally, all insist that this question, ultimate and profound as it may be in its emotional impact, is not at all asked in condemnation. The being, all seem to agree, does not direct the question to them to accuse or to threaten

A City of Fantasy. *American School, Unknown. Oil on canvas.*

As the writer of The Book of Revelation uses word images to describe the heavenly kingdom, so do artists through their creations express realities that transcend the world we see and know.

The National Gallery of Art, Washington, D.C.

them, for they still feel the total love and acceptance coming from the light, no matter what their answer may be. Rather, the point of the question seems to be to make them think about their lives, to draw them out. It is, if you will, a Socratic question, one asked not to acquire information but to help the person who is being asked to proceed along the path to the truth by himself. Let us look at some firsthand accounts of this fantastic being.

(1) I heard the doctors say that I was dead, and that's when I began to feel as though I were tumbling, actually kind of floating, through this blackness, which was some kind of enclosure. There are not really words to describe this. Everything was very black, except that, way off from me, I could see this light. It was a very, very brilliant light, but not too large at first. It grew larger as I came nearer and nearer to it.

I was trying to get to that light at the end, because I felt that it was Christ, and I was trying to reach that point. It was not a frightening experience. It was more or less a pleasant thing. For immediately, being a Christian, I had connected the light with Christ, who said, "I am the light of the world." I said to myself, "If this is it, if I am to die, then I know who waits for me at the end, there in that light."

(2) I got up and walked into the hall to go get a drink, and it was at that point, as they found out later, that my appendix ruptured. I became very weak, and I fell down. I began to feel a sort of drifting, a movement of my real being in and out of my body, and to hear beautiful music. I floated on down the hall and out the door onto the screened-in porch. There, it almost seemed that clouds, a pink mist really, began to gather around me, and then I floated right straight on through

the screen, just as though it weren't there, and up into this pure crystal clear light, an illuminating white light. It was beautiful and so bright, so radiant, but it didn't hurt my eyes. It's not any kind of light you can describe on earth. I didn't actually see a person in this light, and yet it has a special identity, it definitely does. It is a light of perfect understanding and perfect love.

The thought came to my mind, "Lovest thou me?" This was not exactly in the form of a question, but I guess the connotation of what the light said was, "If you do love me, go back and complete what you began in your life." And all during this time, I felt as though I were surrounded by an overwhelming love and compassion.

(3) I knew I was dying and that there was nothing I could do about it, because no one could hear me. . . . I was out of my body, there's no doubt about it, because I could see my own body there on the operating room table. My soul was out! All this made me feel very bad at first, but then, this really bright light came. It did seem that it was a little dim at first, but then it was this huge beam. It was just a tremendous amount of light, nothing like a big bright flashlight, it was just too much light. And it gave off heat to me; I felt a warm sensation.

It was a bright yellowish white—more white. It was tremendously bright; I just can't describe it. It seemed that it covered everything, yet it didn't prevent me from seeing everything around me—the operating room, the doctors and nurses, everything. I could see clearly, and it wasn't blinding.

At first, when the light came, I wasn't sure what was happening, but then, it asked, it kind of asked me if I was ready to die. It was like talking to a person, but a person wasn't there. The light's what was talking to me, but in a *voice*.

Now, I think that the voice that was talking to me actually realized that I wasn't ready to die. You know, it was just kind of testing me more than anything else. Yet, from the moment the light spoke to me, I felt really good—secure and loved. The love which came from it is just unimaginable, indescribable. It was a fun person to be with! And it had a sense of humor, too—definitely!

Further Readings

Beagle, Peter S. *A Fine and Private Place.* 1960. Delightful fantasy in which two ghosts meet at the cemetery and fall in love. The other-worldly couple teaches someone that there is more to living than dying.

Jung, C.G. "Visions" and "On Life After Death" in *Memories, Dreams, Reflections.* 1963. Jung describes his own near-death experience in the first chapter cited, and, in the second, discusses the concept of life after death from a philosophical viewpoint.

Kubler-Ross, Elizabeth, ed. *Death: The Final Stage of Growth.* 1975. A spectrum of viewpoints from rabbis, ministers, doctors, nurses; personal accounts of those near death and their survivors. The book's thesis is that death provides a key to the meaning of human existence.

Montgomery, Ruth. *A World Beyond: A Startling Message from the Eminent Psychic Arthur Ford from Beyond the Grave.* 1971. The author claims to have communicated with Ford after his death through automatic writing. Ford dictated the manuscript in which he describes what happens after death, reincarnation and the fate of famous people he has encountered in the world beyond.

Moody, Raymond A., Jr. *Reflections on Life After Life.* 1977. A sequel to *Life After Life,* in which Moody reports on his continuing research into near-death experiences.

Spraggett, Allen. *The Case for Immortality: The Story of Life After Death.* 1974. The author builds his case by citing evidence from mediums, apparitions, out-of-the-body and near-death experiences and memories of previous lives.

Section 8

CREATING MEANING—ART AND SCIENCE

Many people find it impossible today to discover any coherence or pattern in human experience or in nature. Even the search for some key to the meaning of our existence seems fruitless to them. They reject as wishful thinking the claim of reason, faith or imagination that answers to our deepest questions exist in the unseen realm, or that some future condition after death will compensate for what humanity suffers in this world.

The self-confidence of humankind in its pursuit of meaning was seriously shaken by three significant discoveries over the past five centuries. They contradicted earlier beliefs that humans are a unique focal point in creation and function only according to rational and thus controllable thought. First, it was discovered that our world is not the center of the universe and that there is no reason to think the stars are part of a divine order established for our convenience. Then Darwin (1809-1882) challenged the assumption that the human species is totally distinct in its nature from all other animals. Finally, Freud (1856-1939) brought to light the power exerted by unconscious, irrational forces of the mind, thereby causing us to doubt that our behavior is effectively controlled by our reason.

The result of these shocks to human pretensions was a questioning of the assumption that meaning is to be found in the universe. A renowned physicist stated the problem:

Fiddle maker from the Appalachia region of Georgia.

Standing on our microscopic fragment of a grain of sand, we attempt to discover the nature and purpose of the universe which surrounds our home in space and time. Our first impression is something akin to terror. We find the universe terrifying because of its vast meaningless distances, terrifying because of its inconceivably long vistas of time which dwarf human history to the twinkling of an eye, terrifying because of our extreme loneliness, and because of the material insignificance of our home in space—a millionth part of a grain of sand out of all the seas and in the world. But above all else, we find the universe terrifying because it appears to be indifferent to life like our own: emotion, ambition and achievement, art and religion all seem equally foreign to its plan. (Sir James Jeans, *The Mysterious Universe*).

To some, this doubt about the possibility of discovering meaning has produced a sense of hopelessness. But to others it represents a challenge to be met by human action. Proponents of the second view hold that we cannot expect to discern an ultimate purpose in the universe, but we can *create* meaning in that universe. We may be insignificant in relation to the immensity of nature, but we do have a unique capacity to bestow meaning on an otherwise purposeless universe. We can bring beauty, justice, prosperity, health, pleasure and love into existence and, by doing so, create meaning in our lives and the lives of those who benefit from our actions.

The selections in this session represent a variety of such responses to the human situation. Beethoven, threatened by the loss of his hearing and contemplating suicide, chose to persevere in his musical art despite a devastating affliction. Virginia Woolf's writing gave meaning to her life when threatened by tragic mental breakdown. Lawrence Ferlinghetti reminds us of the risk that he accepts in committing his thoughts to poetry.

The creation of meaning is not limited to the famous. Dorothy Canfield Fisher describes the transformation of one woman's life by the making of a magnificent bedquilt. Perhaps you can think of your own or others' creative work such as dance, music or painting that has reaffirmed your conviction that there is meaning in human accomplishment. Or you might recall some past creative activity that continues to assure you of the value and significance of life.

Science involves another kind of human creativity that we cannot ignore. The great naturalist Charles Darwin compares the satisfaction he felt when his first scientific discovery was published to the joy of the poet. Lewis Thomas in *The Lives of a Cell* describes the exhilaration he experiences in the cooperative endeavor of several scientists engaged in a new discovery. He compares the work of colleagues on a project to the commotion of bees in a disturbed hive, but suggests that their success is like the production of pure honey: "The most powerful and productive of things human beings have learned to do together in many centuries." In your own experience, what shared activity has provided you with emotions akin to those of the scientist? Have you known the satisfaction of creativity with others or only through your own efforts?

For My Brothers

Ludwig van Beethoven
(1770-1827)

The German composer Beethoven initiated the romantic era of serious music, a period marked by freedom of expression and form. His unorthodox musical ideas offended his master, Franz Haydn, a well-known composer of the earlier classical period. Beethoven's insistence on change and innovation led him to compose the music that established his reputation as one of the greatest composers of all time.

Beethoven began to lose his hearing in his late twenties, and by 47 he was completely deaf. In the famous letter excerpted here, he shares with his brothers the anguish he suffered by virtue of his handicap. His music gave him the only meaning he could find in life. He claims that without it he would have ended his life, but "it seemed to me impossible to leave the world until I had brought forth all that I felt was within me." He composed the Ninth Symphony and several other of his best known works after a total loss of hearing.

Oh you men who think or say that I am malevolent, stubborn, or misanthropic, how greatly do you wrong me. You do not know the secret cause which makes me seem that way to you. From childhood on, my heart and soul have been full of the tender feeling of goodwill, and I was ever inclined to accomplish great things. But, think that for six years now I have been hopelessly afflicted, made worse by senseless physicians, from year to year deceived with hopes of improvement, finally compelled to face the prospect of a lasting malady (whose cure will take years or perhaps, be impossible). Though born with a fiery, active temperament, ever susceptible to the diversions of society, I was soon compelled to withdraw myself, to live life alone. If at times I tried to forget all this, oh how harshly was I flung back by the doubly sad experience of my bad hearing. Yet it was impossible for me to say to people, "Speak louder, shout, for I am deaf." Ah, how could I possibly admit an infirmity in the one sense which ought to be more perfect in me than in others, a sense which I once possessed in the highest perfection, a perfection such as few in my profession enjoy or ever have enjoyed. Oh I cannot do it; therefore forgive me when you see me draw back when I would have gladly mingled with you. My misfortune is doubly painful to me because I am bound to be misunderstood; for me there can be no relaxation with my fellow men, no refined conversations, no mutual exchange of ideas. I must live almost alone, like one who has been banished; I can mix with society only as much as true necessity demands. If I approach near to people a hot terror seizes upon me, and I fear being exposed to the danger that my condition might be noticed. Thus it has been during the last six months which I have spent in the country. By ordering me to spare my hearing as much as possible, my intelligent doctor almost fell in with my own present frame of mind, though sometimes I ran counter to it by yielding to my desire for companionship. But what a humiliation for me when someone standing next to me heard a flute in the distance and I heard nothing, or someone heard a shepherd singing and again I heard nothing. Such incidents drove me almost to despair; a little more of that and I would have ended my life—it was only my art that held me back. Ah, it seemed to me impossible to leave the world until I had brought forth all that I felt was within me. So I endured this wretched existence—truly wretched for so susceptible a body, which can be thrown by a sudden change from the best condition to the very worst. Patience, they say, is what I must now choose for my guide, and I have done so—I hope my determination will remain firm to endure until it pleases the inexorable Parcae* to break the thread. Perhaps I shall get better, perhaps not; I am ready. Forced to become a philosopher already in my twenty-eighth year,—oh it is not easy, and for the artist much more difficult than for anyone else. Divine One, thou seest my inmost soul; thou knowest that therein dwells the love of mankind and the desire to do good. Oh fellow men, when at some point you read this, consider then that you have done me an injustice; someone who has had misfortune may console himself to find a similar case to his, who despite all the limitations of Nature nevertheless did everything within his powers to become accepted among worthy artists and men. You, my brothers . . . as soon as I am dead, if Dr. Schmidt is still alive, ask him in my name to describe my malady, and attach this written document to his account of my illness so that so far as is possible at least the world may become reconciled to me after my death. At the same time, I declare you two to be the heirs to my small fortune (if so it can be called); divide it fairly; bear with and help each other. What injury you have done me you know was long ago forgiven. To you, brother Carl, I give special thanks for the attachment you have shown me of late. It is my wish that you may have a better and freer life than I have had. Recommend virtue to your children; it alone, not money, can make them happy. I speak from experience; this was what upheld me in time of misery. Thanks to it and to my art, I did not end my life by suicide— Farewell and love each other—I thank all my friends, particularly Prince Lichnowsky and Professor Schmidt—I would like the instruments from Prince L. to be preserved by one of you, but not to be the cause of strife between you, and as soon as they can serve you a better purpose, then sell them. How happy I shall be if I can still be helpful to you in my grave—so be it. With joy I hasten to meet death. If it comes before I have had the chance to develop all my artistic capacities, it will still be coming

*Fates or destinies (in Roman mythology)

too soon despite my harsh fate, and I should probably wish it later—yet even so I should be happy, for would it not free me from a state of endless suffering? Come when thou wilt, I shall meet thee bravely. Farewell and do not wholly forget me when I am dead; I deserve this from you, for during my lifetime I was thinking of you often and of ways to make you happy—please be so—

Ludwig van Beethoven
(seal)

Heiglnstadt
October 6th
1802

Virginia Woolf was a potent force in the development of the English novel in the early 20th century. Rather than stressing the plot or the interaction between characters in her stories, she dwelt on inner thoughts and feelings, using rich symbolic and visual images. Her unusual style prevented immediate acceptance of her work, and she often had serious doubts about its value. She suffered serious mental breakdowns in 1895 and 1915 and lived in constant fear that she would go mad again. In 1941, suspecting the approach of another attack, she drowned herself.

In these passages from her voluminous diaries, originally written for her private purposes, we see her struggling courageously to complete The Years, *which was ultimately well received by the critics. The excerpts illustrate her distinctive and beautiful use of language. They were edited by her husband, Leonard Woolf, who is frequently referred to as "L."*

Thursday, June 11th

I can only, after two months, make this brief note, to say at last after two months dismal and worse, almost catastrophic illness—never been so near the precipice to my own feeling since 1913—I'm again on top. I have to rewrite, I mean interpolate, and rub out most of *The Years* in proof. But I can't go into that. Can only do an hour or so. Oh but the divine joy of being mistress of my mind again! Now I am going to live like a cat stepping on eggs till my 600 pages are done. I think I can—I think I can—but must have immense courage and buoyancy to compass it. . . .

Tuesday, June 23rd

A good day—a bad day—so it goes on. Few people can be so tortured by writing as I am. Only Flaubert I think. Yet I see it now, as a whole. I think I can bring it off, if I only have courage and patience: take each scene quietly: compose: I think it may be a good book. And then—oh when it's finished!

Not so clear today, because I went to dentist and then shopped. My brain is like a scale: one grain pulls it down. Yesterday it balanced: today dips.

Friday, October 30th

I do not wish for the moment to write out the story of the months since I made the last mark here. I do not wish, for reasons I cannot now develop, to analyse that extraordinary summer. It will be more helpful and healthy for me to write scenes; to take up my pen and describe actual events: good practice too for my stumbling and doubting pen.

183

Can I still "write"? That is the question, you see. And now I will try to prove if the gift is dead, or dormant.

Tuesday, November 3rd

Miracles will never cease—L. actually liked *The Years!* He thinks it so far—as far as the wind chapter—as good as any of my books. I will put down the actual facts. On Sunday I started to read the proofs. When I had read to the end of the first section I was in despair: stony but convinced despair. I made myself yesterday read on to Present Time. When I reached that landmark I said, "This is happily so bad that there can be no question about it. I must carry the proofs, like a dead cat, to L. and tell him to burn them unread." This I did. And a weight fell off my shoulders. That is true. I felt relieved of some great pack. . . .

Wednesday, November 4th

L. who has now read [*The Years*] to the end of 1914, still thinks it extraordinarily good: very strange: very interesting: very sad. We discussed my sadness. But my difficulty is this: I cannot bring myself to believe that he is right. It may be simply that I exaggerated its badness, and therefore he now, finding it not so bad, exaggerates its goodness. If it is to be published, I must at once sit down and correct: how can I? Every other sentence seemed to me bad. But I am shelving the question till he has done, which should be tonight.

Thursday, November 5th

The miracle is accomplished. L. put down the last sheet about 12 last night; and could not speak. He was in tears.

He says it is "a most remarkable book"—he *likes* it better than *The Waves*—and has not a spark of doubt that it must be published. I, as a witness, not only to his emotion but to his absorption, for he read on and on, can't doubt his opinion. What about my own? Anyhow the moment of relief was divine. I hardly know yet if I'm on my heels or head, so amazing is the reversal since Tuesday morning. I have never had such an experience before.

Tuesday, November 10th

On the whole it has gone better this morning. It's true my brain is so tired of this job it aches after an hour or less. So I must dandle it, and gently immerse it. Yes, I think it's good; in its very difficult way.

I wonder if anyone has ever suffered so much from a book as I have from *The Years*. Once out I will never look at it again. It's like a long childbirth. Think of that summer, every morning a headache, and forcing myself into that room in my nightgown; and lying down after a page: and always with the certainty of failure. Now that certainty is mercifully removed to some extent. But now I feel I don't care what anyone says so long as I'm rid of it. And for some reason I feel I'm respected and liked. But this is only the haze dance of illusion, always changing. Never write a long book again. Yet I feel I shall write more fiction—scenes will form. But I am tired this morning: too much strain and racing yesterday.

Monday, November 30th

There is no need whatever in my opinion to be unhappy about *The Years*.

184

It seems to me to come off at the end. Anyhow, to be a taut, real, strenuous book. Just finished it; and feel a little exalted. It's different from the others of course: has I think more "real" life in it; more blood and bone. But anyhow, even if there are appalling watery patches, and a grinding at the beginning, I don't think I need lie quaking at nights. I think I can feel assured. This I say sincerely to myself; to hold to myself during the weeks of dull anticipation. Nor need I care much what people say. In fact I hand my compliment to that terribly depressed woman, myself, whose head ached so often; who was so entirely convinced a failure; for in spite of everything I think she brought it off and is to be congratulated. How she did it, with her head like an old cloth, I don't know. But now for rest. . . .

Thursday, December 31st

There in front of me lie the proofs—the galleys—to go off today, a sort of stinging nettle that I cover over. Nor do I wish even to write about it here.

A divine relief has possessed me these last days—at being quit of it—good or bad. And, for the first time since February I should say my mind has sprung up like a tree shaking off a load. And I've plunged into Gibbon and read and read, for the first time since February, I think. Now for action and pleasure again and going about. I could make some interesting and perhaps valuable notes on the absolute necessity for me of my work. Always to be after something. . . .

Sunday, March 14th

I am in such a twitter owing to two columns in the *Observer* praising *The Years* that I can't, as I foretold, go on with *Three Guineas*. Why I even sat back just now and thought with pleasure of people reading that review. And when I think of the agony I went through in this room, just over a year ago . . . when it dawned on me that the whole of three years' work was a complete failure: and then when I think of the mornings here when I used to stumble out and cut up those proofs and write three lines and then go back and lie on my bed—the worst summer in my life, but at the same time the most illuminating—it's no wonder my hand trembles. What most pleases me though is the obvious chance now since de Selincourt sees it, that my intention in *The Years* may be not so entirely muted and obscured as I feared. . . .

Constantly risking absurdity and death

Lawrence Ferlinghetti
(1919-   )

Lawrence Ferlinghetti belongs to a group of American poets who, since the 1950s, have used their poetry to speak out loudly on social and political ills. Ferlinghetti is distinguished from other poets of social consciousness by his ability to laugh at the craziness of the human condition even as he deplores its darker aspects.

In the poem, "Constantly risking absurdity and death," the author chooses the metaphor of an acrobat to describe the poet as one who must keep a careful balance when he climbs onto the high wire to view and write of the world below. For Ferlinghetti, trying to catch truth and beauty in words seems rather absurd and may make the poet appear like a "charleychaplin man," always taking on tasks that are a bit too big for him.

The poem itself moves across the page like the high-wire performer: Walking forward, then slightly backward, balancing, then forward again.

                    Constantly risking absurdity
                                and death
                        whenever he performs
                                above the heads
                                        of his audience
                    the poet like an acrobat
                                climbs on rime
                                to a high wire of his own making
            and balancing on eyebeams
                                above a sea of faces
                    paces his way
                                to the other side of day
                    performing entrechats
                                and sleight-of-foot tricks
                    and other high theatrics
                                and all without mistaking
                    any thing
                    for what it may not be
            For he's the super realist
                                who must perforce perceive
                    taut truth

FERLINGHETTI

before the taking of each stance or step
in his supposed advance
toward the still higher perch
where Beauty stands and waits
with gravity
to start her death-defying leap
And he
a little charleychaplin man
who may or may not catch
her fair eternal form
spreadeagled in the empty air
of existence.

The Bedquilt

Dorothy Canfield Fisher
(1879-1958)

The writings of Dorothy Canfield Fisher reflect her love for the people and customs of her native New England. She saw integrity and heroism in everyday actions and built her stories, like "The Bedquilt," on an appreciation of those actions. The short story dramatizes the often unseen and unrecognized creative force that exists in people's lives.

Of all the Elwell family Aunt Mehetabel was certainly the most unimportant member. It was in the old-time New England days, when an unmarried woman was an old maid at twenty, at forty was everyone's servant, and at sixty had gone through so much discipline that she could need no more in the next world. Aunt Mehetabel was sixty-eight.

She had never for a moment known the pleasure of being important to anyone. Not that she was useless in her brother's family; she was expected, as a matter of course, to take upon herself the most tedious and uninteresting part of the household labors. On Mondays she accepted as her share the washing of the men's shirts, heavy with sweat and stiff with dirt from the fields and from their own hardworking bodies. Tuesdays she never dreamed of being allowed to iron anything pretty or even interesting, like the baby's white dresses or the fancy aprons of her young lady nieces. She stood all day pressing out a monotonous succession of dish-cloths and towels and sheets.

In preserving-time she was allowed to have none of the pleasant responsibility of deciding when the fruit had cooked long enough, nor did she share in the little excitement of pouring the sweet-smelling stuff into the stone jars. She sat in a corner with the children and stoned cherries incessantly, or hulled strawberries until her fingers were dyed red.

The Elwells were not consciously unkind to their aunt, they were even in a vague way fond of her; but she was so insignificant a figure in their lives that she was almost invisible to them. Aunt Mehetabel did not resent this treatment; she took it quite as unconsciously as they gave it. It was to be expected when one was an old-maid dependent in a busy family. She gathered what crumbs of comfort she could from their occasional careless kindnesses and tried to hide the hurt which even yet pierced her at her brother's rough joking. In the winter when they all sat before the big hearth, roasted apples, drank mulled cider, and teased the girls about their beaux and the boys about their sweethearts, she shrank into a dusky corner with her knitting, happy if the evening passed without her brother saying, with a crude sarcasm, "Ask your Aunt Mehetabel about the beaux that used to come a-sparkin' her!" or, "Mehetabel, how was't when you was in love with

Abel Cummings?" As a matter of fact, she had been the same at twenty as at sixty, a mouselike little creature, too shy for anyone to notice, or to raise her eyes for a moment and wish for a life of her own.

Her sister-in-law, a big hearty housewife, who ruled indoors with as autocratic a sway as did her husband on the farm, was rather kind in an absent, offhand way to the shrunken little old woman, and it was through her that Mehetabel was able to enjoy the one pleasure of her life. Even as a girl she had been clever with her needle in the way of patching bedquilts. More than that she could never learn to do. The garments which she made for herself were lamentable affairs, and she was humbly grateful for any help in the bewildering business of putting them together. But in patchwork she enjoyed a tepid importance. She could really do that as well as anyone else. During years of devotion to this one art she had accumulated a considerable store of quilting patterns. Sometimes the neighbors would send over and ask "Miss Mehetabel" for the loan of her sheaf-of-wheat

design, or the double-star pattern. It was with an agreeable flutter at being able to help someone that she went to the dresser, in her bare little room under the eaves, and drew out from her crowded portfolio the pattern desired.

She never knew how her great idea came to her. Sometimes she thought she must have dreamed it, sometimes she even wondered reverently, in the phraseology of the weekly prayer-meeting, if it had not been "sent" to her. She never admitted to herself that she could have thought of it without other help. It was too great, too ambitious, too lofty a project for her humble mind to have conceived. Even when she finished drawing the design with her own fingers, she gazed at it incredulously, not daring to believe that it could indeed be her handiwork. At first it seemed to her only like a lovely but unreal dream. For a long time she did not once think of putting an actual quilt together following that pattern, even though she herself had invented it. It was not that she feared the prodigious effort that would be needed to get those tiny, oddly shaped pieces of bright-colored material sewed together with the perfection of fine workmanship needed. No, she thought zestfully and eagerly of such endless effort, her heart uplifted by her vision of the mosaic-beauty of the whole creation as she saw it, when she shut her eyes to dream of it—that complicated, splendidly difficult pattern— good enough for the angels in heaven to quilt.

But as she dreamed, her nimble old fingers reached out longingly to turn her dream into reality. She began to think adventurously of trying it out—it would perhaps not be too selfish to make one square—just one unit of her design to see how it would look. She dared do nothing in the household where she was a dependent, without asking permission. With a heart full of hope and fear thumping furiously against her old ribs, she approached the mistress of the house on churning-day, knowing with the innocent guile of a child that the country woman was apt to be in a good temper while working over the fragrant butter in the cool cellar.

Sophia listened absently to her sister-in-law's halting petition. "Why, yes, Mehetabel," she said, leaning far down into the huge churn for the last golden morsels—"why, yes, start another quilt if you want to. I've got a lot of pieces from the spring sewing that will work in real good." Mehetabel tried honestly to make her see that this would be no common quilt, but her limited vocabulary and her emotion stood between her and expression. At last Sophia said, with a kindly impatience: "Oh, there! Don't bother me. I never could keep track of your quiltin' patterns, anyhow. I don't care what pattern you go by."

Mehetabel rushed back up the steep attic stairs to her room, and in a joyful agitation began preparations for the work of her life. Her very first stitches showed her that it was even better than she hoped. By some heaven-sent inspiration she had invented a pattern beyond which no patchwork quilt could go.

She had but little time during the daylight hours filled with the incessant household drudgery. After dark she did not dare to sit up late at night lest she burn too much candle. It was weeks before the little square began to show the pattern. Then Mehetabel was in a fever to finish it. She was too conscientious to shirk even the smallest part of her share of the housework, but she rushed through it now so fast that she was panting as she climbed the stairs to her little room.

Every time she opened the door, no matter what weather hung outside the one small window, she always saw the little room flooded with sunshine. She smiled to herself as she bent over the innumerable scraps of cotton cloth on her work table. Already—to her—they were ranged in orderly, complex, mosaic-beauty.

Finally she could wait no longer, and one evening ventured to bring her work down beside the fire where the family sat, hoping that good fortune would give her a place near the tallow candles on the mantelpiece. She had reached the last corner of that first square and her needle flew in and out, in and out, with nervous speed. To her relief no one noticed her. By bedtime she had only a few more stitches to add.

As she stood up with the others, the square fell from her trembling old hands and fluttered to the table. Sophia glanced at it carelessly. "Is that the new quilt you said you wanted to start?" she asked, yawning. "Looks like a real pretty pattern. Let's see it."

Up to that moment Mehetabel had labored in the purest spirit of selfless adoration of an ideal. The emotional shock given her by Sophia's cry of admiration as she held the work towards the candle to examine it, was as much astonishment as joy to Mehetabel.

"Land's sakes!" cried her sister-in-law. "Why, Mehetabel Elwell, where did you git that pattern?"

"I made it up," said Mehetabel. She spoke quietly but she was trembling.

"No!" exclaimed Sophia. "Did you! Why, I never see such a pattern in my life. Girls, come here and see what your Aunt Mehetabel is doing."

The three tall daughters turned back reluctantly from the stairs. "I never could seem to take much interest in patchwork quilts," said one. Already the old-time skill born of early pioneer privation and the craving for beauty, had gone out of style.

"No, nor I neither!" answered Sophia. "But a stone image would take an interest in this pattern. Honest, Mehetabel, did you really think of it yourself?" She held it up closer to her eyes and went on, "And how under the sun and stars did you ever git your courage up to start in a-making it? Land! Look at all those tiny squinchy little seams! Why, the wrong side ain't a thing *but* seams! Yet the good side's just like a picture, so smooth you'd think 'twas woven that way. Only nobody could."

The girls looked at it right side, wrong side, and echoed their mother's exclamations. Mr. Elwell himself came over to see what they were discussing. "Well, I declare!" he said, looking at his sister with eyes more approving than she could ever remember. "I don't know a thing about patchwork quilts, but to my eye that beats old Mis' Andrew's quilt that got the blue ribbon so many times

at the County Fair."

As she lay that night in her narrow hard bed, too proud, too excited to sleep, Mehetabel's heart swelled and tears of joy ran down from her old eyes.

The next day her sister-in-law astonished her by taking the huge pan of potatoes out of her lap and setting one of the younger children to peeling them. "Don't you want to go on with that quiltin' pattern?" she said. "I'd kind o' like to see how you're goin' to make the grapevine design come out on the corner."

For the first time in her life the dependent old maid contradicted her powerful sister-in-law. Quickly and jealously she said, "It's not a grapevine. It's a sort of curlicue I made up."

"Well, it's nice-looking anyhow," said Sophia pacifyingly. "I never could have made it up."

By the end of the summer the family interest had risen so high that Mehetabel was given for herself a little round table in the sitting room, for *her,* where she could keep her pieces and use odd minutes for her work. She almost wept over such kindness and resolved firmly not to take advantage of it. She went on faithfully with her monotonous house-work, not neglecting a corner. But the atmosphere of her world was changed. Now things had a meaning. Through the longest task of washing milk-pans, there rose a rainbow of promise. She took her place by the little table and put the thimble on her knotted, hard finger with the solemnity of a priestess performing a rite.

She was even able to bear with some degree of dignity the honor of having the minister and the minister's wife comment admiringly on her great proj-ect. The family felt quite proud of Aunt Mehetabel as Minister Bowman had said it was work as fine as any he had ever seen, "and he didn't know but finer!" The remark was repeated ver-batim to the neighbors in the following weeks when they dropped in and ex-amined in a perverse Vermontish silence some astonishingly difficult tour de force which Mehetabel had just finished.

The Elwells especially plumed them-selves on the slow progress of the quilt. "Mehetabel has been to work on that corner for six weeks, comes Tuesday, and she ain't half done yet," they ex-plained to visitors.

They fell out of the way of always ex-pecting her to be the one to run on er-rands, even for the children. "Don't bother your Aunt Mehetabel," Sophia would call. "Can't you see she's got to a ticklish place on the quilt?" The old woman sat straighter in her chair, held up her head. She was a part of the world at last. She joined in the conversation and her remarks were listened to. The children were even told to mind her when she asked them to do some service for her, although this she ventured to do but seldom.

One day some people from the next town, total strangers, drove up to the Elwell house and asked if they could in-spect the wonderful quilt which they had heard about even down in their end of the valley. After that, Mehetabel's quilt came little by little to be one of the local sights. No visitor to town, whether he knew the Elwells or not, went away without having been to look at it. To make her presentable to strangers, the Elwells saw to it that their aunt was bet-ter dressed than she had ever been before. One of the girls made her a pret-ty little cap to wear on her thin white hair.

A year went by and a quarter of the quilt was finished. A second year passed and half was done. The third year Mehetabel had pneumonia and lay ill for weeks and weeks, horrified by the idea that she might die before her work was completed. A fourth year and one could really see the grandeur of the whole design. In September of the fifth year, the entire family gathered around her to watch eagerly, as Mehetabel quilted the last stitches. The girls held it up by the four corners and they all looked at it in hushed silence.

Then Mr. Elwell cried as one speak-ing with authority, "By ginger! That's goin' to the County Fair!"

Mehetabel blushed a deep red. She had thought of this herself, but never would have spoken aloud of it.

"Yes indeed!" cried the family. One of the boys was dispatched to the house of a neighbor who was Chairman of the Fair Committee for their village. He came back beaming, "Of course he'll take it. Like's not it may git a prize, he says. But he's got to have it right off because all the things from our town are going tomorrow morning."

Even in her pride Mehetabel felt a pang as the bulky package was carried out of the house. As the days went on she felt lost. For years it had been her one thought. The little round stand had been heaped with a litter of bright-colored scraps. Now it was desolately bare. One of the neighbors who took the long journey to the Fair reported when he came back that the quilt was hung in a good place in a glass case in "Agricultural Hall." But that meant little to Mehetabel's ignorance of

The National Museum of History and Technology, Smithsonian Institution, Washington, D.C.

Harriet Powers' Bible Quilt. *Appliqué and pieced work.*

Harriet Powers, a black woman who lived on a farm in Georgia, exhibited her quilt at the Athens Cotton Fair of 1886. Using ordinary fabrics, she created a design of her impressions of biblical events. In this detail, according to the Smithsonian description, "Cain goes into the land of Nod to get him a wife. There are bears, leopards, elks and a 'kangaroo hog' but the gem of the scene is an orange-colored calico lion, in the center . . . [who] has a tiny neck and a very meek manner and coy expression, unlike the fierce manner of the original animal."

everything outside her brother's home. She drooped. The family noticed it. One day Sophia said kindly, "You feel sort o' lost without the quilt, don't you, Mehetabel?"

"They took it away so quick!" she said wistfully. "I hadn't hardly had one good look at it myself."

The Fair was to last a fortnight. At the beginning of the second week Mr. Elwell asked his sister how early she could get up in the morning.

"I dunno. Why?" she asked.

"Well, Thomas Ralston has got to drive to West Oldton to see a lawyer. That's four miles beyond the Fair. He says if you can git up so's to leave here at four in the morning he'll drive you to the Fair, leave you there for the day, and bring you back again at night." Mehetabel's face turned very white. Her eyes filled with tears. It was as though someone had offered her a ride in a golden chariot up to the gates of heaven. "Why, you can't *mean* it!" she cried wildly. Her brother laughed. He could not meet her eyes. Even to his easy-going unimaginative indifference to his sister this was a revelation of the narrowness of her life in his home. "Oh, 'tain't so much—just to go to the Fair," he told her in some confusion, and then "Yes, sure I mean it. Go git your things ready, for it's tomorrow morning he wants to start."

A trembling, excited old woman stared all that night at the rafters. She who had never been more than six miles from home—it was to her like going into another world. She who had never seen anything more exciting than a church supper was to see the County Fair. She had never dreamed of doing it. She could not at all imagine what it would be like.

The next morning all the family rose early to see her off. Perhaps her brother had not been the only one to be shocked by her happiness. As she tried to eat her breakfast they called out conflicting advice to her about what to see. Her brother said not to miss inspecting the stock, her nieces said the fancywork was the only thing worth looking at, Sophia told her to be sure to look at the display of preserves. Her nephews asked her to bring home an account of the trotting races.

The buggy drove up to the door, and she was helped in. The family ran to and fro with blankets, woolen tippet, a hot soapstone from the kitchen range. Her wraps were tucked about her. They all stood together and waved goodby as she drove out of the yard. She waved back, but she scarcely saw them. On her return home that evening she was ashy pale, and so stiff that her brother had to lift her out bodily. But her lips were set in a blissful smile. They crowded around her with questions until Sophia pushed them all aside. She told them Aunt Mehetabel was too tired to speak until she had had her supper. The young people held their tongues while she drank her tea, and absent-mindedly ate a scrap of toast with an egg. Then the old woman was helped into an easy chair before the fire. They gathered about her, eager for news of the great world, and Sophia said, "Now, come, Mehetabel, tell us all about it!"

Mehetabel drew a long breath. "It was just perfect!" she said. "Finer even than I thought. They've got it hanging up in the very middle of a sort o' closet made of glass, and one of the lower corners is ripped and turned back so's to show the seams on the wrong side.'"

"What?" asked Sophia, a little blankly.

"Why, the quilt!" said Mehetabel in surprise. "There are a whole lot of other ones in that room, but not one that can hold a candle to it, if I do say it who shouldn't. I heard lots of people say the same thing. You ought to have heard what the women said about that corner, Sophia. They said—well, I'd be ashamed to *tell* you what they said. I declare if I wouldn't!"

Mr. Elwell asked, "What did you think of that big ox we've heard so much about?"

"I didn't look at the stock," returned his sister indifferently. She turned to one of her nieces. "That set of pieces you gave me, Maria, from your red waist, come out just lovely! I heard one woman say you could 'most smell the red roses."

"How did Jed Burgess' bay horse place in the mile trot?" asked Thomas.

"I didn't see the races."

"How about the preserves?" asked Sophia.

"I didn't see the preserves," said Mehetabel calmly.

Seeing that they were gazing at her with astonished faces she went on, to give them a reasonable explanation, "You see I went right to the room where the quilt was, and then I didn't want to leave it. It had been so long since I'd seen it. I had to look at it first real good myself, and then I looked at the others

to see if there was any that could come up to it. Then the people begun comin' in and I got so interested in hearin' what they had to say I couldn't think of goin' anywheres else. I ate my lunch right there too, and I'm glad as can be I did, too; for what do you think?"—she gazed about her with kindling eyes. "While I stood there with a sandwich in one hand, didn't the head of the hull concern come in and open the glass door and pin a big bow of blue ribbon right in the middle of the quilt with a label on it, 'First Prize.' "

There was a stir of proud congratulation. Then Sophia returned to questioning, "Didn't you go to see anything else?"

"Why, no," said Mehetabel. "Only the quilt. Why should I?"

She fell into a reverie. As if it hung again before her eyes she saw the glory that shone around the creation of her hand and brain. She longed to make her listeners share the golden vision with her. She struggled for words. She fumbled blindly for unknown superlatives. "I tell you it looked like—" she began, and paused.

Vague recollections of hymnbook phrases came into her mind. They were the only kind of poetic expression she knew. But they were dismissed as being sacrilegious to use for something in real life. Also as not being nearly striking enough.

Finally, "I tell you it looked real *good*," she assured them and sat staring into the fire, on her tired old face the supreme content of an artist who has realized his ideal.

The Newark Museum, Newark, New Jersey

Brooklyn Bridge *by Joseph Stella (1880-1946). Oil on canvas.*

This painting effectively expresses meaning through art and science. The bridge itself represented a technological breakthrough in design and construction; the artist captured the beauty of the structure's movement and symmetry on canvas. Stella came to America at 19 as an immigrant from Italy. Like many newcomers from Europe he had a special feeling for New York, his place of entry.

Excerpt from

The Autobiography of Charles Darwin and Selected Letters

(Edited by Francis Darwin)

Charles Darwin
(1809-1882)

Darwin was educated at Cambridge University and then spent five years as a naturalist on the Beagle, *a ship engaged in a scientific survey of the coast and islands of South America. It was during this voyage that he first conceived the ideas on evolution published in his* Origin of the Species *in 1859.*

Darwin himself, like many people today, did not think that the theory of evolution was inconsistent with belief in God—though he did not think that this or any other belief could be proved from nature—and called himself an agnostic.

Note the comparison, early in the selection, between scientific achievement and the writing of poetry, and the later reference to his personal loss of aesthetic sensitivity. Consider the ways in which less dramatic contributions to human knowledge and progress may give meaning to the lives of scientists and technicians who never attain public fame.

No pursuit at Cambridge was followed with nearly so much eagerness or gave me so much pleasure as collecting beetles. It was the mere passion for collecting, for I did not dissect them, and rarely compared their external characters with published descriptions, but got them named anyhow. I will give a proof of my zeal: one day, on tearing off some old bark, I saw two rare beetles, and seized one in each hand; then I saw a third and new kind, which I could not bear to lose, so that I popped the one which I held in my right hand into my mouth. Alas! it ejected some intensely acrid fluid, which burnt my tongue so that I was forced to spit the beetle out, which was lost, as was the third one.

I was very successful in collecting and invented two new methods; I employed a labourer to scrape, during the winter, moss off old trees and place it in a large bag, and likewise to collect the rubbish at the bottom of the barges in which reeds are brought from the fens, and thus I got some very rare species. No poet ever felt more delighted at seeing his first poem published than I did at seeing in Stephens' *Illustrations of British Insects,* the magic words, "captured by C. Darwin, Esq."

. . . . .

During my last year at Cambridge, I read with care and profound interest Humboldt's *Personal Narrative.* This work, and Sir J. Herschel's *Introduction to the Study of Natural Philosophy,* stirred up in me a burning zeal to add

197

even the most humble contribution to the noble structure of natural Science.

. . . . .

The voyage of the *Beagle* has been by far the most important event in my life, and has determined my whole career; yet it depended on so small a circumstance as my uncle offering to drive me thirty miles to Shrewsbury, which few uncles would have done, and on such a trifle as the shape of my nose. I have always felt that I owe to the voyage the first real training or education of my mind; I was led to attend closely to several branches of natural history, and thus my powers of observation were improved, though they were always fairly developed.

The investigation of the geology of all the places visited was far more important, as reasoning here comes into play.

On first examining a new district, nothing can appear more hopeless than the chaos of rocks; but by recording the stratification and nature of the rocks and fossils at many points, always reasoning and predicting what will be found elsewhere, light soon begins to dawn on the district, and the structure of the whole becomes more or less intelligible.

. . . . .

The above various special studies were, however, of no importance compared with the habit of energetic industry and of concentrated attention to whatever I was engaged in, which I then acquired. Everything about which I thought or read was made to bear

directly on what I had seen or was likely to see; and this habit of mind was continued during the first years of the voyage. I feel sure that it was this training which has enabled me to do whatever I have done in science.

Looking backwards, I can now perceive how my love for science gradually preponderated over every other taste. During the first two years my old passion for shooting survived in nearly full force, and I shot myself all the birds and animals for my collection; but gradually I gave up my gun more and more, and finally altogether, to my servant, as shooting interfered with my work, more especially with making out the geological structure of a country. I discovered, though unconsciously and insensibly, that the pleasure of observing and reasoning was a much higher one than that of skill and sport. That my mind became developed through my pursuits during the voyage is rendered probable by a remark made by my father, who was the most acute observer whom I ever saw, of a sceptical disposition, and far from being a believer in phrenology; for on first seeing me after the voyage, he turned round to my sisters, and exclaimed, "Why, the shape of his head is quite altered."

. . . . .

As far as I can judge of myself, I worked to the utmost during the voyage from the mere pleasure of investigation, and from my strong desire to add a few facts to the great mass of facts in Natural Science. But I was also ambitious to take a fair place among scientific men,—whether more ambitious or less so than most of my fellow-workers, I can form no opinion.

My chief enjoyment and sole employment throughout life has been scientific work, and the excitement from such work makes me for the time forget, or drives quite away, my daily discomfort.

. . . . .

Whenever I have found out that I have blundered, or that my work has been imperfect, and when I have been contemptuously criticised, and even when I have been overpraised, so that I have felt mortified, it has been my greatest comfort to say hundreds of times to myself that "I have worked as hard and as well as I could, and no man can do more than this." I remember when in Good Success Bay, in Tierra del Fuego, thinking (and I believe that I wrote home to the effect) that I could not employ my life better than in adding a little to Natural Science. This I have done to the best of my abilities, and critics may say what they like, but they cannot destroy this conviction.

. . . . .

I have said that in one respect my mind has changed during the last twenty or thirty years. Up to the age of thirty, or beyond it, poetry of many kinds, such as the works of Milton, Gray, Byron, Wordsworth, Coleridge, and Shelley, gave me great pleasure, and even as a schoolboy I took intense delight in Shakespeare, especially in the historical plays. I have also said that formerly pictures gave me considerable, and music very great delight. But now for many years I cannot endure to read a line of poetry; I have tried lately to read Shakespeare, and found it so intolerably dull that it nauseated me. I have also almost lost my taste for pictures or music. Music generally sets me thinking too energetically on what I have been at work on, instead of giving me pleasure. I retain some taste for fine scenery, but it does not cause me the exquisite delight which it formerly did. On the other hand, novels, which are works of the imagination, though not of a very high order, have been for years a wonderful relief and pleasure to me, and I often bless all novelists. . . .

This curious and lamentable loss of the higher aesthetic tastes is all the odder, as books on history, biographies, and travels (independently of any scientific facts which they may contain), and essays on all sorts of subjects interest me as much as ever they did. My mind seems to have become a kind of machine for grinding general laws out of large collections of facts, but why this should have caused the atrophy of that part of the brain alone, on which the higher tastes depend, I cannot conceive. A man with a mind more highly organised or better constituted than mine, would not, I suppose, have thus suffered; and if I had to live my life again, I would have made a rule to read some poetry and listen to some music at least once every week; for perhaps the parts of my brain now atrophied would thus have been kept active through use. The loss of these tastes is a loss of happiness, and may possibly be injurious to the intellect, and more probably to the moral character, by enfeebling the emotional part of our nature.

. . . . .

On the favourable side of the balance, I think that I am superior to the common run of men in noticing things which easily escape attention, and in observing them carefully. My industry has been nearly as great as it could have been in the observation and collection of facts. What is far more important, my love of natural science has been steady and ardent.

This pure love has, however, been much aided by the ambition to be esteemed by my fellow naturalists. From my early youth I have had the strongest desire to understand or explain whatever I observed,—that is, to group all facts under some general laws. These causes combined have given me the patience to reflect or ponder for any number of years over any unexplained problem. As far as I can judge, I am not apt to follow blindly the lead of other men. I have steadily endeavoured to keep my mind free so as to give up any hypothesis, however much beloved (and I cannot resist forming one on every subject), as soon as facts are shown to be opposed to it. Indeed, I have had no choice but to act in this manner, for with the exception of the Coral Reefs, I cannot remember a single first-formed hypothesis which had not after a time to be given up or greatly modified. This has naturally led me to distrust greatly, deductive reasoning in the mixed sciences. On the other hand, I am not very sceptical,—a frame of mind which I believe to be injurious to the progress of science. A good deal of scepticism in a scientific man is advisable to avoid much loss of time, [but] I have met with not a few men, who, I feel sure, have often thus been deterred from experiment or observations, which would have proved directly or indirectly serviceable.

. . . . .

My habits are methodical, and this has been of not a little use for my particular line of work. Lastly, I have had ample leisure from not having to earn my own bread. Even ill-health, though it has annihilated several years of my life, has saved me from the distractions of society and amusement.

Therefore, my success as a man of science, whatever this may have amounted to, has been determined, as far as I can judge, by complex and diversified mental qualities and conditions. Of these, the most important have been—the love of science—unbounded patience in long reflecting over any subject—industry in observing and collecting facts—and a fair share of invention as well as of common-sense. With such moderate abilities as I possess, it is truly surprising that I should have influenced to a considerable extent the belief of scientific men on some important points.

The Lives of a Cell

Lewis Thomas
(1913-   )

In the following excerpt, the author sketches a picture of scientists working together to achieve a discovery about the natural world. Whatever the focus on the search, it arouses intense enthusiasm, singleness of purpose and an experience of shared creativity. The satisfaction they derive from making a discovery and from working cooperatively contributes substantially to the meaning they find in life.

Lewis Thomas, a physician, biologist and author, has served on the faculty of several university medical schools, including Yale's department of pathology. He is currently president of Memorial Sloan-Kettering Cancer Center in New York City.

I don't know of any other human occupation, even including what I have seen of art, in which the people engaged in it are so caught up, so totally preoccupied, so driven beyond their strength and resources.

Scientists at work have the look of creatures following genetic instructions; they seem to be under the influence of a deeply placed human instinct. They are, despite their efforts at dignity, rather like young animals engaged in savage play. When they are near to an answer their hair stands on end, they sweat, they are awash in their own adrenalin. To grab the answer, and grab it first, is for them a more powerful drive than feeding or breeding or protecting themselves against the elements.

It sometimes looks like a lonely activity, but it is as much the opposite of lonely as human behavior can be. There is nothing so social, so communal, so interdependent. An active field of science is like an immense intellectual anthill; the individual almost vanishes into the mass of minds tumbling over each other, carrying information from place to place, passing it around at the speed of light.

There are special kinds of information that seem to be chemotactic [related to movement toward or away from a chemical substance]. As soon as a trace is released, receptors at the back of the neck are caused to tremble, there is a massive convergence of motile minds flying upwind on a gradient of surprise, crowding around the source. It is an infiltration of intellects, an inflammation.

There is nothing to touch the spectacle. In the midst of what seems a collective derangement of minds in total disorder, with bits of information being scattered about, torn to shreds, disintegrated, deconstituted, engulfed, in a kind of activity that seems as random and agitated as that of bees in a disturbed part of the hive, there suddenly emerges, with the purity of a slow phrase of music, a single new piece of truth about nature.

In short, it works. It is the most powerful and productive of the things human beings have learned to do together in many centuries, more effective than farming, or hunting and fishing, or building cathedrals, or making money.

It is instinctive behavior, in my view, and I do not understand how it works. It cannot be prearranged in any precise way; the minds cannot be lined up in tidy rows and given directions from printed sheets. You cannot get it done by instructing each mind to make this or that piece, for central committees to fit with the pieces made by the other instructed minds. It does not work this way.

What it needs is for the air to be made right. If you want a bee to make honey, you do not issue protocols on solar navigation or carbohydrate

National Gallery of Art, Washington, D.C.

Self-Portrait *by Paul Gauguin (1848-1903). French. Oil on wood.*

In this self-portrait, Gauguin attempts to define himself through art: He is wearing the halo of sainthood, yet he appears between the apples and the snake, biblical symbols of temptation. Gauguin began painting for relaxation, but his art soon became an obsession. He abandoned his job and family to seek an exotic, unspoiled place to pursue his passion. The natives of Tahiti are the subjects of his most famous works.

chemistry, you put him together with other bees (and you'd better do this quickly, for solitary bees do not stay alive) and you do what you can to arrange the general environment around the hive. If the air is right, the science will come in its own season, like pure honey.

There is something like aggression in the activity, but it differs from other forms of aggressive behavior in having no sort of destruction as the objective.

While it is going on, it looks and feels like aggression: get at it, uncover it, bring it out, grab it, it's mine! It is like a primitive running hunt, but there is nothing at the end of it to be injured. More probably, the end is a sigh. But then, if the air is right and the science is going well, the sigh is immediately interrupted, there is a yawping new question, and the wild, tumbling activity begins once more, out of control all over again.

Further Readings

Bronowski, J. *The Ascent of Man*. 1973. Man's cultural evolution and the development of science. How man's "imagination, his reason, his emotional subtlety and toughness make it possible for him not to accept the environment but to change it."

Capra, Fritjof. *The Tao of Physics*. 1975. An exploration of the parallels between modern physics and Eastern mysticism by a research physicist. Relation of the world view emerging from theoretical high-energy physics to the mystical traditions of Hinduism, Buddhism, Taoism, Zen and the I Ching.

McLeish, John A.B. *The Ulyssean Adult: Creativity in the Middle and Later Years*. 1976. How the older adult can lead an active and creative life. Chapter 7, "Ulysseans in Action," is especially thought provoking.

May, Rollo. *The Courage to Create*. 1975. An analyst discusses creativity in the arts and in life.

Pirsig, Robert M. *Zen and the Art of Motorcycle Maintenance*. 1974. Novel of a modern man in search of himself. Explores the relationship between persons and the machines they create.

Thomas, Lewis. *The Medusa and the Snail: More Notes of a Biology Watcher*. 1979. Witty and insightful commentary on the human genius for making mistakes, on cloning, life and death, warts, Montaigne and much more.

Section 9

CREATING MEANING— SACRIFICE AND SERVICE

This final section is a continuation of the previous one. Here we consider another way in which people create meaning: By devoting themselves to the good of others. In the last section we considered examples of aesthetic and intellectual creativity in the face of meaninglessness. Now we look at ethical creativity—actions widely recognized as bestowing value through the exercise of sympathy, generosity and self-sacrifice.

Albert Camus, one of the most influential writers of this century, gave serious thought to the problem of meaning. He regarded the human predicament as one of absurdity—an inexplicable and isolated oddity in the midst of a purposeless universe. Yet in his life, and in his plays and stories, Camus affirmed a courageous humanity, achieving dignity by refusing to accept the pointlessness of existence. His characters take upon themselves the burden of humankind's loneliness and choose to create meaning by sharing the fate of others. D'Arrest in "The Growing Stone" is such a character, who shares both a literal and figurative burden. He does not carry the stone to the church, its intended destination, but to a humble home where he finds a place with the poor and "a fresh beginning in life."

Albert Schweitzer was another major influence on our times. Outstanding in theology, music and science, he chose to dedicate himself totally to medical missionary work in the west African nation of Gabon. For this service, he was awarded the 1952 Nobel Peace Prize. His basic principle of action was "reverence for life"—a concern he extended to ants and flies, indeed, to all creatures. Schweitzer thought of himself as a Christian

---

The Mother *by Charles White (1918-1979). Sepia ink on paper.*

Charles White devoted his career to interpreting the American Negro. His figures have strength, dignity and a sculpture quality.

in that he derived his ideals from Jesus. But he rejected the doctrine of the divinity of Christ and found all the traditional explanations of the ultimate meaning of life inadequate. "All thinking," he wrote, "must renounce the attempt to explain the universe. We cannot understand what happens in the universe." Yet he himself accepted the responsibility to "maintain life at the highest point of development—my own life and other life—by devoting myself to it in help and love." And he created meaning for himself and for thousands of others by his dedication to the needy sick of Africa. Can Schweitzer's greatness be measured by the numbers of people he served or by his wholehearted assistance to people?

While these heroic examples from literature and life may inspire us, they may also blind us to the uncounted examples of creative living in the everyday world. A television station in a large northeastern city, through its annual Jefferson awards, attempts to honor a few of the people whose "unselfish helping of others goes largely unrecognized" and who work "to improve the life of other citizens without thought of personal reward." The example of a recent nominee for the award, described in this section, illustrates the kind of meaningful existence many citizens live without fanfare. The man described was 65 years old at the time of the nomination and had undergone surgery for cancer two years previously. What examples of quiet self-sacrifice have you known? Does the life of someone like Tom Hogan create meaning by its own inherent quality, or does its significance depend on the context of the kind of religious faith that Hogan himself possesses?

It is an old Jewish custom for parents to draw up an "ethical will" for their children, setting out the ideals they would like to see them live by. A modern example of such a will is included in this session. You might consider spending some time formulating a similar type of document that could be called a Testament of Meaning. The latter may be more difficult to write because one's perspective on ultimate reality is less easy to express than one's basic ethical standards. But experience shows that people often learn a lot about themselves in attempting this task. It is suggested, therefore, that you write out—as if for your children or grandchildren—a brief statement on how and why you find meaning in life, or at least the direction of your search.

The Saint Louis Art Museum

Country School *by Winslow Homer (1836-1910). Oil on canvas.*

Excerpt from

The Growing Stone

Albert Camus
(1913-1960)

In this short story, D'Arrast, a successful French engineer, is driven by his chauffeur Socrates to a poverty-stricken town to consult with officials about building a jetty to prevent flooding by the river. He meets a ship's cook who tells him of a promise he made years before in gratitude for his escape from drowning. That night the cook dances so late at the celebration of the local saint's day that he is unable to fulfill his vow.

A frequent theme of Camus is reflected in D'Arrast's initial impression that the cook's promise is "absurd"—but one that the engineer has to take upon himself in compassion. An equally important connection is suggested between D'Arrast's comment to Socrates: "Yes, you see, I never found my place" (suggestive of the restlessness of humankind lost in a meaningless universe) and his final welcome in the native house where he finds a place: "Sit down with us."

Camus manifested a "tumultuous happiness" in identifying with the underprivileged. In this story, what might appear to be a dead-end—the involvement of an internationally known engineer in the petty affairs of a dismal backwater—becomes a critical opportunity to create meaning. The chance will pass if D'Arrast does not respond to the situation that has been "waiting patiently for him at the end of the world."

In the little Garden of the Fountain, mysterious and pleasant under the fine rain, clusters of exotic flowers hung down along the lianas among the banana trees and pandanus. Piles of wet stones marked the intersection of paths on which a motley crowd was strolling. Half-breeds, mulattoes, a few gauchos were chatting in low voices or sauntering along the bamboo paths to the point where groves and bush became thicker and more impenetrable. There, the forest began abruptly.

D'Arrast was looking for Socrates in the crowd when Socrates suddenly bumped him from behind.

"It's holiday," he said, laughing, and clung to D'Arrast's tall shoulders to jump up and down.

"What holiday?"

"Why, you not know?" Socrates said in surprise as he faced D'Arrast. "The feast of good Jesus. Each year they all come to the grotto with a hammer."

Socrates pointed out, not a grotto, but a group that seemed to be waiting in a corner of the garden.

"You see? One day the good statue of Jesus, it came upstream from the sea. Some fishermen found it. How beautiful! How beautiful! Then they washed it here in the grotto. And now a stone grew up in the grotto. Every year it's the feast. With the hammer you break, you break off pieces for blessed happiness. And then it keeps growing and you keep breaking. It's the miracle!"

They had reached the grotto and could see its low entrance beyond the waiting men. Inside, in the darkness studded with the flickering flames of candles, a squatting figure was pounding with a hammer. The man, a thin gaucho with a long mustache, got up and came out holding in his open palm, so that all might see, a small piece of moist schist, over which he soon closed his hand carefully before going away. Another man then stooped down and entered the grotto.

D'Arrast turned around. On all sides pilgrims were waiting, without looking at him, impassive under the water dripping from the trees in thin sheets. He too was waiting in front of the grotto under the same film of water, and he didn't know for what. He had been waiting constantly, to tell the truth, for a month since he had arrived in this country. He had been waiting—in the red heat of humid days, under the little stars of night, despite the tasks to be accomplished, the jetties to be built, the roads to be cut through—as if the work he had come to do here were merely a pretext for a surprise or for an encounter he did not even imagine but which had been waiting patiently for him at the end of the world. He shook himself, walked away without anyone in the little group paying attention to him, and went toward the exit. He had to go back to the river and go to work.

But Socrates was waiting for him at the gate, lost in voluble conversation with a short, fat, strapping man whose skin was yellow rather than black. His head, completely shaved, gave even more sweep to a considerable forehead. On the other hand, his broad, smooth face was adorned with a very black beard, trimmed square.

"He's champion!" Socrates said by way of introduction. "Tomorrow he's in the procession."

The man, wearing a sailor's outfit of heavy serge, a blue-and-white jersey under the pea jacket, was examining D'Arrast attentively with his calm black eyes. At the same time he was smiling, showing all his very white teeth between his full, shiny lips.

"He speaks Spanish," Socrates said and, turning toward the stranger, added: "Tell Mr. D'Arrast." Then he danced off toward another group. The man ceased to smile and looked at D'Arrast with outright curiosity.

"You are interested, Captain?"

"I'm not a captain," D'Arrast said.

"That doesn't matter. But you're a noble. Socrates told me."

"Not I. But my grandfather was. His father too and all those before his father. Now there is no more nobility in our country."

"Ah!" the Negro said, laughing. "I understand; everybody is a noble."

"No, that's not it. There are neither noblemen nor common people."

The fellow reflected; then he made up his mind.

"No one works? No one suffers?"

"Yes, millions of men."

"Then that's the common people."

"In that way, yes, there is a common people. But the masters are policemen or merchants."

The mulatto's kindly face closed in a frown. Then he grumbled: "Humph! Buying and selling, eh! What filth! And with the police, dogs command."

Suddenly, he burst out laughing.

"You, you don't sell?"

"Hardly at all. I make bridges, roads."

"That's good. Me, I'm a ship's cook. If you wish, I'll make you our dish of black beans."

"All right."

The cook came closer to D'Arrast and took his arm.

"Listen, I like what you tell. I'm going to tell you too. Maybe you will like."

He drew him over near the gate to a damp wooden bench beneath a clump of bamboos.

"I was at sea, off Iguape, on a small coastwise tanker that supplies the harbors along here. It caught fire on board. Not by my fault! I know my job! No, just bad luck. We were able to launch the lifeboats. During the night, the sea got rough; it capsized the boat and I went down. When I came up, I hit the boat with my head. I drifted. The night was dark, the waters are vast, and, besides, I don't swim well; I was afraid. Just then I saw a light in the distance and recognized the church of the good Jesus in Iguape. So I told the good Jesus that at his procession I would carry a hundred-pound stone on my head if he saved me. You don't have to believe me, but the waters became calm and my heart too. I swam slowly, I was happy, and I reached the shore. Tomorrow I'll keep my promise."

He looked at D'Arrast in a suddenly suspicious manner.

"You're not laughing?"

"No, I'm not laughing. A man has to do what he has promised."

The fellow clapped him on the back.

"Now, come to my brother's, near the river. I'll cook you some beans."

"No," D'Arrast said, "I have things to do. This evening, if you wish."

"Good. But tonight there's dancing and praying in the big hut. It's the feast for Saint George." D'Arrast asked him if he danced too. The cook's face hardened suddenly; for the first time his eyes became shifty.

"No, no, I won't dance. Tomorrow I must carry the stone. It is heavy. I'll go this evening to celebrate the saint. And then I'll leave early."

"Does it last long?"

"All night and a little into the morning."

He looked at D'Arrast with a vaguely shameful look.

"Come to the dance. You can take me home afterward. Otherwise, I'll stay and dance. I probably won't be able to keep from it."

"You like to dance?"

"Oh, yes! I like. Besides, there are cigars, saints, women. You forget everything and you don't obey any more."

"There are women too? All the women of the town?"

"Not of the town, but of the huts."

The ship's cook resumed his smile. "Come. The Captain I'll obey. And you will help me keep my promise tomorrow."

D'Arrast felt slightly annoyed. What did that absurd promise mean to him? But he looked at the handsome frank face smiling trustingly at him, its dark skin gleaming with health and vitality.

"I'll come," he said. "Now I'll walk along with you a little."

. . . . .

When D'Arrast, his head in the vise of a crushing migraine, had awakened after a bad sleep, a humid heat was weighing upon the town and the still forest. He was waiting now under the hospital portico, looking at his watch, which had stopped, uncertain of the time, surprised by the broad daylight and the silence of the town. The almost clear blue sky hung low over the first dull roofs. Yellowish urubus,* transfixed by the heat, were sleeping on the house across from the hospital. One of them suddenly fluttered, opened his beak, ostensibly got ready to fly away, flapped his dusty wings twice against his body, rose a few inches above the roof, fell back, and went to sleep almost at once.

The engineer went down toward the town. The main square was empty, like the streets through which he had just walked. In the distance, and on both sides of the river, a low mist hung over the forest. The heat fell vertically, and D'Arrast looked for a shady spot. At that moment, under the overhang on one of the houses, he saw a little man gesturing to him. As he came closer, he recognized Socrates.

"Well, Mr. D'Arrast, you like the

_____
*vultures.

ceremony?"

D'Arrast said that it was too hot in the hut and that he preferred the sky and the night air.

"Yes," Socrates said, "in your country there's only the Mass. No one dances." He rubbed his hands, jumped on one foot, whirled about, laughed uproariously. "Not possible, they're not possible." Then he looked at D'Arrast inquisitively. "And you, are you going to Mass?"

"No."

"Then, where are you going?"

"Nowhere. I don't know."

Socrates laughed again. "Not possible! A noble without a church, without anything!"

D'Arrast laughed likewise. "Yes, you see, I never found my place. So I left."

"Stay with us, Mr. D'Arrast, I love you."

"I'd like to, Socrates, but I don't know how to dance." Their laughter echoed in the silence of the empty town.

"Ah," Socrates said, "I forget. The Mayor wants to see you. He is lunching at the club." And without warning he started off in the direction of the hospital.

"Where are you going?" D'Arrast shouted.

Socrates imitated a snore. "Sleep. Soon the procession." And, half running, he resumed his snores.

The Mayor simply wanted to give D'Arrast a place of honor to see the procession. He explained it to the engineer while sharing with him a dish of meat and rice such as would miraculously cure a paralytic. First they would take their places on a balcony of the Judge's house, opposite the church, to see the procession come out. Then they would go to the town hall in the main street leading to the church, which the penitents would take on their way back. The Judge and the Chief of Police would accompany D'Arrast, the Mayor being obliged to take part in the ceremony. The Chief of Police was in fact in the clubroom and kept paying court to D'Arrast with an indefatigable smile, lavishing upon him incomprehensible but obviously well-meaning speeches. When D'Arrast left, the Chief of Police hastened to make a way for him, holding all the doors open before him.

Under the burning sun, in the still empty town, the two men walked toward the Judge's house. Their steps were the only sound heard in the silence. But all of a sudden a firecracker exploded in a neighboring street and flushed on every roof the heavy, awkward flocks of bald-necked urubus. Almost at once dozens of firecrackers went off in all directions, doors opened, and people began to emerge from the houses and fill the narrow streets.

The Judge told D'Arrast how proud he was to receive him in his unworthy house and led him up a handsome baroque staircase painted chalky blue. On the landing, as D'Arrast passed, doors opened and children's dark heads popped out and disappeared at once with smothered laughter. The main room, beautiful in architecture, contained nothing but rattan furniture and large cages filled with squawking birds. The balcony on which the Judge and D'Arrast settled overlooked the little square in front of the church. The crowd was now beginning to fill it, strangely silent, motionless under the heat that came down from the sky in almost visible waves. Only the children ran around the square, stopping abruptly to light firecrackers, and sharp reports followed one another in rapid succession. Seen from the balcony, the church with its plaster walls, its dozen blue steps, its blue-and-gold towers, looked smaller.

Suddenly the organ burst forth within the church. The crowd, turned toward the portico, drew over to the sides of the square. The men took off their hats and the women knelt down. The distant organ played at length something like marches. Then an odd sound of wings came from the forest. A tiny airplane with transparent wings and frail fuselage, out of place in this ageless world, came in sight over the trees, swooped a little above the square, and, with the clacking of a big rattle, passed over the heads raised toward it. Then the plane turned and disappeared in the direction of the estuary.

But in the shadow of the church a vague bustle again attracted attention. The organ had stopped, replaced now by brasses and drums, invisible under the portico. Black-surpliced penitents came out of the church one by one, formed groups outside the doors, and began to descend the steps. Behind them came white penitents bearing red-and-blue banners, then a little group of boys dressed up as angels, sodalities of Children of Mary with little black and serious faces. Finally, on a multicolored shrine borne by leading citizens sweating in their dark suits, came the effigy of the good Jesus himself, a reed in his hand and his head crowned with thorns, bleeding and tottering above the crowd that lined the steps.

When the shrine reached the bottom of the steps, there was a pause during which the penitents tried to line up in a semblance of order. Then it was that D'Arrast saw the ship's cook. Bare from the waist up, he had just come out under the portico carrying on his bearded head an enormous rectangular block set on a cork mat. With steady tread he came down the church steps, the stone perfectly balanced in the arch formed by his short, muscular arms. As soon as he fell in behind the shrine, the procession moved. From the portico burst the musicians, wearing bright-colored coats and blowing into beribboned brasses. To the beat of a quick march, the penitents hastened their step and reached one of the streets opening off the square. When the shrine had disappeared behind them, nothing could be seen but the cook and the last of the musicians. Behind them, the crowd got in motion amidst exploding firecrackers, while the plane, with a great rattle of its engine, flew back over the groups trailing behind. D'Arrast was looking exclusively at the cook, who was disappearing into the street now and whose shoulders he suddenly thought he saw sag. But at that distance he couldn't see well.

Through the empty streets, between closed shops and bolted doors, the Judge, the Chief of Police, and D'Arrast reached the town hall. As they got away from the band and the firecrackers, silence again enveloped the town and

already a few urubus returned to the places on the roofs that they seemed to have occupied for all time. The town hall stood in a long, narrow street leading from one of the outlying sections to the church square. For the moment, the street was empty. From the balcony could be seen, as far as the eye could reach, nothing but a pavement full of potholes, in which the recent rain had left puddles. The sun, now slightly lower, was still nibbling at the windowless façades of the houses across the street.

They waited a long time, so long that D'Arrast, from staring at the reverberation of the sun on the opposite wall, felt his fatigue and dizziness returning. The empty street with its deserted houses attracted and repelled him at one and the same time. Once again he wanted to get away from this country; at the same time he thought of that huge stone; he would have liked that trial to be over. He was about to suggest going down to find out something when the church bells began to peal forth loudly. Simultaneously, from the other end of the street on their left, a clamor burst out and a seething crowd appeared. From a distance the people could be seen swarming around the shrine, pilgrims and penitents mingled, and they were advancing, amidst firecrackers and shouts of joy, along the narrow street. In a few seconds they filled it to the edges, advancing toward the town hall in an indescribable disorder—ages, races, and costumes fused in a motley mass full of gaping eyes and yelling mouths. From the crowd emerged an army of tapers like lances with flames fading into the burning sunlight. But when they were close and the crowd was so thick under the balcony that it seemed to rise up along the walls, D'Arrast saw that the ship's cook was not there.

Quick as lightning, without excusing himself, he left the balcony and the room, dashed down the staircase, and stood in the street under the deafening sound of the bells and firecrackers. There he had to struggle against the crowd of merrymakers, the taper-bearers, the shocked penitents. But, bucking the human tide with all his weight, he cut a path in such an impetuous way that he staggered and almost fell when he was eventually free, beyond the crowd, at the end of the street. Leaning against the burning-hot wall, he waited until he had caught his breath. Then he resumed his way. At that moment a group of men emerged into the street. The ones in front were walking backward, and D'Arrast saw that they surrounded the cook.

He was obviously dead tired. He would stop, then, bent under the huge stone, run a little with the hasty step of stevedores and coolies—the rapid, flat-footed trot of drudgery. Gathered about him, penitents in surplices soiled with dust and candle-drippings encouraged him when he stopped. On his left his brother was walking or running in silence. It seemed to D'Arrast that they took an interminable time to cover the space separating them from him. Having almost reached him, the cook stopped again and glanced around with dull eyes. When he saw D'Arrast—yet without appearing to recognize him—

he stood still, turned toward him. An oily, dirty sweat covered his face, which had gone gray; his beard was full of threads of saliva; and a brown, dry froth glued his lips together. He tried to smile. But, motionless under his load, his whole body was trembling except for the shoulders, where the muscles were obviously caught in a sort of cramp. The brother, who had recognized D'Arrast, said to him simply: "He already fell." And Socrates, popping up from nowhere, whispered in his ear: "Dance too much, Mr. D'Arrast, all night long. He's tired."

The cook advanced again with his jerky trot, not like a man who wants to progress but as if he were fleeing the crushing load, as if he hoped to lighten it through motion. Without knowing how, D'Arrast found himself at his right. He laid his hand lightly on the cook's back and walked beside him with hasty, heavy steps. At the other end of the street the shrine had disappeared, and the crowd, which probably now filled the square, did not seem to advance any more. For several seconds, the cook, between his brother and D'Arrast, made progress. Soon a mere space of some twenty yards separated him from the group gathered in front of the town hall to see him pass. Again, however, he stopped. D'Arrast's hand became heavier. "Come on, cook, just a little more," he said. The man trembled; the saliva began to trickle from his mouth again, while the sweat literally spurted from all over his body. He tried to breathe deeply and stopped short. He started off again, took three steps, and tottered. And suddenly the stone slipped onto his shoulder, gashing it, and then forward onto the ground, while the cook, losing his balance, toppled over on his side. Those who were preceding him and urging him on jumped back with loud shouts. One of them seized the cork mat while the others took hold of the stone to load it on him again.

Leaning over him, D'Arrast with his bare hand wiped the blood and dust from his shoulder, while the little man, his face against the ground, panted. He heard nothing and did not stir. His mouth opened avidly as if each breath were his last. D'Arrast grasped him around the waist and raised him up as easily as if he had been a child. Holding him upright in a tight clasp with his full height leaning over him, D'Arrast spoke into his face as if to breathe his own strength into him. After a moment, the cook, bloody and caked with earth, detached himself with a haggard expression on his face. He staggered toward the stone, which the others were raising a little. But he stopped, looked at the stone with a vacant stare, and shook his head. Then he let his arms fall at his sides and turned toward D'Arrast. Huge tears flowed silently down his ravaged face. He wanted to speak, he was speaking, but his mouth hardly formed the syllables, "I promised," he was saying. And then: "Oh, Captain! Oh, Captain!" and the tears drowned his voice. His brother suddenly appeared behind him, threw his arms around him, and the cook, weeping, collapsed against him, defeated, with his head thrown back.

D'Arrast looked at him, not knowing what to say. He turned toward the crowd in the distance, now shouting again. Suddenly he tore the cork mat from the hands holding it and walked toward the stone. He gestured to the others to hold it up and then he loaded it almost effortlessly. His head pressed down under the weight of the stone, his shoulders hunched, and breathing rather hard, he looked down at his feet as he listened to the cook's sobs. Then with vigorous tread he started off on his own, without flagging covered the space separating him from the crowd at the end of the street, and energetically forced his way through the first rows, which stood aside as he approached. In the hubbub of bells and firecrackers he entered the square between two solid masses of onlookers, suddenly silent and gaping at him in amazement. He advanced with the same impetuous pace, and the crowd opened a path for him to the church. Despite the weight which was beginning to crush his head and neck, he saw the church and the shrine, which seemed to be waiting for him at the door. He had already gone beyond the center of the square in that direction when brutally, without knowing why, he veered off to the left and turned away from the church, forcing the pilgrims to face him. Behind him, he heard someone running. In front of him mouths opened on all sides. He didn't understand what they were shouting, although he seemed to recognize the one Portuguese word that was being constantly hurled at him. Suddenly Socrates appeared before him, rolling startled eyes, speaking incoherently and pointing out the way to the church behind him. "To the church! To the church!" was what Socrates and the crowd were shouting at him. Yet D'Arrast continued in the direction in which he was launched. And Socrates stood aside, his arms raised in the air comically, while the crowd gradually fell silent. When D'Arrast entered the first street, which he had already taken with the cook and therefore knew it led to the river section, the square had become but a confused murmur behind him.

The stone weighted painfully on his head now and he needed all the strength of his long arms to lighten it. His shoulders were already stiffening when he reached the first streets on the slippery slope. He stopped and listened. He was alone. He settled the stone firmly on its cork base and went down with a cautious but still steady tread toward the huts. When he reached them, his breath was beginning to fail, his arms were trembling under the stone. He hastened his pace, finally reached the little square where the cook's hut stood, ran to it, kicked the door open, and brusquely hurled the stone onto the still glowing fire in the center of the room. And there, straightening up until he was suddenly enormous, drinking in with desperate gulps the familiar smell of poverty and ashes, he felt rising within him a surge of obscure and panting joy

that he was powerless to name.

When the inhabitants of the hut arrived, they found D'Arrast standing with his shoulders against the back wall and eyes closed. In the center of the room, in the place of the hearth, the stone was half buried in ashes and earth. They stood in the doorway without advancing and looked at D'Arrast in silence as if questioning him. But he didn't speak. Whereupon the brother led the cook up to the stone, where he dropped on the ground. The brother sat down too, beckoning to the others. The old woman joined him, then the girl of the night before, but no one looked at D'Arrast. They were squatting in a silent circle around the stone. No sound but the murmur of the river reached them through the heavy air. Standing in the darkness, D'Arrast listened without seeing anything, and the sound of the waters filled him with a tumultuous happiness. With eyes closed, he joyfully acclaimed his own strength, he acclaimed, once again, a fresh beginning in life. At that moment, a firecracker went off that seemed very close. The brother moved a little away from the cook and, half turning toward D'Arrast but without looking at him, pointed to the empty place and said: "Sit down with us."

Excerpt from

Out of My Life and Thought

Albert Schweitzer
(1875-1965)

Albert Schweitzer, Alsatian scholar and missionary, earned doctorates in music, theology and medicine. As a theologian, he wrote an epoch-making book on the life of Jesus. As a musician, he was recognized as one of the renowned interpreters of Bach's organ music. Schweitzer began the study of medicine at 30, after deciding to become a jungle doctor. As the clouds of war were gathering on the continent, he and his wife left Europe for Africa in 1913. He remained in Gabon for the rest of his life, except for visits to Europe to raise money for his hospital, and one lecture in the United States.

In the following selection from his autobiography, Schweitzer describes the decisions and actions that led him to a life of service and gives advice to others who might be contemplating a similar total commitment.

On October 13th, 1905, a Friday, I dropped into a letter box in the Avenue de la Grande Armée in Paris, letters to my parents and to some of my most intimate acquaintances, telling them that at the beginning of the winter term I should enter myself as a medical student, in order to go later on to Equatorial Africa as a doctor. In one of them I sent in the resignation of my post as principal of the Theological College of St. Thomas, because of the claim on my time that my intended course of study would make.

The plan which I meant now to put into execution had been in my mind for a long time, having been conceived as long ago as my student days. It struck me as incomprehensible that I should be allowed to lead such a happy life, while I saw so many people around me wrestling with care and suffering. Even at school I had felt stirred whenever I got a glimpse of the miserable home surroundings of some of my schoolfellows and compared them with the absolutely ideal conditions in which we children of the parsonage at Günsbach lived. While at the university and enjoying the happiness of being able to study and even to produce some results in science and art, I could not help thinking continually of others who were denied that happiness by their material circumstances or their health. Then one brilliant summer morning at Günsbach, during the Whitsuntide holidays—it was in 1896—there came to me, as I awoke, the thought that I must not accept this happiness as a matter of course, but must give something in return for it. Proceeding to think the matter out at once with calm deliberation, while the birds were singing outside, I settled with myself before I got up, that I would consider myself justified in living till I was thirty for science and art, in order to devote myself from that time forward to the direct service of humanity. Many a time already had I tried to settle what meaning lay hidden for me in the saying of Jesus! "Whosoever would save his life shall lose it, and whosoever shall lose his life for My sake and the Gospels shall save it." Now the answer was found. In addition to the outward, I now had inward happiness.

What would be the character of the activities thus planned for the future was not yet clear to me. I left it to circumstances to guide me. One thing only was certain, that it must be directly human service, however inconspicuous the sphere of it.

I naturally thought first of some activity in Europe. I formed a plan for taking charge of abandoned or neglected children and educating them, then making them pledge themselves to help later on in the same way children in similar positions. When in 1903, as warden of the theological hostel, I moved into my roomy and sunny official quarters on the second floor of the College of St. Thomas, I was in a position to begin the experiment. I offered my help now here, now there, but always unsuccessfully. The constitutions of the organizations which looked after destitute and abandoned children made no provision for the acceptance of such voluntary cooperation. For example, when the Strasbourg orphanage was burnt down, I offered to take in a few boys, for the time being, but the superintendent did not even allow me to finish what I had to say. Similar attempts which I made elsewhere were also failures.

. . . . .

One morning in the autumn of 1904 I found on my writing table in the college one of the green-covered magazines in which the Paris Missionary Society reported every month on its activities. A certain Miss Scherdlin used to put them there knowing that I was specially interested in this society on account of the impression made on me by the letters of one of its earliest missionaries, Casalis by name, when my father read them aloud at his missionary services during my childhood. That evening, in the very act of putting it aside that I might go on with my work, I mechanically opened this magazine, which had been laid on my table during my absence. As I did so, my eye caught the title of an article: *Les Besoins de la Mission du Congo* ("The needs of the Congo Mission").

It was by Alfred Boegner, the president of the Paris Missionary Society, an Alsatian, and contained a complaint that the mission had not enough workers to carry on its work in the Gaboon, the northern province of the Congo Colony. The writer expressed his hope that his appeal would bring some of those "on whom the Master's eyes already rested" to a decision to offer themselves for this urgent work. The conclusion ran: "Men and women who can reply simply to the Master's call, 'Lord, I am coming,' those are the people whom the Church needs." Having finished the article, I quietly began my work. My search was over.

. . . . .

Latchkey is one of countless voluntary groups through which persons can share the gift of themselves with others.

As a man of individual action, I have since that time been approached for my opinion and advice by many people who wanted to make a similar venture, but only in comparatively few cases have I taken on me the responsibility of giving them immediate encouragement. I often had to recognize that the need "to do something special" was born of a restless spirit. Such persons wanted to dedicate themselves to larger tasks because those that lay nearest did not satisfy them. Often, too, it was evident that they had been brought to their decisions by quite secondary considerations. Only a person who can find a value in every sort of activity and devote himself to each one with full consciousness of duty, has the inward right to take as his object some extraordinary activity instead of that which falls naturally to his lot. Only a person who feels his preference to be a matter of course, not something out of the ordinary, and who has no thought of heroism, but just recognizes a duty undertaken with sober enthusiasm, is capable of becoming a spiritual adventurer such as the world needs. There are no heroes of action: only heroes of renunciation and suffering. Of such there are plenty. But few of them are known, and even these not to the crowd, but to the few.

. . . . .

Of all the will for the ideal which exists in mankind only a small part can be manifested in action. All the rest is destined to realize itself in unseen effects, which represent, however, a value exceeding a thousandfold and more that of the activity which attracts the notice of the world. Its relation to the latter is like that of the deep sea to the waves which stir its surface. The hidden forces of goodness are embodied in those persons who carry on as a secondary pursuit the immediate personal service which they cannot make their life work. The lot of the many is to have as a profession, for the earning of their living and the satisfaction of society's claim on them, a more or less soulless labor in which they can give out little or nothing of their human qualities, because in that labor they have to be little better than human machines. Yet no one finds himself in the position of having no possible opportunity of giving himself to others as a human being. The problem produced by the fact of labor being today so thoroughly organized, specialized, and mechanized depends only in part for its solution on society's not merely removing the conditions thus produced, but doing its very best to guard the rights of human personality. What is even more important is that sufferers shall not simply bow to their fate, but shall try with all their energy to assert their human personality amid their unfavorable conditions by spiritual activity. Anyone can rescue his human life, in spite of his professional life, who seizes every opportunity of being a man by means of personal action, however unpretending, for the good of fellow men who need the help of a fellow man. Such a man enlists in the service of the spiritual and good. No fate can prevent a man from giving to others this direct human service side by side with his life work. If so much of such service remains unrealized, it is because the opportunities are missed.

That everyone shall exert himself in that state of life in which he is placed, to practice true humanity toward his fellow men, on that depends the future of mankind.

Nomination of Tom Hogan for Service Award

In 1976, a television station in a major northeastern city noted that news reports featured stories of crime, corruption and delinquency, while many ordinary citizens were quietly devoting their lives to the service of others without receiving any recognition. The station decided to establish an annual service award and asked viewers to write nomination letters. Over 800 letters were received, from which five award recipients were selected. The following letter, nominating the 1978 award-winner, describes the activities of a 65-year-old man who has found meaning in life through serving others. Names have been changed to avoid embarrassment.

Tom Hogan serves as a friend to those who don't have any friends.

For the past year and a half he has had a paid position as crisis counselor for the Youth Development Center (the parent organization for People in Trouble) for 35 hours a week. However, he works every day, seven days a week, from 8:30 a.m. to 11:00 p.m. and until midnight on weekends because of his dedication. Prior to his present position, Tom was a lathe operator for 20 years at a local factory. During this time he managed to volunteer for about 20 hours a week with various programs. A list of his volunteer activities follows:

—For twenty years he has been active in Alcoholics Anonymous, and has been on 24-hour call at the state central service, ready to help anyone with a drinking problem.
—He has worked in Volunteers in Probation, helping troubled youths and their families.
—He was one of the first volunteers at People in Trouble and is largely responsible for the program's success.
—He is a volunteer in corrections, and helped to set up the AA groups at the prison. He is also on the external Board of Directors of the National Prison Reform Association.
—He is a former member of the local Community Action board of directors and resigned only because he resided in the wrong census tract.
—He is the parish social worker for St. James Church, where he assisted troubled parishioners with their problems.
—He has formed and conducted two Alateen groups (children whose parents are alcoholics).
—At the prison he helps prisoners set up job interviews at the time of their release, delivers messages to prisoners' families, and helps deserving prisoners in their attempts to get paroled.
—He helped to form the "Easy Does It" club for couples with alcohol problems. Since the club's function was to provide the members with alternative week-end activity, Tom taught himself how to call square dances and volunteered his services each weekend for five years.

While the above is the factual data of Tom's total commitment to a life of service, perhaps a few examples of the way he functions in these roles will help to explain why I think he is so worthy.

One day while he was manning the telephone at People in Trouble, a woman called who had a myriad of problems. She was 28 years old, black and had a housing problem, for starters. Her husband was in prison; she had two young children, and she couldn't find any housing she could afford. At the time, she was living with her mother who told her she had to get out immediately because she couldn't stand having the children underfoot. Tom found them a place to stay that night, and went out and brought them to the house. The next morning he brought them to a more permanent residence that he found for them.

One of the children needed open-heart surgery; the child's mother was concerned that the child was not baptized before the operation. So Tom arranged for Father John of St. James Church to perform the baptism. He also got the daughter a white dress and the boy a suit for the occasion. Then it turned out they needed godparents. So—you guessed it—Tom and his wife are now the godparents of the two children. Meanwhile, he found permanent housing for the family.

As he was leaving the woman's apartment after getting them settled, walking to his car, an intoxicated 60-year-old man literally fell on him and asked for a dime to call the medical center. Tom said, "Save your money. I'll drive you there." Tom took the man down to the medical center to the detoxification unit. For the next ten days, he visited him and tried to work out a plan for him after he got out. The man had two artificial legs, and had become almost a drunken recluse. Tom managed to settle him in a rooming-house, and to draw him into activities. The last we heard, he was doing fine, and while his drinking problem was not cured, it had been greatly reduced.

An Ethical Will

Anonymous

The following document is direct and simple, two characteristics that outweigh its unsophisticated literary style. Members of a study group in Rhode Island, many relatively young, were asked one day to pretend they were dying and to write a will. In it they were to tell their descendants the expectations they had for them: Virtues to be developed, religious practices to be observed and attitudes to be nurtured.

Dearest children,

From the time you were just little babies, Daddy and I have tried to show you what was really important in this world, to us and for you, not by mere words but more important by our deeds. I hope you will always remember this way of life through which we all found such a feeling of joy and family togetherness.

We tried to let you know why it was so important to be an honest human being. First, by always being honest with yourself, you cannot help but be honest and honorable to others. Be proud of yourself, not only in who and what you are, but also in what you do to make the world a more decent world for others less fortunate than you. Be compassionate and charitable to them and try to share what you have in a real way with those who can benefit by your caring. Fight for what you believe in, and though your path may not be an easy one, know that your concern adds strength to others who need it as well as adding strength to yourself.

Remember how important our Jewishness was to us. Our day-to-day living was enriched by our living as

Jews—from the joyous celebration of Shabbat [Sabbath] with Kiddush [blessing of the wine] and kindling the candles to Seders [Passover meals] to building a Sukkah [booth to celebrate], eating Bachser and all the rest! Try to observe as many of the mitsvot [commandments] as you can, as are meaningful to you. Remember that by observing them you are also re-cementing your ties to all the Jews in history; and never forget your history, through which Jews—some of them—have survived. It is so very much for this reason that you must remember how important your being Jewish must be to you—and to the survival of the Jewish People. Think of Eretz Yisrael often, and now as you give up your allowance money to plant trees in Israel, so continue to be generous to her in an even more meaningful way. Remember how much Israel means to us as Jews.

Remember to always study, not just for book reports or piano or guitar lessons as you do now, or soon in college to prepare for your role in life, but even more as you grow older. Never grow too old to learn. Realize how much there is to know. For when you stop studying or lose the desire to learn, a part of you is lost too. Our tradition stresses "Torah L'shma"—Torah for the Love of Torah. I don't mean to limit you with Torah, but Torah is still the greatest guide to a better life that I know of.

Our family has always had what we called "togetherness." We have loved together, laughed together, cried together, played together, fought together. We always cared about each other. Do you remember how the other two of you would "gang up" on me when I reprimanded one of you?! As you grow up, you may move far away from each other, and with families of your own you probably will teach your children the important things you learned as children. Try to be open to

their "generation gap" views as I tried to, for the world is not static, but human understanding is constant. Remember not to take for granted your relationship with Daddy, your brothers and sisters; take time, make time to call, to visit, to share your new families with each other.

If, as you read this now or in the years to come, you ask yourself, "Why is Mom writing us all this? We already know it—this is what she's taught us, this is how we have always lived and are still trying to live now," then I will be thankful for having been so fortunate.

With all my love,

Mother

Further Readings

Addams, Jane. *Twenty Years at Hull-House*. 1938. Jane Addams, who devoted her life to caring for the underprivileged and oppressed, describes the founding of the world-famous Chicago settlement house.

Herriot, James. *All Creatures Great and Small*. Rev. edition, 1973. True story of a veterinarian whose courage, warmth and humor lend a special quality to his service in his rural community. Also, two sequels: *All Things Wise and Wonderful* and *All Things Bright and Beautiful*.

Lasch, Christopher. *Culture of Narcissism: American Life in an Age of Diminishing Expectations*. 1979. Lasch analyzes American society and concludes that we have become preoccupied with self. A strong and provocative critique of the "me" generation.

Lash, Joseph. *Eleanor: The Years Alone*. 1972. Eleanor Roosevelt gave herself joyously in service to others. The biography shows how her sympathy, vitality and intellect had a profound influence on national life.

ACKNOWLEDGMENTS

Thanks are extended to Katherine Leonard of the Montgomery County Public Library, Bethesda, Maryland, for the researching and compilation of "Further Readings" which appear at the end of each section of *The Search for Meaning*.

Grateful acknowledgment is made to the holders of copyrights and publishers named below for permission to reprint the selections in this collection:

"A Father Sees His Son Nearing Manhood." From *The People, Yes* by Carl Sandburg, copyright 1936 by Harcourt, Brace Jovanovich, Inc.; renewed 1964 by Carl Sandburg. Reprinted by permission of the publisher.

From pp. 100-103 "The Second Tree from the Corner" in *The Second Tree from the Corner* by E. B. White. Copyright 1947, © 1975 by E. B. White. Reprinted by permission of Harper & Row, Publishers, Inc.

From *Thank You All Very Much* by Margaret Drabble, by permission of William Morrow & Company, Inc., Publishers. Copyright © 1973 by Margaret Drabble.

Excerpt reprinted by permission of Grosset & Dunlap, Inc. from *A Death In the Family* by James Agee, copyright © 1957 by The James Agee Trust, copyright renewed © 1985 by Mia Agee.

"On Being a Grandmother" from *Blackberry Winter* by Margaret Mead. Copyright © 1972 by Margaret Mead. Used by permission of William Morrow & Company.

From *The Names* by N. Scott Momaday. Copyright © 1976 by N. Scott Momaday. Reprinted by permission of Harper & Row, Publishers, Inc.

From *All Real Life is Meeting*, by J. H. Oldham. Reprinted by permission of The Seabury Press. Every effort has been made to reach the current copyright holder.

"Sexuality and Personality." From *Sexual Deviation* by Anthony Storr. © Anthony Storr, 1964. Reprinted by permission of A.D. Peters & Co. Ltd.

"We Are Transmitters" and "Terra Incognita." From *The Complete Poems of D. H. Lawrence*. Copyright © 1964, 1971 by Angelo Ravagli and C. M. Weekley, Executors of the Estate of Frieda Lawrence Ravagli. Reprinted by permission of Viking Penguin Inc.

"The Family Meadow." Copyright © 1965 by John Updike. Reprinted from *The Music School* by John Updike, by permission of Alfred A. Knopf, Inc.

Reproduced by permission of the American Anthropological Association from *Autobiography of a Papago Woman*, 1936. Not for further reproduction.

From "Home Sickness" by George Moore. Reprinted from *The Untilled Field* by permission of Mr. J. C. Medley and Conlin Smythe Ltd., Gerrards Cross, Buckinghamshire, England.

"I Have a Dream." Copyright © 1963 by Martin Luther King, Jr. By permission of Joan Daves.

ILLUSTRATION CREDITS

The researching of the pictures was done by Ann Freud, Picture Research, Washington, D.C.

Cover: *The Thinker*. Auguste Rodin. National Gallery of Art, Washington. Gift of Mrs. John W. Simpson.

2—From *The First Jewish Catalog*, published by The Jewish Publication Society of America.

5, 14, 33, 36-37, 133—*The Labyrinth* by Robert Vickrey, 1951. Casein on composition board. 32 x 48 inches. Purchase with funds from the Juliana Force Purchase Award 52.6; *Conversation* by Henry Schnakenberg, 1930. Oil on canvas. 50¼ x 36 inches. Gift of Gertrude Vanderbilt Museum of American Art. 31.338; *Mirror of Life* by Henry Koerner, (alternate title "Lebensspiegel"), 1946. Oil on composition board. 36 x 42 inches. Purchase 48.2; *The Subway* by George Tooker, 1950. Egg tempera on composition board. 18⅛ x 36⅛ inches. Purchase with funds from the Juliana Force Purchase Award 50.23; *Despair* by Hugo Robus, 1927. Bronze. 12¾ x 10 x 13 inches. Purchase 40.23. Collection of Whitney Museum of American Art.

11—*The Nooning* by Winslow Homer. Oil on canvas. 13⁵⁄₁₆ x 19¾ inches. Wadsworth Atheneum, Hartford. The Ella Gallup Sumner and Mary Caitlin Sumner Collection.

22—*The Banjo Lesson* by Henry O. Tanner. Collection of Hampton University's Museum.

30, 56, 116, 124, 204—*Family Group* by Henry Moore (66.3610). Gift of Joseph H. Hirshhorn, 1966; *The Bus Riders* by George Segal (66.4506). Gift of Joseph H. Hirshhorn, 1966; *Woman and Little Girl in Front of the Sun* by Joan Miro (72.203). Gift of Joseph H. Hirshhorn, 1972; *Construction #107* by Jose De Rivera (72.91). Gift of Joseph H. Hirshhorn, 1972; *The Mother* by Charles White (66.5533). Gift of Joseph H. Hirshhorn, 1966. Hirshhorn Museum and Sculpture Garden, Smithsonian Institution.

41, 86-87, 172-173, 202—*The Kiss* by Edvard Munch. Rosenwald Collection; *Peaceable Kingdom* by Edward Hicks. Gifts of William & Bernice Chrysler Garbisch; *A City of Fantasy*, American School, Unknown. Gift of Edgar William & Bernice Chrysler Garbisch; *Self-Portrait* by Paul Gauguin. (1814). Chester Dale Collection. Collection of The National Gallery of Art, Washington, D.C.

44,142—*Washington Square (A Holiday in The Park)* by William Glackens. (1913). 24⅝ x 18½ inches (ruled margins of drawing). Gift of Abby Aldrich Rockefeller; *Christina's World* by Andrew Wyeth. (1948). 32 ¼ x 47¾ inches. Collection of The Museum of Modern Art, New York.

49,91,157—"Bean Day Festival" photograph by Russell Lee; "Picnickers Along Highway 12A" photograph by Jack Delano; "Violin and Broomstraws" photograph by Carl Fleischauer, American Folklife Center. The Library of Congress.

53—*Delaware Doll Dance* by Ruthe Balock Jones. U.S. Department of the Interior, Indian Arts and Crafts Board.

65—Courtesy of Wide World Photos, Inc.

71—*Assembly Church* by Prentiss Hottel Taylor 1974. 44.21. National Museum of American Art, Smithsonian Institution. Gift of Irina A. Reed.

79—*The Luncheon of the Boating Party* by Pierre Auguste Renior. Courtesy of The Phillips Collection, Washington, D.C.

93—*The Residence of David Twining* by Edward Hicks. Abby Aldrich Rockefeller Folk Art Center, Williamsburg, VA. Courtesy of The Colonial Williamsburg Foundation.

102—"Boy in Dinosaur Track." Neg. #319835. Courtesy of the American Museum of Natural History.

104—Death Valley "Sand Dunes Near Stovepipe Wells." National Park Service. Photo by George A. Grant.

110-111—"Boy Communicating With Sculpture From The Luba People, Zaire." Eliot Elisofon Archives. National Museum of African Art, Smithsonian Institution.

126—"Pennsylvania Train Yard, Baltimore," circa 1945, A. Aubrey Bodine. Courtesy A. Aubrey Bodine Estate handled by Kathleen Ewing Gallery, Washington, D.C.

140—*The Fall of Icarus* by Pieter Brueghel. SCALA/Editorial Photocolor Archives, Inc.

147—*The Blind Botanist* by Ben Shahn. Courtesy the Wichita Art Museum, The Roland P. Murdoch Collection.

150—USDA—Forest Service.

157—Photo by Carl Fleischauer, American Folklife Center, Library of Congress.

176—Photograph from *Foxfire 4* edited by Eliot Wigginton. Copyright © 1973, 1974, 1975, 1976, 1977 by The Foxfire Fund, Inc. Reproduced by permission of Doubleday, a division of Bantam, Doubleday, Dell Publishing Group, Inc.

189, 191, 193—*Harriet Powers' Bible Quilt*. Division of Textiles, Smithsonian Institution, photo no. 75-2988.

196—*The Bridge* by Joseph Stella. Courtesy of the Collection of the Newark Museum.

207—*The Country School* (1871) by Winslow Homer (1836-1910). From the collection of The Saint Louis Art Museum.

219—NCOA Senior Center Latchkey Program.